Knuckler

Knuckler

MY LIFE WITH BASEBALL'S MOST CONFOUNDING PITCH

Tim Wakefield

with

Tony Massarotti

Foreword by

Phil Niekro

HOUGHTON MIFFLIN HARCOURT
Boston · New York
2011

Copyright © 2011 by Tim Wakefield

For information about permission to reproduce selections from this book,
write to Permissions, Houghton Mifflin Harcourt Publishing Company,
215 Park Avenue South, New York, New York 10003.

www.hmhbooks.com

Library of Congress Cataloging-in-Publication Data
Wakefield, Tim.
Knuckler : my life with baseball's most confounding pitch / Tim Wakefield with Tony Massarotti.
p. cm.
Summary: "The story of one of baseball's most unlikely successes — a knuckleball pitcher who
has outlived, outmatched, and outsmarted the dancing pitch" — Provided by publisher.
ISBN 978-0-547-51769-8 (hardback)
1. Wakefield, Tim. 2. Baseball players — United States — Biography. 3. Pitchers (Baseball) — United
States — Biography. 4. Pitching (Baseball) — Anecdotes. I. Massarotti, Tony. II. Title.
GV865.W3347A3 2011
796.357092 — dc22 2010049848

Book design by Brian Moore

Printed in the United States of America

DOC 10 9 8 7 6 5 4 3 2 1

For my grandfather, Lester, my biggest fan, who passed away right after I was drafted and never got the chance to watch me play professionally; for Red Sox fans, who have given me support, love, and understanding over the past 16 years and who understand me and the knuckler; and for my wife, Stacy, for her support, love, and sacrifices through the grind of the many seasons that we've been married. She provides a true testament to how strong an athlete's wife needs to be while we dedicate our time to our profession. She has been my rock through it all. I love you. (TW)

For Natalie, who continues to stand by the world's biggest knucklehead. (TM)

Foreword

•

WE'RE A SMALL group to begin with, so when I tell you that Tim Wakefield is one of the best knuckleballers of all time, I suppose that leaves some room for interpretation. So what I'll tell you instead is that Tim has been one of the best *pitchers* in the game for a long time, just so that nobody gets bug-eyed from focusing on the knuckleball for too long.

We're different, of course. Sometimes it feels like people see us as freaks or oddities. But I've always thought that an effective knuckleballer brings so much more to the table than a conventional pitcher, and Tim is a great example of that. Look at all of the things he's done over his career. He's been a starter and a closer, and he's pitched long relief, middle relief, and set-up. I bet there isn't a pitcher in the game who has done all of those things during the time he's been in the big leagues. I'm not sure how the Red Sox look at him, but I don't know where the Red Sox would be if he hadn't been on their pitching staff for the last 16 years.

Let's make this clear: knuckleballers aren't superstars. Tim, especially, was rarely the kind of pitcher who got front-page billing during any year, but when the season ended, I bet the Red Sox and everyone else looked up and gave thanks that they had him. The numbers are one thing—and those speak for themselves. But one thing I told Tim early on is that he needed to have his spikes and glove ready every day, because a knuckleballer is always in a position to help. We can pitch in between starts, on short rest, on no rest. He did that as well as anyone. He's been like a 26th man for the Red Sox during his entire time there.

Here's something else I told Tim early in his career, when he was learning about the knuckleball, learning to trust it: "If you ever lose confidence in this thing, they're going to have to bring you to the hospital." He looked at me and asked why. And that's when I told him: "Because they're going to have take my size 11 shoe out of your ass."

Tim laughed at that, but I'm proud of what he's become during his career, on the field and off. He's as good a person as he is a pitcher. I could see that he had potential from the first time I saw him pitch, in the 1992 playoffs against the Atlanta Braves team that I played with almost my entire career. Tim was with Pittsburgh then. I remember watching the game from the stands and seeing Tim's knuckleball floating in slow motion, and I remember thinking, *This kid is good.* I had no idea then that we'd end up meeting, that the Red Sox would ask me to help, that I'd become like a mentor to him, and that we'd eventually become peers.

As knuckleballers, we really have only ourselves to rely on. Nobody else understands the pitch the way that we do. I had the chance to pitch with Hoyt Wilhelm for a brief time with the Braves in 1969, and I remember speaking with Wilbur Wood during the 1970s about the challenges of pitching on short rest. Guys like Wilhelm, Tom Candiotti, Charlie Hough—we're all in the same small fraternity. I was especially lucky because one of those guys was my real brother, Joe. We all connect with each other in way that only we can understand, and I think we're all as proud of the others' careers as we are of our own.

People ask me sometimes about the future of the knuckleball, about where the pitch is going, and I'll tell you the same thing I tell them: I'm not sure. But isn't that right? We don't always know where the pitch is going. We just throw it and trust it. Baseball evaluators certainly don't go out scouting for knuckleballers, but I'm sure the pitch will endure.

It always does. I'm not sure who will be the next guy to throw it effectively or where that is going to be, but someone will throw it and hand it on to the next guy, the way Wakefield has for the last two decades or so.

And when that guy comes along, I know he'll learn something from Tim Wakefield the way Tim learned from me, Joe, and the others, because Tim stopped being a student of the knuckleball a long time ago.

And he became a teacher.

Phil Niekro
Autumn 2010

Introduction

●

THE KNUCKLEBALL, I know, is a big part of the story. It's a big part of who I am. But I've never really thought of myself as being different, not really, not in comparison to other pitchers and certainly not in comparison to the people who come watch us play.

What I am, I believe, is someone who got a bunch of second chances and took advantage of them, who persevered through adversity. I hope that comes through as much as anything else in this book. I think there are lessons in that for all of us. I know there were for me.

People look at the knuckleball differently than they do other pitches — they're fascinated by it. I understand why. People have asked me all kinds of questions about the knuckleball over the years — how I grip it, why it does what it does, whether I ever get frustrated by it. That last question is one I've always found interesting, because people sometimes talk about it as if it were a person, as if I had a relationship with it. No one would ever ask Pedro Martinez about his changeup or Josh Beckett about his curveball the same way they ask me about my knuckleball, but I also understand there are differences. If one pitch isn't working for those guys, they can try something else. I really can't.

For roughly 20 years as a professional pitcher, I've thrown the knuckle-ball on almost every pitch. It's worked for me most of the time. When it hasn't, I've simply chalked it up to the balancing forces of baseball, the way any pitcher would.

I don't resent the knuckleball. In fact, it's quite the opposite. I *love* the knuckleball. It has given me a long career to be proud of and pro-vided for my wife, Stacy, and two children, Trevor and Brianna. It's allowed me to meet people I might never have met, experience things I might never have been able to experience, and help people in ways I might never have been able to help.

Before I joined the Red Sox in 1995, I thought my career might be over. I was still learning about the knuckleball, and I knew almost nothing about Boston or about the Red Sox other than what I had learned from one of my college roommates, Tom Krystock, who was a Red Sox fan. Tom was from Connecticut and convinced me to go with him to Fenway Park, where we took in a handful of games. I never imagined then that Boston and Fenway would become my home, that I would pitch in nearly 300 games there and be part of two world championship teams. And I never imagined that Boston would accept me the way it has, that the people there would welcome me as part of their community, that Boston would be as much a home to me as Melbourne, Florida, where I grew up and played college baseball.

Sometime during my career in Boston—I can't remember exactly when—someone asked one of my teammates, Derek Lowe, about what it was like to pitch at Fenway Park. What made Fenway differ-ent? Derek told them that when he pitched in other, bigger stadiums, he would look into the stands and see colors. But at Fenway, when he stood on the mound, he would look into the crowd and see *faces*. I al-ways thought that was a great way to describe how special it is to pitch at Fenway Park, for the Red Sox and for their fans. The experience is just more intimate. To me, Boston always has felt like a neighbor-hood more than a city, the kind of place, like *Cheers*, where everybody knows your name and you know theirs. It's one of the things I love most about playing there. People talk about "Red Sox Nation" all the time now, but it really is true. To me, the Red Sox and their fans are a *community* unlike any other in sports, and I've been blessed to be a part of it. I've invested in Boston during my time there, and I feel like Boston has invested in me.

In that way, especially, I've been very fortunate. Over the course of baseball history, other knuckleballers have had their own communities too. Hoyt Wilhelm. Phil and Joe Niekro. Wilbur Wood. Charlie Hough and Tom Candiotti. The list goes on. I've had the chance to meet most of those guys and to talk to them about the knuckler, to share an experience that has made us some of the most unique pitchers in baseball history. The knuckleball has taken us all through some unpredictable dips and turns, but we all owe everything we've accomplished to a pitch that, to me, is unlike any other in baseball.

I hope this book gives you some idea as to what it has been like to live with the knuckleball for the last 20 years or so.

And I hope you enjoy the journey as much as I have.

Tim Wakefield
Autumn 2010

Knuckler

One

•

He's so consistent with a pitch that's not consistent. You look up in the sixth or seventh inning and he's got a chance to win.

— *Red Sox manager Terry Francona speaking about Tim Wakefield, March 2010*

ON JUNE 8, 2010, with one out in the seventh inning of his 538th career appearance with the Boston Red Sox, Tim Wakefield familiarly stood on the pitcher's mound, glove resting near his left hip, right arm comfortably hanging at his side, as he peered in toward home plate. He was already behind in the count, two balls and no strikes. As Indians slugger Russell Branyan settled into the batter's box at Progressive Field in downtown Cleveland, Wakefield eased back and spun on his right foot, reaching into his glove for the pitch that would soon make him the all-time innings leader in Red Sox history, an achievement far more commendable than most anyone would care to acknowledge.

A knuckleball? No, no, no — not in this case — and perhaps there is a good measure of irony in that. In recording the 8,329th out of his 16-year Red Sox career — more outs than any other pitcher in the history of a storied franchise — Wakefield threw a *fastball* clocked at 73 miles per hour, inducing a pop-up that safely landed in the glove of teammate and shortstop Marco Scutaro. That was it. That was the instant when Wakefield reached precisely 2,776⅓ innings, literally a fraction more than the 2,776 recorded by longtime Red Sox ace Roger Clemens, adding further accomplishment to a workmanlike career during which his most significant contributions had often been disguised and one in which he had negotiated and endured the whims, eccentricities, and unpredictable dips and turns of baseball's most maddening, mystifying, and unpredictable pitch.

Even against Branyan, after all, Wakefield had to work around the knuckleball as much as he relied on it, resorting to his oxymoronic *fast*ball, which barely qualified for a speeding ticket, to record the out that distinguished him from every other pitcher who had worn the Boston uniform — from Clemens to Cy Young to Curt Schilling, Pedro Martinez, Babe Ruth, and beyond.

"He's a very unassuming guy, but he's been the glue that's held that pitching staff together for a long time. That's a fact," said former Red Sox general manager Dan Duquette, who brought Wakefield to Boston in 1995, when the pitcher's career seemed to be in ruins. "He's the consummate organization man. He was always available to the team. He made a huge contribution to the team and to the community."

For Red Sox general manager Theo Epstein, who inherited Wakefield upon taking over the Red Sox GM position in November 2003 and would re-sign him to a succession of contracts, it was Wakefield's connection with fans that was most striking.

"There's something about a knuckleballer that generates empathy in fans," Epstein said. "Even though it couldn't be further from the truth, it's just hard to shake the thought that, 'Hey, he's only throwing 68 [miles per hour] — that could be me out there!' Fans don't feel that way about guys who throw 95 [mph]. Between the knuckler, his 'everyman' demeanor, and his incredible contributions to the community, it's no surprise that Wake is a favorite of so many fans. Unfortunately, for many of the same reasons, the quality of his on-field contribution often gets overlooked. He's had a great career — one that anybody would be proud of — and has been an essential ingredient on some really good teams. Aside from all the records and being part of two world championship clubs, that paradox is what stands out about Wake's legacy to me. For a guy who was often underrated and sometimes overlooked, he was completely loved and embraced by Red Sox fans. That means a lot."

Indeed, for an array of reasons, Wakefield grew to be loved in Boston, a very traditional, guarded, and skeptical city where self-promotion is frowned upon, social responsibility is stressed, and group thinking is encouraged. As surely as Wakefield became part of the Red Sox in 1995, he also became part of the *city*. He routinely participated in charitable endeavors for the Jimmy Fund and Boston Children's Hospital as surely as he did for the Space Coast Early Intervention Center in his native Melbourne, Florida. At the end of the 2010 major league baseball season, Wakefield had finally won the award for which he had been nominated *seven times*: the prestigious and comprehensive Roberto Clemente Award. Named for the philanthropic Hall of Famer who began his career in Pittsburgh, like Wakefield, this annual award goes to the major leaguer who "best exemplifies the game of baseball, sportsmanship, community involvement, and the individual's contribution to his team."

The Red Sox, too, recognized this quality in Wakefield as surely as anyone. When the team mailed out a brochure highlighting its community contributions in 2010, Wakefield was the first player featured in it; on a similar billboard overlooking the Massachusetts Turnpike, Wakefield was the only player pictured.

"He has a wonderful reputation in baseball," said commissioner Allan "Bud" Selig. "We take for granted all the really decent human beings we have in the major leagues. Tim Wakefield ranks at the top of the list."

Amid all of that, of course, Wakefield also distinguished himself as a *pitcher*, no small feat given his reliance on the schizophrenic knuckler, which can destroy careers as easily — or perhaps *more* easily — as it can build them. By definition, the knuckleball is fickle. The knuckleball is wild. The idea is to relinquish almost all control and unleash the knuckleball in such a manner that its natural tendencies take hold, allowing the pitch to crazily float, flutter, and, ultimately, flummox.

The risks are enormous, and the rewards potentially great.

In his 16 seasons as a member of the Red Sox, Wakefield did not merely pitch more innings than any pitcher in franchise history; he also made more starts. He frequently sacrificed himself for the greater good while simultaneously winning more games than all but two pitchers in Red Sox history, Cy Young and Roger Clemens—the former the namesake of baseball's greatest pitching honor, the latter a pitcher who won that award a record seven times—proving that you could be a team player *and* be celebrated individually, the sports world's equivalent of *think globally, act locally*. Tim Wakefield was proof that you could be true to yourself by being true to your team, that success with something perceived as warily as the knuckleball was really just a matter of perspective.

"It just means that I've persevered," Wakefield said when asked to reflect on his career and accomplishments. "I've started, relieved, closed. I'm kind of proud that I've been able to do a lot and pitch in a lot of games. It means a lot, but I really don't think it has sunk in yet.... I think things can get overlooked when somebody stays in one place for a long time. You get young guys who come in, and they're like, 'He's old,' but let's look at *why* he's been here so long. I think that gets overlooked sometimes, to be honest with you."

In fact, as Wakefield climbed to the top of the Red Sox record book during his final seasons, his career achievements became more like items on a checklist and less like mileposts worthy of recognition. In 2009, for instance, after making the 380th start of his Red Sox career, Wakefield stood with his uniform top unbuttoned in a corner doorway of an emptying conference room at historic Fenway Park following a relatively methodical 8–2 dispatching of the Florida Marlins that had improved his record to a sparkling 9–3. As he approached his 43rd birthday, he was having another good year and was on the way to his first career appearance at the All-Star Game. Wakefield had enjoyed other, similar runs during his Red Sox career—some better, some worse—but the end result was almost always a remarkable consistency that Red Sox fans, above all others, seemed to appreciate. And yet, in this case and many others, almost nobody was aware that Wakefield had just made the 380th start of his Red Sox career, two shy of Clemens's club record of 382. It was an achievement far more worthy of recognition than anyone had taken the time to acknowledge.

In the end, after all, what real difference did two starts make? In a career marked by 380 starts, two games signified a difference of roughly 0.5 percent. Whether Wakefield finished at 380 or 382 games started, the conclusion was the same. His legacy had been forged. He had become, against all odds, part of the background, one of the most reliable and dependable pitchers in baseball history, particularly given that he pitched in a city and for a franchise that frequently devoured its own.

The Red Sox have been part of the culture in Boston for well over a century, their history defined by everything from pure heartbreak (most frequently) to unfiltered glory (more recently). Consequently, loyal followers of the team have prided themselves a great deal on perseverance, grit, determination. Red Sox fans have long since learned to show up for work the next day, no matter what, and they have memorized all of the clichés that celebrate the most noteworthy achievements. *Slow and steady wins the race. When the going gets tough, the tough get going. Focus on the journey, not on the destination.* In retrospect, no one more perfectly reflected those qualities than Wakefield, who had resurrected his career on more than one occasion and who continued to push forward — methodically, deliberately, undeterred.

And yet, when it came to instances like this and many others, Wakefield's achievements seemed to materialize out of thin air. Red Sox fans, too, sometimes could be distracted by the flash and glitz of the stars who came and went — men like Clemens, Mo Vaughn, Nomar Garciaparra, Manny Ramirez, David Ortiz. The list went on and on. Even Boston seemed to take Wakefield for granted sometimes, to overlook him entirely, to forget that the most commendable achievements can take place over years and years and years, like a steady, continuous construction project.

And then, one day, there it was.

Baseball was something of a religion in Boston, where the Red Sox, especially, were a passion, obsession, addiction, and psychosis all wrapped into one. ("Sometimes I almost wonder if it's a sickness," Wakefield chuckled.) The game was seen as a true test of endurance, where consistency and longevity reflected an ability both to perform and to survive. The Red Sox were dissected and analyzed over and over again, especially by those who deemed themselves to be card-carrying members of *Red Sox Nation,* a fan base that sometimes seemed as widespread as Islam. All of that should have made Wakefield an obvious focus as he moved toward the end of an accomplished, hard-working career defined by resourcefulness and resiliency, if for no other reason than the fact that Boston was the kind of place where even the smallest sacrifices were recognized by a Red Sox following that typically paid great care to detail.

With Wakefield, however, his career was greater than any individual year. By the end, a man who rarely received top billing had compiled a résumé that was, in many ways, like no other in team history.

"I think I've stayed under the radar my whole career. I've never gotten too high or too low — that has helped me [survive]," Wakefield said. "I think there are a couple of reasons I have a connection with people here. I think I bust my butt and never make excuses, and I think they appreciate that. I think I care about the team more than I care about myself. I think I put the team first, and I think that's very much appreciated by the fans because they get that side of it. And I just think, from a philosophy standpoint, outside of baseball, I think they get that side of me, too. I care about the community, like everybody else. I care about the neighborhood. I give my time. I care about the community that I live in and the community that supports us on a daily basis.

"I've tried to stay humble for as long as I can," he said.

Indeed, while maintaining a healthy dose of humility — the knuckler, too, will do that to a man — Wakefield had long since decided that he wanted to pitch in no other place than Boston, where he felt the aforementioned connection from the moment he arrived. He saw Boston as far more intimate than many of the bigger America cities — "It's more of a blue-collar, deep-rooted neighborhood that cares about its own," he said — and that was, of course, how he saw himself. The glitz of New York or Los Angeles never really lured him. The idea of a nomadic existence never really appealed. In an age when professional athletes frequently were urged to market their services, to take the best deal available, Wakefield was an absolute anachronism, a man whose values left him terribly out of place. In those instances when free agency beckoned, Wakefield flirted with homier, more comfortable places

like Minneapolis — the Minnesota Twins, too, had a family-type environment — than he did with bigger, louder metropolitan areas. He
grew up in Melbourne, Florida. He began his career in Pittsburgh. For
Wakefield, Boston was the perfect landing spot, a place where the fans
took their baseball seriously, but where citizenship mattered. More
than anything else in his career, Wakefield had always wanted to *belong*. As such, he had never really tried to leave Boston, and the Red
Sox had never really looked to dispose of him. They had built the kind
of gold-watch relationship that had generally ceased to exist elsewhere
in baseball.

"I just don't understand how some people can separate the personal
side of it," he said.

As much as anyone else, Tim Wakefield saw himself as the last of a
dying breed.

By the time Wakefield concluded 2009 and signed what looked to
be a final, two-year contract that would keep him with the Red Sox
through the 2011 baseball season, he was one of a unique group of major league players — and not solely because he was one of the few in
history to have mastered the knuckleball. Wakefield was one of only
19 pitchers in baseball history to have spent at least 15 seasons with
a single franchise; along with the incomparable New York Yankees
closer Mariano Rivera, he was one of only two active pitchers in the
game (and the only starter) to have remained with the same team since
the start of the 1995 season. And somewhat incredibly, Wakefield had
spent more time with the Red Sox than any pitcher in the history of the
organization, an accomplishment that only grew in magnitude when
one considered that Wakefield did so while making the journey with
his impulsive knuckler, a pitch that frequently operates as if it has a
mind of its own and one that had caused him as much angst and anxiety as it gave him dignity and delight.

By that point, Wakefield had long since accepted the fact that the
knuckleball was as much a part of him as the wins and the innings, the
number 49 he wore on his back, and the mustache and goatee he had
sported throughout his stint with the Red Sox. The knuckler could
inspire both wonder and fear. The knuckleball had produced some of

Wakefield's most glorious successes and some of his most gut-wrenching failures, and he had long since learned to make peace with the pitch and accept its flaws.

Along the way, the Red Sox and their fans learned to do the same with the knuckleball as well as with the man who had brought it to them.

"I think a lot of it is the pitch. I really do. It *is* me," Wakefield said when asked about the identity and legacy he built in Boston. "It's what's gotten me to where I am. It's hard to separate that. My biggest thing is — and you hear me say this every spring training when people say, 'What are your goals?' — I want to give the team innings. I mean, results — yeah, I'd love to win 20 games. I'd love to do that. But my job is to go out there and keep us in the game as long as possible. And I think I've proven that over time, if you go back historically and look at my career."

To do that, with Tim Wakefield as with anyone else, we have to go back to the beginning, to things that happened long before he came along, things he had absolutely nothing to do with.

That Wakefield would succeed in Boston, of all places, was as unforeseeable as the knuckleball is unpredictable. For the large majority of their history, the Red Sox were an organization defined by power hitters and heartbreaking failure, not necessarily in that order. By the time Wakefield arrived in Boston in late May 1995, Clemens had only just begun to alter the organization's lineage of royalty — a *pitcher,* of all beings, now ruled the Red Sox — and Boston was a championship-starved baseball town so desperate for a winner that the slightest bit of failure prompted irrational, illogical thinking and responses.

The Red Sox and their followers were willing to try anything by then, but they were just as quick to dismiss it.

The sale of Babe Ruth to the rival New York Yankees in 1920 served as the proverbial fork in the road at which the Red Sox had clearly made the wrong turn, but the history of the organization after 1920 was marked not by failure so much as by torture. In the 86 years from 1919 to 2003, a period during which the Red Sox failed to win even a single championship, the team had qualified for the postseason ten times and made four trips to the World Series, losing all four chances at a title in the maximum seven games. The Red Sox were always good enough to contend and flawed enough to fail—qualities that made them the perfect landing place for someone like Wakefield, whose career had followed a similar track thanks to the unreliable nature of his favorite pitch. When he was good, Wakefield could be very, very good. But when he was bad, he could be very, very bad.

And sometimes he could be both within a matter of seconds.

The Red Sox had taken on their identity long before Wakefield's arrival, however, thanks largely to Ted Williams, the Hall of Fame left fielder who debuted in 1939 and remained with the club through 1960. Beginning with "The Kid"—and Williams was, in some ways, a boy king—the Red Sox had assembled a line of royalty like few organizations in professional sports. Williams batted .327 with 31 home runs and 145 RBI as a 20-year-old *rookie* in 1939, launching a truly legendary career that produced a .344 career average and 521 home runs despite time lost to serve his country during World War II and the Korean War. He became a truly iconic figure in American history and was widely regarded in the baseball world as the greatest hitter who ever lived. Williams's Red Sox played in just one World Series, losing to the St. Louis Cardinals in 1946, and it was during his career that the Red Sox began to take on the identity of their star player. That problem would plague them for decades.

As much as baseball is a team sport, after all, the nature and pace of the game spotlight individual responsibilities and talents. The spectator's eye needs only to follow the ball. As analysts scrutinize individual performances after the game, they often lose track of the larger objectives. In baseball, sacrifices are easily overshadowed, particularly in the absence of group success.

"I went through the bad years there. I remember when, on a Friday night, you were lucky to have 10,000 people in the stands," said Hall of Famer and Red Sox great Carl Yastrzemski, who succeeded Williams in left field. "If you didn't go three-for-four or something like that, you could throw meat up into the stands and they would have devoured it. I mean, God, it was tough to play."

Once Williams retired, the Red Sox became Yastrzemski's team, and then the property of Jim Rice when Yaz left. Like Williams, both Yastrzemski and Rice were left fielders and accomplished hitters whose individual performances would land them in the Hall of Fame; like Williams, each played an entire career without winning a World Series championship. All three players spent their entire careers playing for a Red Sox organization owned by Thomas A. Yawkey, his wife, Jean, or the Yawkey Trust, which endured well beyond the deaths of the Yawkeys. Tom Yawkey drew much criticism for how the Red Sox seemed to coddle their star players. Aside from being the last organization in baseball to integrate, the Red Sox often were accused of operating with a country club mentality, a suggestion that the inmates ran the asylum. The perception that the elite players often had more power than the manager for whom they played created both great instability in the manager's office at Fenway Park and a culture that placed the individual before the team. Beginning in 1948 — just short of the midpoint of Williams's career — the Red Sox would not have a single manager last as long as five consecutive full seasons until after the turn of the century, and that was hardly a coincidence. In the Fenway Park clubhouse that served as both a sanctuary and a locker room for Red Sox players, the Red Sox had a clear hierarchy. Williams handed his crown to Yastrzemski, who handed it to Rice, and so forth. The organization was segregated on many levels.

Those policies began to change in the late 1980s, but only because Rice placed the scepter in the hands of a pitcher instead of a positional player. Clemens made his debut for the team as a highly touted rookie in 1984, but he did not fully blossom until 1986, the last productive year of Rice's career. Just as Rice was about to begin fading, Clemens ascended. Triggered by a historic 20-strikeout performance against the Seattle Mariners on April 29, 1986, Clemens raced off to an unforgettable 14–0 start that season and finished the year at a sterling 24–4, winning both the Most Valuable Player Award (his first and only) and the Cy Young Award (his first of seven) while bringing the Red Sox *this close* to a victory over the New York Mets in the 1986 World Series. Though the Sox ultimately failed — again in seven games after a crushing collapse in Game 6 — there was nonetheless a sentiment that the

Red Sox had entered a new era in their history built on the young, bullish Clemens, the kind of ace and cornerstone pitcher the Red Sox had so often lacked.

Clemens, in fact, frequently referred to pitching as having been "a second-class citizen" before his rise to power in Boston — and he was right.

Following his breakthrough season of 1986, Clemens spent ten more seasons in Boston and won two more Cy Young Awards (1987, 1991), which only added to the individual awards won by Williams (American League MVP in 1946 and 1949), Yastrzemski (AL MVP in 1967), and Rice (AL MVP in 1978). The Red Sox qualified for the postseason three more times during Clemens's stint with the team — in 1988, 1990, and 1995 — but they never again reached the World Series. Clemens left the team via free agency following the 1996 season in what proved to be a landmark change in the club's history — unlike Williams, Yastrzemski, and Rice, Clemens would not play his entire career in Boston. Under a bold and controversial general manager named Dan Duquette, the Red Sox seemed to be intent on reclaiming the rule of their own kingdom after having let their players run roughshod for a good chunk of the century. (For what it's worth, one Boston sports columnist called Duquette "Dictator Dan" throughout his tenure with the team.)

In keeping with a Red Sox tradition established prior to World War II, however, the Red Sox continued to operate more like an aristocracy, the regal Clemens starting his own line of kings. This time the royal bloodline of the Boston clubhouse ran not to left field but rather to the pitcher's mound. One year to the day after Clemens snubbed the Red Sox to sign with the Toronto Blue Jays, Duquette acquired Pedro Martinez from the Montreal Expos in a blockbuster trade. Just as Williams begot Yastrzemski, who begot Rice, Clemens begot Martinez, who begot Curt Schilling, who begot Josh Beckett, who begot Jon Lester. Along the way, the Red Sox finally changed owners and, thankfully, cultures, transitioning from a team that overvalued its superstars to one that preached the team concept and togetherness, commitment and dedication.

Having arrived during the final days of the Clemens years, Tim

Wakefield was the only member of the Boston organization who had been there to see it all. And only people like Duquette saw Wakefield for what he was: "the glue that's held that pitching staff together for a long time."

Truth be told, Tim Wakefield already could have been, should have been, and would have been the winningest pitcher in Red Sox history were it not for the simple fact that he was asked, along the way, to serve as the club's emergency response unit. For the bulk of Wakefield's career in Boston, he often was asked to pitch on short rest, to pitch out of the bullpen between starts, to fill gaps, to plug holes. Whether in the regular season or the postseason, Wakefield almost always was the man on the other end of the line when a Red Sox manager — particularly when he had just decided it was time to dial 9-1-1 — picked up his dugout phone and called the bullpen.

For that, Wakefield had his knuckleball to thank.

Or perhaps blame.

Knuckleball pitchers are regarded by most baseball historians as nothing more than .500 pitchers, which is to say, they lose as frequently as they win. In fact, given the difficulty of harnessing the pitch and the disproportionate number of those who have failed trying to do so, many knuckleballers have lost *more* than they won, and many never reached the major leagues at all. Only the good ones have been fortunate enough to tread water and spend some time at the highest level of baseball played in the world. Only the great ones have endured and won more than they lost to become members of one of the more exclusive fraternities in sports.

In 2010, at the end of his 18th major league season and his 16th with the Red Sox, Wakefield owned a career record of 193–172, a winning percentage of .529 that most teams would have eagerly embraced. (In baseball a .529 winning percentage translates into an 85–77 season, a record that most teams would consider a success.) And yet, even that simplest of truths, a .529 winning percentage, could not quantify Wakefield's contributions to the Red Sox, especially in a baseball world where managers, coaches, fans, and teammates had learned to become as wary of the knuckleball's whims as Wakefield himself.

In baseball more than any other sport, the games are connected, which is to say that one can affect the next. On June 10, 1996, for example, the struggling Red Sox were in the midst of a bad losing streak that had required manager Kevin Kennedy to rely heavily on his relief pitchers, who had been worked to the bone. He sent Wakefield out to the mound with a very unappealing and demanding task — to remain in the game come hell or high water. Wakefield subsequently allowed 16 hits and eight runs while issuing three walks and throwing a whopping 158 pitches in an 8–2 Red Sox defeat that was not nearly that competitive, all because the Red Sox quite simply needed someone to take a bullet so that they could get their house in order.

Having had the opportunity to catch their breath, the Red Sox came out to win four straight and five of their next six games, a winning streak for which Wakefield was largely responsible but for which he received almost no credit. His individual statistics suffered. The team benefited.

That was just one of many such instances in which Wakefield made similar sacrifices.

Since statisticians in baseball officially began counting pitches in 1988, Wakefield and his knuckleball have produced the two highest single-game pitch totals in any major league game. On April 27, 1993, as a member of the Pirates, Wakefield threw an astonishing 172 pitches in 10 innings of a 6–2 win over the Atlanta Braves; on June 5, 1997, he threw 169 pitches in 8⅔ innings of a 2–1 win for the Red Sox over the Milwaukee Brewers. Wakefield remained the only pitcher to appear twice among those named in the top ten pitch counts since 1988 — again, he owned numbers one and two — and the ninth performance on the list belonged to longtime knuckleballer Charlie Hough, who threw 163 pitches in 11 innings of a 1–0 win for the Texas Rangers over the Seattle Mariners on June 29, 1988.

And then there was this: during Wakefield's career in the major leagues, he had made 37 regular-season or postseason starts on short rest (three days or fewer) — more than any other pitcher in baseball. During that same period of time, no other Red Sox pitcher had started more than six games on short rest, all while Sox aces Clemens, Martinez, Schilling, and Beckett combined for three such starts (all by Clemens). That statistic offers great evidence for those who believe that Wakefield often was made into a sacrificial lamb, particularly during an age when pitchers were treated more and more like delicate crystal than strong, young, full-blooded American farm boys.

In the modern baseball era, much to the chagrin of veteran pitchers who played prior to, say, 1985, major league pitchers generally are regarded as valuable assets and treated accordingly. Where teams once operated with four-man pitching rotations to negotiate the season—a starter would work every fourth day with three days of rest in between—the schedule has now been adjusted to incorporate a fifth starter, providing every pitcher with an extra day of rest. With costs escalating rapidly, especially for pitching—in 2009 the going rate for pitching was somewhere in the neighborhood of $1 million *per win*—teams have begun to protect their arms and, more specifically, their investments. By reducing the number of starts per pitcher per season from 40 or 41 to 32 or 33, teams can get more out of their pitchers over the long run—or so they believe. (This point is still contested by some.) The end result has been a culture in which pitchers are handled with great care. The resulting reduction in the number of starts per season *and* the number of pitches per start has created a rather peculiar business model in which pitchers are asked to do less while being paid more.

Unless, of course, you happen to be a knuckleballer. Faced with a knuckler, teams generally throw caution to the wind and operate as if from another era.

If this suggests a certain willingness among conventional baseball decision-makers to abuse knuckleballers in some form—and it does—then it also suggests a willingness on the part of the pitchers to do whatever is necessary to contribute, to endure, to succeed. As hypnotizing as the knuckleball can be to hitters, the pitch fosters humility in those who have dared to befriend it. As surely as Wakefield survived the ups and downs of a relationship with the pitch, the same has been true of Hough, Phil Niekro, and fellow knuckleballers like Wilbur Wood and Hoyt Wilhelm, among others. To a man, knuckleballers have never wanted anything more than to be treated like any other player, which has almost universally resulted in a willingness to sacrifice themselves for the greater good.

"He's not really any different than any other pitcher in the major leagues," said Wakefield's father, Steve, who taught his son the pitch. "He's going to have his good days and he's going to have his bad days."

Countered Phil Niekro, who is in the Hall of Fame: "Most knuckleball pitchers, if you go back and look—and Tim's very good at this—they can start for you, they can be a long man, they can be a middle man, and they can close for you. Tim's done all of that. I don't know if there's another pitcher that's done what he's done for one organization."

For Tim Wakefield in particular, that willingness helped change the culture in a Red Sox organization that had long since gone astray.

And along the way it made him one of the most unique and extraordinary success stories in team history. If his ability to harness the knuckler made him, in some ways, like any other successful pitcher in the major leagues, his commitment to the pitch made him a most unusual exception.

Two

·

Like some cult religion that barely survives, there has always
been at least one but rarely more than five or six devotees throwing the knuckleball in the big leagues . . . . Not only can't pitchers control it, hitters can't hit it, catchers can't catch it, coaches
can't coach it, and most pitchers can't learn it. The perfect pitch.

— *Ron Luciano, American League umpire from 1969 to 1979*

W**ITH THE KNUCKLEBALL,** the debate between perception and reality begins at its core: the grip. In most
cases, the pitch has little to do with the knuckles at all.
Far more often than not, baseball's most complex pitch is thrown from
the fingertips, positioned between the thumb, index, and middle fingers as if it were a credit card being held up for display. The knuckles
are what people *see,* but they are, like many things associated with the
pitch, an illusion.

Just the same, the term *knuckleball* has become an accepted part of
the American lexicon, synonymous with almost anything that lacks
spin and moves in an unpredictable, unsettling fashion. In football, for
example, a punt or kick returner might speak of handling a *knuckleball*
kicked by a cleated punter or kicker; the poorest free-throw shooters
in the National Basketball Association are usually those who put decidedly little backspin on the ball and shoot, as their coaches will tell
you, *knuckleballs.* In soccer, a goaltender might face the unenviable
task of saving a ball redirected with just the right amount of touch that
the ball stops spinning altogether, *knuckling* its way toward the goal.

Even tennis players, on rare occasions, can fire off a forehand or backhand return, only to see the ball *knuckle* right back as the result of an unusual convergence of spin and counterspin.

In baseball, of course, the absence of any spin on the ball is achieved by design, at least by the pitcher, though the skill is far more difficult than it sounds. (Fielders, too, sometimes speak of balls hit at them that *knuckle.*) That simplest of facts about the knuckleball is why relatively few people can throw it, and fewer still can throw it effectively. Proper delivery of the knuckleball requires absolutely no spin — or very, very little, because even the slightest deviance from that requirement can render the pitch entirely useless.

In effect, every pitch with the knuckleball can be a proverbial roll of the dice.

"If it spins at all," Wakefield said succinctly, "it basically doesn't work."

In the most complex sense, according to everyone from physicists to knuckleball cultists, the knuckleball succeeds through an array of physical realities, many of them triggered by the red stitching that se-cures the cover of a baseball (also known as the laces). There is ample talk of airflow, vortexes, and wind swirls — mind-numbing physical terms that would cause the average person's eyes to glaze over as if try-ing to follow the path of the pitch itself. Curious minds ranging from Robert Adair, a professor emeritus at Yale and author of *The Physics of Baseball,* to Dave Clark, a baseball fan and author of a playful work entitled *The Knucklebook,* have taken a turn at explaining the physics behind the pitch, though the simplest explanation goes something like this:

When the knuckleball is thrown properly, air deflects off the laces and slides around the ball to the top, bottom, and sides. The rear of the ball generally remains untouched. And because the shape of the laces deflects balls at varying speeds, the combination of factors can cause instability in the movement — the kind of turbulence, on extreme lev-els, that can cause an airplane to rumble unsteadily through patches of rough air.

Wakefield, for his part, typically planted his fingertips just below the area of the stitching that he described as the *horseshoe,* a patch of white typically adorned by the official logo for Major League Baseball. (Baseballs are stitched in such a way that the laces resemble a pair of horseshoes connected at the two tips on the open end.) The grip allowed for the stitches to run across the top and down the sides of the ball's front side, effectively directing wind in all directions and creating an entirely unpredictable journey.

Wakefield's version of the physics: "Aerodynamically, when you throw it without any spin, it seems to catch the air and there's a vacuum, or a pocket of air behind the ball, that causes it to move around."

And when it moves, as any major league player will tell you, the challenge of hitting it or catching it can be arduous.

In fact, baseball lore is filled with amusing tales and anecdotes about the knuckler, which has caused more than its share of angst for pitchers, catchers, hitters, coaches, and managers alike. Hall of Fame first baseman Willie Stargell, who played for the Pittsburgh Pirates, once suggested that the challenge of throwing strikes with a knuckleball was "like throwing a butterfly with hiccups across the street into your neighbor's mailbox." Richie Hebner, a highly regarded hitter who played much of his career in Philadelphia, once said that trying to hit a knuckleball was "like eating soup with a fork." Longtime catcher and baseball wit Bob Uecker once scoffed at the notion that catching the knuckleball was difficult, arguing that a catcher merely had to "wait [until] it stops rolling, then go to the backstop and pick it up."

Not surprisingly, then, the knuckleball has always been met with a great deal of skepticism, particularly by managers, executives, and evaluators who often enough are at a loss to explain how the knuckleball works and, just as often, why it sometimes does not. Red Sox manager Terry Francona, who managed Wakefield at the end of the pitcher's career, often remarked that the hardest part of handling Wakefield came when it was time to remove him from the game, primarily because the usual indicators did not apply. With conventional pitchers, Francona noted, fatigue is often apparent to the trained eye, and pitch totals have far greater meaning. Toward the end of his stint with the Red Sox, for example, ace Pedro Martinez usually became ineffective anytime he exceeded 100 pitches, the count that put Francona and Red Sox pitching coaches on high alert. But with a knuckleballer like Wakefield, a pitch count of 30 could be just as revealing as 130 — in other words, neither number was particularly revealing at all.

As Clark notes in *The Knucklebook*: "For a knuckleballer, a pitch count of 150 is not a problem — unless it's the first inning."

Adding to everyone's mistrust of the pitch is its schizophrenic nature: the knuckleball can oscillate between effectiveness and ineffectiveness as if possessing multiple personalities. The change can come abruptly and without notice. Whether the result of humidity, wind, or maybe nothing at all, the knuckleball can move dramatically on one pitch and do relatively little on the next, giving managers little advance warning that a pitcher is about to implode. More so than some other pitches, a poorly thrown knuckleball is susceptible to two outcomes in particular — walks and home runs — and any combination of elements can rapidly turn a stable, successful pitching performance into what baseball people might refer to as a *stinker*.

And there is quite simply no way to prepare for it.

Beyond that, because the knuckleball is thrown relatively slowly — Wakefield's knuckler, for instance, was often clocked at 60 to 68 miles per hour, or 25 to 30 miles an hour slower than the average major league fastball — an array of side effects can make even the most accomplished, highly respected, and astute managers sweat.

Said Jim Leyland, who has overseen nearly 3,000 major league games (including some during the early years of Wakefield's career) and is regarded as one of the best managers in baseball history: "One of the reasons is that with runners on base, it's a very tough pitch to catch and you're always worried about it getting away [for passed balls]. You're always holding on tight. Another thing is, even while a guy like Wakefield is really quick to the plate, a lot of guys will still run, try to steal, because the pitch is thrown so much slower and because it's hard to handle."

Add the threat of stolen bases and passed balls to the walks and home runs and what you have, for any manager, is a recipe for a nervous breakdown. Almost to a man, managers are control freaks, and most tend to treat and interpret the knuckleballer the way a young,

single man might regard an attractive, successful single woman in a
bar.

Psycho.

So they do the instinctive thing.

They run in the opposite direction.

Bill Lajoie has spent a lifetime in professional baseball as a player,
scout, and executive, amassing more than 50 years of experience that
have made him one of the most widely respected and highly regarded
evaluators in the history of the game. During a career that began as
a minor league player with the Baltimore Orioles in 1956, Lajoie has
played or worked for franchises in Baltimore, Brooklyn, Los Angeles,
Washington, New York, Minnesota, Cincinnati, Detroit, Atlanta,
Milwaukee, Boston, and Pittsburgh. Through it all, Lajoie has remained
one of the most open-minded men in baseball, someone whose thirst
for the game is so great that he deems any and all perspectives worth
considering.

In 2003, the year that marked his 69th birthday, Lajoie served as an
adviser and special consultant to Theo Epstein, then a 29-year-old in
his first season as general manager of the Boston Red Sox. As much as
the Red Sox hired Lajoie to counterbalance the new, progressive ways
of analytical baseball thinking that someone like Epstein had come to
represent — perpetuated by the Michael Lewis book *Moneyball,* statistical analysis in baseball, or *sabermetrics,* had become the rage — Lajoie
found himself as eager to learn *from* Epstein as he was to impart wisdom to his young boss.

"I've had a saying all my life: believe your eyes. But your eyes are
also looking at a [computer] screen now, and that can help you," said
Lajoie. "This is a great challenge for me — to understand this concept
and to put it to use. I think anybody will tell you I'm making a con-
certed effort to understand. I hope everybody does. It would be easy
for me to sit back and say, 'Bullshit,' but I'm going to learn more about
this game. So why not do it?"

And yet, when it comes to the knuckleball, Bill Lajoie admitted that
he probably has been as biased against the pitch as most any other
conventional thinker in the game.

Of course, in an age when baseball is a multibillion-dollar operation and jobs are at stake on a daily basis, most baseball evaluators
are unwilling to gamble their careers on something so fickle as the
knuckleball. In the eyes of most baseball evaluators, the skills of the
game's positional players have always been measured in five *tools:* arm
strength, speed, fielding, hitting for average, and hitting for power. (A
player who grades well in all five areas is said to be a *five-tool player.*)
With pitchers, the breakdown has always been far simpler. While
evaluators look for pitchers with relatively smooth mechanics or de-
liveries — the smoother the delivery of the pitch, the less the strain on
the arm and the greater the likelihood of a healthy, long, and productive career — the first objective is always the same: power. The harder
a pitcher can throw, the greater is his margin for error and the better
are his chances for success. Even a pitcher with a straight fastball has a
chance of succeeding if he possesses above-average or higher velocity;
baseball history is littered with fireballers who were good enough to
enjoy fairly long careers despite being relatively mediocre pitchers.

After all, someone will almost always take a gamble on a pitcher
with a power arm that can produce baseball's omnipotent weapon: the
strikeout.

Beyond power, a pitcher is graded on the quality of his secondary
pitches — the curveball, changeup, and slider — as well as the supple-
mentary areas of movement, control, and command, the last two of
which are often mistakenly interchanged. (If *control* is the general
ability to throw the ball over the plate, then *command* is the ability to
harness a pitch's lateral and vertical *movement.* A diving or darting target, after all, is always harder to hit.) Combine all three elements with
some measure of velocity and what you have is something akin to Greg
Maddux, a craftsman who won 355 games and pitched more than 5,000
innings with a fluid delivery and an uncanny ability to pierce the strike
zone from an array of angles, or Pedro Martinez, a harder-throwing
power pitcher who commanded an array of secondary pitches so devastating that his 1999 and 2000 seasons forever will remain among the
greatest pitching performances in baseball history.

Now compare all of those pitching assets to the general description of knuckleballers, all of whom throw with almost no power and

possess questionable degrees of command and control. The knuckle-baller throws his pitch, upward of 90 percent of the time, with only one real asset: movement that is often unpredictable or unreliable. In the end, what a manager or scout is left with is a 65-mile-an-hour pitch that can move a lot, a little, or not at all, a list of options that leaves relatively little room for success. The knuckler that moves too much cannot be harnessed or caught; the knuckler that moves too little will be transported to faraway places by opposing hitters as if shipped via Federal Express. Thus, the successful knuckleballer has to walk a tightrope between two dangerous places — self-destruction and certain doom.

"Everybody's looking for power. That's the one thing that remains constant," said Leyland, who has spent nearly a half century in profes-sional baseball as a player, coach, and manager. "I think some of it is just the nature of our game."

As such, while the list of people who have attempted to throw the knuckleball is fairly extensive, the true, successful knuckleballers in baseball history have been relatively few and far between. The origins of the pitch trace back to the early part of the 20th century — there are varying theories as to who, precisely, invented the knuckle-ball — but the concept of throwing a ball without spin is hardly unique. Somewhere along the line, in their never-ending attempt to confuse hitters and disrupt their timing, pitchers recognized that throwing a ball without spin can be extremely effective, mostly as the result of a sharp, downward movement just before the ball reaches home plate. Over the course of baseball history, pitchers have accomplished this in a number of ways, ranging from wrapping the entire hand around the ball (if they can) and holding it deep in the hand — the *palmball,* which is thrown to the plate almost like a shot put — or sticking the ball in the gap between the index and middle fingers — the *forkball* or, later, the *split-fingered fastball.* Regardless of the precise name, the concept was the same.

Remove the spin.

And watch the ball dance.

The knuckleball took its name from the earliest grip: a pitcher would place his thumbs under the ball, then press it against the uppermost knuckles on his index and ring fingers. This method has morphed into the far more common fingertip-grip of the present day — again, the grip that Wakefield uses — though the objective is the same. By holding the ball against the knuckles or by the fingertips, most (if not all) of the friction is eliminated upon release, allowing the ball to travel to the desired target with little or no spin.

"It's kind of a push with your arm and your wrist," said Lajoie. "It's a push rather than a speed thing."

For a scout like Lajoie — and for that matter, a baseball manager or traditional evaluator like Leyland — the concept of a *push* can be difficult to grasp, if only because power and speed are so ingrained in any baseball evaluator's thinking. As a longtime scout, Lajoie can remember occasions when, seated in the traditional scouts' seats behind home plate for a night game, a pitcher would throw with such great arm speed that Lajoie could see a brief burst of perspiration spray from his arm. The phenomenon is visible only at night, when the perspiration reflects in the stadium lights, but it's as sure an indication as any that a pitcher is throwing with great velocity.

Radar guns often can be unnecessary.

"I remember blinking the first time I saw that," Lajoie recalled of the perspiration spray. "And then the ball was past me."

Thus, the question persists: if power is so highly regarded in baseball, why would anyone invest in a knuckleballer at all?

The answer: innings.

Lots of 'em.

On the whole, most people see the game of baseball from the wrong perspective. Final outcomes are reported in the form of scores like 4–3, 7–2, and 6–5 when they could just as easily be reported as 3–4, 2–7, and 5–6. Baseball, after all, is the only game in which the *defense* controls the ball. The idea is to prevent runs as much as to score them. Some would argue that run prevention is the far greater goal of the competition.

That explains why pitching has been, is, and always will be the most valuable commodity in the game, the simplest foundation upon which any formula for success is built.

Without pitching, quite simply, a team has virtually no chance to win consistently.

Given that fundamental truth, the pitcher's simplest objective is the out. To win any regulation game, a team must record three per inning, 27 in all. For as much emphasis as has been placed on pitching statistics over the years — wins, for example, can be terribly misleading because they reflect a *team* accomplishment more than an individual one — certain elements of the game have been taken for granted and glossed over for so long that their meaning has been lost. Outs and, thus, innings are chief among them. During the course of a major league season, the average team totals somewhere in the neighborhood of 1,440 innings pitched, which translates into 4,320 outs per season. Those outs typically are distributed among the members of a pitching staff that undergoes constant change throughout the course of the year. Injured pitchers are replaced by healthy ones, and ineffective pitchers by the potentially more successful. In the end, in the modern era, the successful pitchers on any team record somewhere between 600 and 750 outs per year, placing their innings total somewhere between 200 and 250.

In 2009, during a major league season in which 664 pitchers recorded at least one out — this included some positional players forced to pitch in one-sided losses so as to preserve the health of the real pitchers — a mere 36 pitched 200 innings or more. That number translates into 1.2 pitchers for each of the 30 major league teams. Those 36 pitchers had earned run averages (ERAs) ranging from 2.48 to 5.04, and they pitched for teams that were good, bad, and everywhere in between. While their salaries ranged from the current major league minimum ($424,000 per season for Washington Nationals newbie John Lannan) to a whopping total of more than $23 million per year (for decorated New York Yankees ace C. C. Sabathia), the large majority of those pitchers earned millions of dollars per season and ranked among the highest-paid pitchers in baseball.

To the teams, the innings are what matter as much as anything. The outs are what they will pay for.

And there is nothing an effective knuckleballer can give a team more than a mountain of outs.

"Basically, the game of baseball is a .500 game," said Lajoie, noting that most players and teams lose as much as they win over any significant length of time. "I think it's the innings that become more important with a knuckleball pitcher and the frequency with which he can be used when you evaluate the contribution he can make to a staff."

In the end, it all adds up to the same thing: Outs. Longer outings. Shorter rest. More outs. In the baseball world, knuckleballers are marathoners capable of short sprints in between outings. Sometimes they can run one marathon after the next. And even though there have been only a few select pitchers in baseball history who have effectively thrown the pitch, the payoff has been huge for the teams with the good fortune to have had a knuckleballer on their staff.

Consider: since the start of the 1970 season, a major league pitcher has thrown as many as 330 innings in a season only 11 times; six of them were knuckleballers. (Right-hander Phil Niekro and left-hander Wilbur Wood each accomplished the feat three times.) Since Walter Johnson retired in 1927, no pitcher in the history of the game — including the ageless Nolan Ryan — has thrown more innings (or recorded more outs) than Niekro, who pitched 5,404 innings over the course of 24 full seasons, totaling 16,212 outs and *averaging* slightly more than 225 innings per season. During his career, Niekro finished among the league's top 10 pitchers in innings 11 times; for five consecutive years in the early 1970s, Wood finished in the top *five* of American League hurlers in innings pitched; and in the 1980s, after being named a full-time starting pitcher for the first time in his career, knuckleballer Charlie Hough ripped off a stretch of 12 consecutive seasons during which he totaled just under 2,745 innings and averaged 229 innings pitched, a total that placed him among the most valuable pitchers in baseball.

As for Tim Wakefield, whose career included stints as both a starter and a reliever, his value was infinitely higher in the former role. During his nine full seasons as a starting pitcher for the Red Sox, Wakefield pitched 1,810 innings, an average of slightly more than 201 innings per season during an era when most other pitchers were asked to pitch less, when some were protected to a fault, and when conventional pitchers broke down more frequently while being asked to do *less*.

"With the importance of innings pitched, why the hell hasn't there been more effort to teach this pitch?" asked Lajoie. "Hell, everybody throws a slider. To me, it should be part of a program where you pick certain guys to experiment with. Why not? The length of career is unbelievable on [knuckleballers].

"We have an unwritten rule in baseball: a guy with a good arm who plays a position and can't hit, you almost always try him as a pitcher before releasing him," Lajoie continued. "There is no reason in hell that we can't take a fully coordinated, athletically gifted person who loves baseball and put him in a program where he might be able to develop [as a knuckleballer]. Wakefield is actually getting to the point where he is the last of a dying breed."

Indeed, while the knuckleball will always exist, the population seems to be dwindling. By late in the 2009 season, New York Mets right-hander R. A. Dickey had boosted his fledgling career by joining the list of knuckleballers and was just starting to be regarded as a true knuckleballer who relied on the pitch the large majority of the time. But the knuckleball was being increasingly looked upon as a trick pitch. Few pitchers were throwing it and fewer were teaching it.

As Tim Wakefield approached the end of his career, a long and distinguished line of knuckleballers seemed to be fading with him.

The roots of the knuckleball can be traced back to the early 20th century and perhaps beyond, and knuckleball historians are often quick to mention the Hall of Fame career of knuckleballer Jesse Haines, who won 210 games for the St. Louis Cardinals from 1920 to 1937. And yet, almost all knuckleball discussions begin and end with Hoyt Wilhelm, who won 143 games and saved 227 others while pitching for nine organizations during a 21-year career that ranged from 1952 to 1972.

Wilhelm lived to the age of 80 before dying in 2002. He left behind a career that disproved many theories about the knuckler — specifically that the pitch cannot be as effective at the *end* of the game as it is at the beginning, something Wakefield also would prove — and spawned a lineage of knuckleballers that began with left-hander Wilbur Wood.

"As far as I'm concerned," Wood said of Wilhelm, "he was the king of the pitch."

A New England native who turned 69 late in 2010, Wilbur Forrester Wood was affectionately known as "Wilbah" during a high school career in Belmont, Massachusetts, a suburb of Boston where r's are forever optional and w's are in great supply. As an amateur, Wilbur Wood was a conventional pitcher who won a lot of games. He signed with the Red Sox as a free agent in 1960 and made his major league debut in 1961, though, as he put it, his fastball "was a few yards too short." Wood had dabbled some with the knuckleball as a youngster because his father was an amateur pitcher who threw a palmball, a spinless pitch that captured his son's attention.

"It had no rotation the way he threw it," Wood said of his father's palmball. "Who doesn't want to be like Dad?"

And so son emulated father.

Sort of.

After a relatively undistinguished career with the Red Sox and Pittsburgh Pirates from 1961 to 1965 — he went a combined 1–8 in the major leagues before spending all of 1966 in the minors — Wood was traded from the Pirates to the Chicago White Sox during the off-season prior to the 1967 season. Wood cost Chicago a soon-to-be-30-year-old pitcher named Juan Pizarro, but the White Sox believed that Wood had a great upside as a knuckleballer, particularly if he had the proper guidance and tutelage to harness what was regarded as one of the game's most intriguing weapons.

As it was, the White Sox had the perfect mentor for Wood, an aging, longtime reliever who was coming off a 1966 season during which he went 5–2 with a 1.66 ERA and six saves despite having turned 44 that July.

His name was Hoyt Wilhelm.

For Wood, who was still just 25 entering the 1967 season, the opportunity to serve as an apprentice to someone like Wilhelm was an extraordinary opportunity — and for multiple reasons. For one, Wood was running out of chances. For another, aside from being "the king of the knuckleball," as Wood put it, Wilhelm was one of the few men in baseball history who understood the challenges and nuances of the pitch and could provide Wood with a vital support group of one.

"The way my career was going, I had to do something or I had to pack it up and go home," Wood said. "It was great because you had someone [in Wilhelm] to talk to. A lot of pitching coaches and managers, they don't know a lot about the knuckleball. It's not like they can talk to you about it like it's a curveball or a slider. They don't know that much about it. Johnny Sain [the team pitching coach who won 20 games in a season four times as a pitcher with the Boston Braves] was one of the best pitching coaches around. He came right out and said, 'I can't help you with the knuckleball.' Especially in the beginning, it really helped [having Wilhelm as an adviser] because I had someone to talk to when things were going wrong."

In 1967, during his first season with the White Sox, and pitching largely as a relief pitcher, Wood appeared in 51 games and had by far his best major league season, going 4–2 with a 2.45 ERA and four saves. A year later, with Wilhelm still watching closely — Chicago had the most unusual potential to summon knuckleballers out of its bullpen from both the left *and* right sides — Wood pitched in a major league–leading 88 games while going 13–12 with a 1.87 ERA and 16 saves. Following that season, the White Sox lost the then-46-year-old Wilhelm to the Kansas City Royals via the major league expansion draft, though by then the student had learned enough from the teacher to have become equipped with his own diagnostics program.

From 1968 to 1970, during a span covering three full major league seasons, nobody pitched in more major league games than Wilbur Wood — and the competition wasn't even close. While going 32–36 ("Basically, the game of baseball is a .500 game"), Wood made an impressive 241 appearances, 33 more than his next-closest peer. While posting a 2.50 ERA and amassing 52 saves, Wood pitched precisely 400⅓ innings — also the highest total in baseball among all relief pitchers. Wood had developed into such a force that, following the 1970 campaign, the White Sox did a very logical thing.

They increased his workload.

And they made him a starter.

Over the next five seasons, from 1971 to 1975, Wood started 224 games, more than any pitcher in baseball, and won 106, more than any pitcher in the game except eventual Hall of Famer Jim "Catfish" Hunter. Of his 224 starts, an incredible 199 came on fewer than four days of rest. (The next-closest man on the list, power left-hander Mickey Lolich, made 140 starts on fewer than four days.) During those five seasons, Wood ranked among the major league leaders with a 3.08 ERA. He recalled regularly pitching two games a *week* — the first in a weekly Sunday doubleheader and then, on just two days of rest, another on the following Wednesday. For a salary that ended up in the range of $125,000 per season during the most productive years of his career, Wood essentially did the work of two modern pitchers, who might earn somewhere in the neighborhood of $10 million — or more — *each*.

"I went through a period where I pitched on Sunday and Wednesday for about two and a half years," Wood recalled. "I was filling two spots because of the doubleheader. The team didn't have to find another starter," he explained, and at a time when three days of rest was customary for pitchers, "that kept everybody else on a four-day rotation."

Indeed, for as much as Wood gave the White Sox, the benefit to the team was even greater. Because Wood was taking up so much of the workload as well as pitching on short rest, the White Sox could handle everyone else on the pitching staff with greater care and boost their productivity.

Along the way, Wood's durability became the stuff of legend, particularly during a 1973 season in which he led the league with 359⅓ innings pitched, a total of 17⅓ innings *fewer* than the mind-numbing 376⅔ innings he pitched in 1972 and the highest total in baseball history since World War I. (Of the five highest single-season innings totals posted since 1919, Wood's 1972 and 1973 seasons rank as numbers 1 and 5.) During a doubleheader against the New York Yankees on July 20, 1973, Wood accomplished the rare feat of starting both games of a doubleheader, something no pitcher has accomplished since. And while White Sox manager Chuck Tanner remembered starting Wood in the second game solely because Wood did not record an out among the six batters he faced in the first inning of the first game — as it happened, the White Sox lost both games — no manager today would even consider such a maneuver under similar circumstances for fear of injuring a pitcher in whom his bosses had made a multimillion-dollar investment. The idea of such caution made Wood chuckle.

"I've said this to enough people, but I don't think they throw enough," Wood said of today's pitchers, be they knuckleballers or conventional pitchers. "I could not pitch every five or six days and have the same command or feel. I'd be lost, to be honest with you."

Still just 34 — prime years for a knuckleballer — Wood was on his way to having another typically productive season in 1976 when he took the mound for his seventh start of the season on May 9 at Tiger Stadium in Detroit. Paired against Detroit Tigers right-hander Joe Coleman, Wood had a 2–0 lead with two outs and the bases empty in the bottom of the sixth inning when outfielder Ron Leflore lined a pitch back to the mound. Unable to prevent the drive from striking his left knee — because he threw left-handed, Wood's glove was on his right hand — Wood suffered a shattered kneecap that ended his season, stripping the White Sox of a man who had recorded 5,214 outs since the start of the 1971 baseball season.

Though Wood returned to pitch 290⅔ more innings during his career, he was never the same after the injury, and he pitched his last major league game in 1978 as a member of the White Sox. In his career, he pitched a total of 2,684 innings and won 164 games, all but one of them for the White Sox. Wood's success brought him full circle and made him a resource for other budding knuckleballers. He played in an era before baseball salaries exploded to the current, life-altering levels, and so he spent many years outside of the game working conventional jobs to support his family. Nevertheless, Wood remembered discussing by phone the challenge of pitching on two days of rest with a right-hander named Phil Niekro. The two still have never met. Other friends and colleagues have also called Wood from time to time, usually because they need his advice or counseling on a pitch that has perplexed some of baseball's best traditional minds throughout its history.

In 1994, for example, former teammate Pete Vuckovich called Wood from Buffalo, where Vuckovich was serving as the pitching coach for the Buffalo Bisons, the Triple A affiliate of the Pittsburgh Pirates. The Bisons were working with a frustrated young knuckleballer searching to unlock the secrets of the knuckler, and Vuckovich wanted to know if Wood would be willing to visit with the pitcher.

The young man's name was Tim Wakefield.

"I was working selling pharmaceuticals at the time, and I only had two weeks of vacation," Wood recalled. "He said, 'I'd like you to come to Buffalo and work with Tim.' I said, 'Pete, that'd be great, but I only get two weeks of vacation, and my wife teaches school. I'm not sure she'd like to come to Buffalo during the summer. If you were in Florida, it would be a different situation.'"

Alas, following a successful 11-year career as a major league pitcher — albeit a conventional one — Pete Vuckovich was on his own.

And he had no answers for Wakefield.

Philip Henry Niekro is that rarest of rare beings, and not solely because Niekro is in the Hall of Fame, or because he won 318 games, or because he threw a knuckleball. What makes Niekro different as much as anything else is that he essentially was a knuckleballer from conception. He did not learn the pitch as a novelty, adopt it as a way to revive a dying career, or reluctantly commit to it because he had an arm injury. Niekro learned the knuckleball the way Tiger Woods learned golf — from childhood. He is the closest thing baseball has ever had to a true knuckleballing prodigy.

For that reason, no other knuckleballer in baseball will ever be known as "Knucksie."

"My father was a coal miner. I have [newspaper] clippings of him from when he was 16, 17, or 18, when he used to pitch [recreationally]. He hurt his arm, and another pitcher taught him the knuckler. He taught me how to hold it, and that was it," Niekro recalled. "He really didn't know what it was or where it was going to get me.

"When I retired in 1987, I was still trying to master it," Niekro continued. "I was still trying to figure out what it does or why it does what it does. It never does the same thing twice."

And yet, to the extent that any pitcher has ever been able to control the knuckler and command it — to know exactly what it is going to do and when it is going to do it — nobody has had more success than Niekro.

During a 24-year major league career that ranged from 1964 to 1987, Niekro made 716 starts (ranking fifth most all-time) and posted a 3.35 ERA, finishing four times in the top 10 of the league ERA leaders. Twelve times he finished among the top 10 pitchers in the league in wins. He went to five All-Star Games and in four seasons led the league in innings.

Niekro was, in short, everything a knuckleballer had ever been, could be, or will be again.

Nonetheless, as is almost always the case with any knuckleballer (or, for that matter, pitcher) who benefited from the baseball equivalent of a big break, Phil Niekro had to overcome certain obstacles during his career. He pitched through much of the minor leagues as a reliever, a role he continued after being called up to the Braves for the first time in 1964. Niekro remained in the bullpen until 1967. In the middle of that season, the Braves traded catcher, first baseman, and outfielder Gene Oliver to the Philadelphia Phillies for a colorful and defensive-minded catcher, Bob Uecker, who was nearing the end of his career. Uecker would bat just .146 in 62 games for the Braves before being released at season's end, but what he taught Phil Niekro helped launch one of the great knuckleballing careers of all time by delivering a message to Niekro that has since been delivered to scores of young pitchers seeking to establish their place in the game.

Trust your stuff.

In Niekro's case, that meant investing fully in the knuckleball.

Prior to 1967, Niekro remembered, there was still a great deal of trepidation with regard to the knuckler, particularly with men on base. Managers didn't trust it. Catchers would not call for it. That all changed with Uecker, who recognized the brilliance of Niekro's knuckler and was willing to call it at anytime, all the time, no matter the circumstances and the consequences be damned. As much as anyone who ever caught Niekro, Uecker understood that everything in baseball comes with a trade-off — throwing a fastball often comes at the cost of the curve, for instance — and that the trade-off with the knuckleball could be well worth it.

Said Niekro of his career before Uecker arrived, "There were situations where they had to take me out of games because catchers wouldn't call it in certain situations. When Uecker came over, he didn't care. He said, 'I'm going to call that pitch in situations where other guys won't.'"

Indeed, as accomplished as Atlanta's starting catcher was at the time, he admitted to harboring a certain uneasiness when it came time to handle Niekro's knuckleball. From 1966 to 1968, Atlanta's catcher was none other than Joe Torre, who hit 252 home runs during an 18-year career and later would manage the New York Yankees to four World Series titles in five years during an accomplished run as a major league manager. But when he talked about handling the knuckler, even Torre seemed to remember the pitch as more of a headache inducer than an out producer, a sentiment shared by a range of catchers throughout history.

Mused Torre: "Once the Braves traded for Uecker, I was off the hook."

And Niekro, for his part, was off and running.

After Uecker's first start with the Braves on June 9, 1967, Niekro would go on to have a 10–7 season with three saves and a 1.90 ERA in 165⅔ innings over 23 appearances (20 starts). The Braves went 15–8 anytime he threw a single pitch. Uecker allowed 25 passed balls in 59 games with the Braves — and Niekro finished as the National League leader in ERA, the only time in his 24-year career he accomplished that feat.

From that point forward, over the final 20 years of his career, Niekro made 695 starts for the Braves — more than any pitcher in baseball — and just 44 relief appearances while winning an additional 301 games. By that point, Niekro's younger brother, Joe, looking to jump-start his fledgling major league career, had also incorporated the knuckler into his repertoire. Over the next 22 years, he would win 221 games (with 204 losses) and pitch 3,584⅓ innings, bringing the Niekro family contribution to major league baseball to an astonishing 539 victories and 8,988⅓ innings, the latter of which translates into 26,965 outs.

Five years younger than his older brother, Joe Niekro had a far more traditional baseball upbringing, playing in Little League and the Colt Leagues; these opportunities had not been open to his older brother. ("My first organized game was as a freshman in high school," Phil Niekro said.) As Joe Niekro grew to be six-foot-one and roughly 200 pounds, he built a pitching arsenal around a fastball and curveball, a combination that made him a third-round selection of the Chicago Cubs in 1966. (Phil Niekro was undrafted.) Joe Niekro spent six years pitching for the Cubs, San Diego Padres, and Detroit Tigers before he turned 28 years old, at which point the Atlanta Braves claimed him off waivers and reunited him with his older brother, who did for his younger brother what Bob Uecker had done for him.

"[Joe] was about to retire," Phil Niekro recalled. "He had been with about two or three clubs, and he said he wanted to try the knuckleball because they wouldn't let him throw it in [those other places]. I said, 'Joe, take it out of your pocket, you've got to do it.'"

Taking his brother's advice, Niekro spent two years as a reliever with the Braves, who then sold Joe Niekro to the Houston Astros, who used the younger Niekro almost exclusively as a reliever in 1975. They began the next year shuttling Joe Niekro to and from their bullpen, but he produced the kind of results that finally forced them to make him a full-time starter. In eight seasons from 1977 to 1984, Joe Niekro went 125–92 — older brother Phil went 122–105 during the same stretch — while ranking fourth in all of baseball in innings pitched (1,851), behind only four-time Cy Young Award winner Steve Carlton of the Philadelphia Phillies, his big brother (of course), and Montreal Expos right-hander Steve Rogers. In 1979, while going 21–11 with a 3.00 ERA, Joe Niekro was selected to his only All-Star Game, something his brother accomplished five times. Traditional baseball's concerns about the knuckler reared their ugly heads at those All-Star Games.

In their six All-Star appearances, the Niekro brothers faced just four batters, all by Phil. For all that the knuckleballing brothers accomplished during their careers, for all that the knuckleball had proven it could accomplish, there were still those who did not trust it on the grandest stages, who wanted nothing to do with a pitch that could confound pitchers and managers to the point of fear.

With the knuckleball, after all, some level of discrimination is almost always part of the story.

Three

●

Knuckleballs suck.

*— Geno Petralli, former catcher, after a particularly
tough night with knuckleballer Charlie Hough*

L IKE MOST PEOPLE on the receiving end of the knuckleball,
Tim Wakefield initially treated the pitch with skepticism, frustration, and distrust. Neither Wakefield nor his father, Steve,
remembers exactly how old Wakefield was when Steve started throwing knuckleballs to Tim and his sister, Kelly, while playing catch in the
yard of their home in Melbourne, Florida, but both generally agree
that Tim was probably seven or eight, maybe on the verge of starting
Little League. What they also agree upon, with absolute certainty, is
the way Tim reacted to the pitch that would serve as the foundation for
a long and productive major league career. He despised it.

Wakefield would come home from school or his father would return from playing softball, and the son wanted to play catch with his
father. Wakefield enjoyed those times until the Norman Rockwell moment fell apart when his father began throwing the knuckleball, a pitch
Wakefield found impossible to catch — which, of course, was all part of
Steve Wakefield's plan.

Dad, stop that.

"You know, as a father, I never refused to play catch with him or
even Kelly," said a chuckling Steve Wakefield, an accomplished high
school sprinter who later played softball as an adult. "It's something

that I felt like I had to do. I robbed my kids of a lot of things because I was so dedicated to softball, so if he asked me to go out in the yard and play catch, I always said yes. But then he'd want to play and play and play, so I started throwing knuckleballs at him. He didn't like it. Eventually he'd say, 'Okay, I've had enough.'"

And so, at an early age, Tim Wakefield learned that the knuckleball could be a *weapon,* something used to fluster people, even make them quit.

Had enough yet?

By the time Wakefield began throwing knuckleballs himself as a teenager—his father, of course, had shown him the grip—the pitch had become nothing more than a toy for him, something to be played with to help pass the time. Wakefield looked at the pitch like he might have looked at a Frisbee. He admitted that, in the beginning, he saw the pitch the same way almost everyone else does—as if it were a magic trick or a party stunt. He would throw it to teammates while playing catch and getting his arm loose before games, sometimes during pregame warm-ups if he was scheduled to pitch, but almost never in competition and never with the idea that it was a real option.

Of course, Wakefield was nowhere near the major leagues then. He was still a boy growing up in Melbourne, Florida, a city of 75,000 people located halfway up the east coast of the Florida peninsula, midway between West Palm Beach and Daytona. His father Steve worked the early shift from 3:00 to 11:00 AM, designing circuits as a draftsman for the Harris Corporation, an innovation and electronics firm that also eventually employed Wakefield's mother, Judy, as a purchaser and professional assistant. The message was clear: the Wakefields woke up every day and did their jobs, no matter what the hours were, no matter what outside influences might have been pulling at them. Mom and Dad both went to work. Everything needed to get done at one point or another, so there was no point in quibbling over petty issues, over who did what.

Besides playing catch with his father in the backyard of their home—where the knuckleball became part of his repertoire early in life—Wakefield went to public schools as a child, and like most boys who spent mornings, afternoons, and evenings thinking about baseball, he liked to hit. He *wanted* to hit. It was the most enjoyable part of the game and something to look forward to. Unless he was pitching, the time he spent in the field, on defense, could be dull and seemingly endless. Many years later, Judy Wakefield still had memories of Tim going out into the yard, toting a plastic bat and ball. Standing in the back yard of the home that the Wakefields bought in 1969 — and where they still reside — Tim would hit the ball over the house and into the front yard. He then would scamper around to the front, toss the ball up in the air again, and hit it over the roof and into the backyard. He would continue the practice, hitting the ball over and over — effectively playing a game of tennis with himself, albeit with the instruments he would employ throughout the rest of his life — until he got bored or tired or it got too dark.

"Every day," Judy Wakefield said by way of describing her son's affection for the game. Baseball "was his life" even at a young age. "He played his first game at five [years old]," she recalled. "He played T-ball, and then he never stopped. I think he played every year after that. We could see in Little League [that he was advanced]. He just kept getting better."

During the 1960s, 1970s, and 1980s, there were no major league teams in Florida, but the state was home to some of the better college programs in the country and the weather was conducive for baseball. In the late winter and early spring, major league teams trained throughout the state. Minor league clubs were scattered about Florida, a good many of them in the Class A Florida State League, where teams sent draftees and prospects to begin playing in the earlier stages of their development. From Little League through high school and college, the baseball season in Florida was much longer than in most other parts of the country, a fact that paid obvious dividends for the boys and girls raised there who dreamed about playing outdoor sports.

If Tim Wakefield wanted to play baseball almost every day, he could — and he did. There was nothing to prevent him from doing so. Like other boys growing up in California, Arizona, Texas, and Florida — states that would produce nearly half of all professional players drafted or signed during the 30-year period from 1965 to 1994, the period during which Wakefield grew up—Wakefield had the advantage of endless practice time to reinforce his obsession with baseball. In short, Tim Wakefield grew up in a baseball hotbed that allowed him to develop and cultivate his talents even though, until the early 1990s, the state of Florida still lacked something that it desperately wanted, something that would further validate its place as a baseball breeding ground.

A major league team.

Wakefield adopted the Atlanta Braves as his team of choice, largely because the Braves were the closest major league team to Melbourne. His favorite player was Dale Murphy, the multitalented Braves slugger who won consecutive Most Valuable Player Awards in 1982 and 1983 and who had slowly matured into one of the most complete players in baseball. During his prime, Murphy was a Gold Glove outfielder and elite hitter who once stole as many as 30 bases in a season, a man whose skills were so comprehensive that he could do just about anything on a baseball diamond. Murphy had caught and played in both the infield and the outfield, he could hit for average and power, and he could run, throw, and play defense. Murphy played hard and played hurt, and his durability was legendary. During the heart of his career, an 11-year period that began in 1980 and ran through 1990, Murphy never missed more than eight games in any season, and at one point he played four consecutive seasons in which he appeared in the maximum 162 games.

Dale Murphy, like Steve Wakefield, almost never missed a day of work.

And like Tim Wakefield would later prove on the pitcher's mound, Murphy could contribute to his team at a number of different positions and with a number of different skills.

That's who I want to be.

Wakefield was a skilled athlete as a boy and teen in Melbourne, having inherited the athletic ability of his father (though Steve Wakefield never played baseball). Wakefield's sister Kelly also was innately athletic, though she later lost interest in the game—she played softball for a time — and in sports altogether. For Wakefield, the opposite was true. With baseball in particular, there was no such thing as too much. By the time he reached his midteens, Wakefield was one of the better players at Eau Gallie High School in Melbourne, the same high school that major leaguer Prince Fielder would later attend. His previous coaches had utilized his advanced skills at two of the more important positions on the diamond: like most major leaguers in their youth, Wakefield had pitched and played shortstop. That changed some at Eau Gallie, where coach Ken Campbell started playing Wakefield at first base because the team had a better shortstop. Wakefield also continued to pitch, albeit without really using the knuckleball. He would throw the pitch while playing catch with his teammates and sometimes dared to unveil it in a game "if we were winning like 10–0 or something." The pitch was not seen by anyone, however, as something *serious* and was regarded more as a novelty.

By the time he graduated from high school, Wakefield was slotted as a Division 2–caliber college talent; he had the skill, but lacked some of the size, that would have made him an elite Division 1 college player. His options were relatively limited, particularly when Brevard Community College was the only program to offer him a baseball scholarship. BCC was an established junior college baseball program in Melbourne, and enrolling there allowed Wakefield to remain close to home. The idea was that he would distinguish himself at BCC, continue to develop, and maybe transfer to a bigger college program like Miami or Tampa or Florida after his sophomore year. In the short term, the comfort of being close to home could help him, something that would prove to be true over the course of his career.

It means something to me to be here.

Of course, as is usually true with most anything involving the knuckleball and those with the skill to unleash it, things did not go entirely according to plan.

For Tim Wakefield, the dips and turns were about to begin.

In Florida — or more accurately, throughout the warm-weather regions of the United States — college baseball is a year-round sport. There is no real off-season. Teams work out and practice during the fall semester, making preparations for the start of the official season in spring. Baseball is serious business in Florida. Practice time is seen as instrumental in the development and success of a player, and so baseball was immediately part of Wakefield's curriculum at BCC.

At the time, the coach at Brevard Community College was a man named Ernie Rosseau, a native of Nyack, New York, who had attended Satellite High School in Satellite Beach, Florida, and played college baseball years earlier at Florida Tech, located in Melbourne. Rosseau had spent four seasons as an outfielder in the minor league system of the St. Louis Cardinals, where he climbed as high as Double A. Rosseau's college coach, Les Hall, remembered Rosseau as tough, hard-nosed, and "demanding," the kind of player who almost certainly would go on to become a coach if and when his playing career ended.

As a coach, unsurprisingly, Rosseau took the same aggressive approach he had brought to the game as a player, a philosophy that generally worked for him and produced a long, accomplished career, including a pair of junior college national championships and job opportunities with an assortment of major league organizations.

In Wakefield's case, however, the coach and the player disagreed from the start. Wakefield thought that his scholarship meant something, that having been recruited entitled him to a spot on the team. In Rosseau's eyes, that was the furthest thing from the truth. Wakefield remembered showing up at the first day of team workouts in the fall and recognizing that most every other player at BCC was just as good as he was — if not better — and that a starting position on the team was not a given. The change made him uneasy. He suddenly had the feeling that he was not wanted. The transition to college and the challenge of winning a starting position were both far more difficult than Wakefield had imagined, and so between the fall and spring semesters he did something he never imagined himself doing. He quit the baseball team.

Wakefield's inability to cope undoubtedly was a reflection of his immaturity at that stage of his life as much as it was a comment on

Rosseau, whom Wakefield would later come to respect. In retrospect, he would see that he had made a mistake.

It just didn't work out. I was immature. Those kinds of things happen.

After remaining at BCC as a student for the balance of his freshman year, Wakefield resumed playing baseball for an assortment of select teams in the Melbourne area, including a team in a summer league for 16- to 18-year-olds. His decision to leave the BCC team had reached Hall, the same man who had coached Rosseau years earlier and who happened to be friendly with Steve Wakefield. Hall was the head coach at the Florida Institute of Technology — known today as Florida Tech — a school that played its games in the Sunshine State Conference, then regarded as one of the better Division 2 baseball conferences in the country.

Through his wife, who had been a teacher at Melbourne High School, Hall knew of Steve Wakefield's standing as a track athlete in local history, and he certainly knew of Tim Wakefield's baseball career at Eau Gallie. Hall initially had not spent a great deal of time trying to recruit Wakefield out of high school because he felt he had little opportunity of securing him; Wakefield's long-term goal at the time had been to transfer to a bigger Division 1 program, and Hall thought he would have seemed like a misfit among a collection of Florida Tech players who were students first and athletes second.

"Back then, Florida Tech was known for its engineering program," Hall, 74, said in the fall of 2010. "The [students there] wanted to be engineers. They didn't want to be baseball players.

"Tim wasn't really a pitcher then. He was a position player, and he was very good. He was a natural athlete. He could play all kinds of sports."

Florida Tech offered Wakefield a number of possibilities, all of them attractive. Because he had never played in a game at BCC, Wakefield could make the jump without using a year of his athletic eligibility, effectively becoming a *redshirt* freshman in the fall of 1985. (Though a sophomore under academic guidelines, he would qualify as a freshman athletically and still possess four years of eligibility.) Wakefield would get a better education at Florida Tech, he could still be close to home, and there remained the possibility that if he blossomed, he could transfer to a bigger program where he might be able to advance his playing career.

And finally, at a place like Florida Tech, Wakefield could effectively start right away to get the playing time he needed to develop.

This is more my speed.

Hall, for his part, knew that Wakefield could excel at Division 2, and Wakefield took very little time to prove him right. Wakefield's addition to the team had an immediate and profound impact on the performance of the Florida Tech squad: the school's program went, in the words of the coach, "from mediocre to very good" almost overnight. In the spring of 1986, Wakefield still had yet to mature physically, but he was so eager and willing to do whatever Hall asked that he fit in immediately.

"His first year at Florida Tech, we were short of pitchers at one point," Hall recalled. "We were playing a national schedule, and it was a nonconference game, so I was looking for options. We needed to save our pitching [for more important games], so he volunteered to pitch. He was throwing in the bullpen, and he threw a knuckleball, and the kid who was catching him couldn't handle it. I remember him looking at Tim and saying, 'I don't think we should use that pitch, it's not very good.'"

In fact, though relatively no one recognized it at the time, the opposite was true.

Tim Wakefield's knuckleball was *too* good.

Still, Hall also regarded the pitch as nothing more than a party trick at the time, and in fact he fully believed that Wakefield's future rested in his abilities as a hitter. Hall recalled a game against Bethune-Cookman College during one of Wakefield's first seasons in which he belted a home run to right-center field that caught everyone's attention — "It was a bomb," mused Hall — and not solely for the distance the ball traveled. Wakefield, according to Hall, was a pull hitter in college. As a right-handed hitter, Wakefield's power was primarily to the left side of the field. At any level, for a right-handed batter, hitting a ball out to *right-center* required an exceptional amount of strength, discipline, and hand-eye coordination. The mechanics had to be perfect. And if a player could demonstrate that kind of ability consistently, he possessed the kind of exceptional talent that might draw the attention of professional scouts.

"He worked hard at it," Hall said of Wakefield's commitment to hitting. "He loved to hit. That's what he really liked. He was a good first baseman, too, but hitting—that's what he really liked to do."

And that is also what Tim Wakefield did well.

Between his freshman and sophomore years, a period that coincided with his physical maturation—and remember, Wakefield effectively had the academic standing of a sophomore heading into his junior year, meaning he was a year older than many of his classmates—he fully invested in working out. When he returned to school in the fall, he was bigger and stronger than he had ever been. Wakefield struggled with the academics at Florida Tech—"I almost failed out of school," he said—but the baseball began coming more and more easily to him, to the point where he started to be recognized as a local phenom. In Wakefield's second season at Florida Tech, in the spring of 1987, he was compared routinely to a first baseman from the University of Tampa, Tino Martinez, a local prodigy who had played his high school baseball at Jefferson High School in Tampa. During the same spring, while Martinez was hitting 24 home runs for Tampa, Wakefield hit 22—in 48 games, no less—for Florida Tech. Local fans and media gave intense coverage to the two blossoming talents in the area—one batting left-handed (Martinez), one batting right-handed (Wakefield)—and the future for each seemed extremely bright.

By the spring of 1988 Martinez was seen as one of the best players in the country, but Tim Wakefield still was seen as a developing prospect, if for no other reason than the fact that he had matured later. For hitters especially, size and strength are important assets because the pitching gets more challenging at every level of development. The average velocity with which pitches are thrown increases dramatically at the professional levels. Off-speed pitches change direction far more acutely—and at higher speeds. The transition from aluminum bats (used in college) to wooden bats (used in professional play) is another major adjustment. Players like Martinez were seen as virtual can't-miss prospects because they hit everything and anything from a young age — and for power — whereas someone like Wakefield was still regarded as something of a *project*.

Nonetheless, Tim Wakefield knew he had a chance to be drafted.

In June 1988, following a junior season in which he hit 13 more homers and raised his career total to a school record 40 — the record still stands — the Pittsburgh Pirates grabbed Wakefield in the eighth round of the draft with the 200th overall selection. (Martinez, by contrast, was the 14th overall player taken, in the first round, by the Seattle Mariners.) Wakefield was elated. He wanted to turn pro immediately. Steve and Judy Wakefield were similarly excited about the prospect of their son becoming a major leaguer — "You're always hopeful, but that's a big dream," Judy Wakefield said — and there was little doubt that Tim would sign relatively quickly. Hall, for one, remembered advising Wakefield throughout the process, but Florida Tech was hardly a baseball factory and the experience was new for all of them.

"I was at his house with his mom and his dad when he signed with the Pirates," Hall recalled. "I remember during the process [of negotiations], Tim turned to me and said, 'What do you think I should do?' I said, 'Tim, I don't know, but I'll tell you one thing: don't take the first offer.'"

With some minor haggling, Wakefield negotiated a deal with the Pirates that guaranteed him a signing bonus of just $15,000 and ensured that the Pittsburgh organization would pay for the balance of his schooling, if and when Wakefield returned to college. At the time, the Wakefields believed that was a good deal for an eighth-round selection, because it ensured their son some security in the event that his major league career did not work out. Wakefield himself, of course, was certain that signing with the Pirates would eventually produce a major league career, a typical expectation for a young man approaching his 22nd birthday. He had excelled everywhere he played. On the baseball diamond, he was as confident in his abilities as anyone. Wakefield never stopped to consider that he was one of thousands of minor league players who aspired to make it to the major leagues and that the odds were overwhelmingly stacked against him. He never considered failure or even hardship.

During the summer of 1988, along with his parents, Tim Wakefield made the trip from Melbourne to Bradenton, across the flatness of the Florida peninsula, entirely unsure of what to expect. Baseball was an adventure now. He would be competing against dozens of other prospects and draft picks just like him. The Pirates had selected 66 players in the 1988 draft, and those who had signed quickly were asked to report to extended spring training at Pittsburgh's training facility along the Gulf Coast. As the newest members of the Pirates organization arrived, all of them with the hope of making it to the major leagues, Wakefield felt like a college freshman at BCC again, showing up for school amid a mountain of cardboard boxes, packing tape, and wild uncertainty.

How we got here doesn't matter. We're all the same now. Nobody is going to give me anything.

"Everybody was even. Everybody was good," Wakefield said. "It was a lot like the switch I made from high school to college. It was a huge adjustment."

In the grand scheme of any baseball career, extended spring training, in or around the time of the draft, qualifies as the major league equivalent of freshman orientation, or perhaps matriculation. The idea is to get everyone acclimated to a new environment, new life, new existence. The minor league structure subsequently allows teams to assign players to new locations immediately, and players are assigned according to their level of skill. Some begin at higher levels and some at lower levels, but all generally are faced with the same responsibilities. The idea is to show up every day, work hard, get better, and advance to the next level.

Truth be told, Tim Wakefield did not need long to learn that his hitting skills were short, that the power he demonstrated in college would not translate to the next level, that the journey would be difficult. As a starting point, the Pirates assigned Wakefield to their affiliate in the New York–Penn League at Watertown, New York, a transitional league designed to help assimilate amateurs to a professional life. The New York–Penn League is the lowest level of minor league play — Class A — and it plays a *short* season of roughly 75 games. Because the season typically begins in June and runs through the summer, teams can immediately place those players from the annual June draft who signed quickly and showed the capability to play right away.

At Watertown, Wakefield's first career hit as a professional was a home run in a game during which he went 3-for-4, a performance that might have launched the career of one of the game's great hitters had it not been for the simple fact that, in Wakefield's words, "it was all downhill from there." Wakefield had trouble adjusting to the wooden bats — years later he would playfully explain his difficulties by telling people that he was "allergic to wood" — but the problem caused him quite a bit of consternation at the time. And living in New York felt much different to him than living near the campuses of BCC or Florida Tech. Compared with his transitions in college — to BCC and then to Florida Tech — Wakefield saw the start of his career as something far more real, more permanent, more intimidating.

This is my job now.

He remembered feeling alone when his parents drove him to Bradenton for extended spring — "They basically just dropped me off and left — and I don't mean that negatively," he said — and he felt even more isolated after being assigned to Watertown.

Nobody here knows me.

He was earning a mere $700 per month. Along with a pair of teammates whom he had just met, Wakefield rented a room in the house of an elderly woman for $50 a week. He rode a bike to and from the stadium. He remembered his parents being "horrified" at these arrangements when they first came to visit him, though Wakefield was too young and too inexperienced to know any better.

All in all, the start of Wakefield's professional career was hardly what he had envisioned, particularly when reality further intruded.

Shortly after arriving at Watertown, Wakefield learned of the death of his grandfather, Lester Wakefield, with whom he had shared an extremely close relationship. His grandfather had been battling cancer, and Wakefield remembered being "devastated" by his death. He always had been able to confide in his grandfather, to speak to him, to share things with him. Hall was among those who described Lester Wakefield as "Tim's best friend," and with his death, Wakefield spent a good deal of his first official camp dwelling on what he had lost instead of the opportunity he had gained. He found it impossible to focus on baseball.

"It was really the first time I had to deal with something like that," Wakefield said of Lester's death. "He was somebody who came to all my games, and he took me fishing all the time. It was my first time away from home. I don't remember if it was my mom or my dad who called me with the news, but I flew to Virginia and met up with an aunt and uncle, who drove me home. Those two or three days were a complete fog. I was depressed. Having to leave early and go back to work was very difficult."

Along with baseball and fishing, Lester Wakefield shared something else with his grandson: music. Lester enjoyed playing the guitar, and he had spent some time trying to teach the skill to Tim before he died. The lessons never were completed. When Wakefield inherited the guitars his grandfather left behind, he committed himself to completing the teaching that his grandfather could not. And he did indeed teach himself to play the guitar, a skill he would never lose. Wakefield took a certain amount of gratification in that accomplishment, a sense of fulfillment from having applied some of the lessons his grandfather taught him, and not just with the guitar.

You have more talent than you think you do. You can adjust. You can still succeed.

Just the same, Wakefield's return to Watertown was a struggle: it was immediately evident that he would ultimately fail as a hitter, that the level of competition had exceeded his talent. In 54 games at Watertown, Wakefield went 30-for-159 — a .189 average — with just nine extra-base hits. Pitchers overpowered him. He could not make good contact consistently. Even in Class A, pitchers threw much harder than they did in college, and the crispness of their breaking pitches did not compare.

Had Wakefield been able to hit some home runs despite a low batting average, the Pirates might have seen value in his talents. There was always latitude for a power hitter—who might grow in plate discipline and contact—because, quite simply, power cannot be taught. Nevertheless, the early signs were beyond discouraging—and for obvious reasons. If Tim Wakefield could not hit the pitching at Watertown, he certainly would not be able to hit the pitching in Boston, Chicago, New York, or Los Angeles—not now, not ever. A few months at Watertown hardly qualified as a final verdict on Wakefield's abilities, but it was an indication that he had farther to travel than anyone might have guessed.

Wakefield returned home for the winter disappointed by his first professional season, and neither his performance nor his prognosis improved the following spring. He went back to Bradenton in February, when the Pirates began minor league camp, and he failed to make *any* of the club's affiliates out of spring training. He was caught in the netherworld between the lowest levels of minor league baseball and the highest level of amateur play, a no-man's-land that sends the large majority of aspiring professional baseball players off to lives filled with bar stools, beer taps, gas stations, mail rooms, public works, and office jobs. Wakefield was effectively relegated to the *practice squad* of professional baseball—Bradenton served as the "Land of Misfit Toys" for those struggling minor leaguers who were waiting for someone, somewhere, to suffer from an injury or extended failure.

For many of the players in extended spring training, the days could be a torturous exercise in frustration. There was the time before and after baseball, and then there was the time during. Wakefield was among those players who anxiously showed up at camp, put on their uniforms, and took the field not knowing how many more days they would be asked back. After the workouts, they got out of uniform and left with the same concerns. In between, Wakefield worked out and played in loosely structured games against players in other organizations living the same existence, the time they spent on the field often remaining as enjoyable as it had ever been. The baseball was fun. Baseball was the reason they were there. Baseball was why they lined up and tossed the ball back and forth to one another, throwing curveballs and screwballs and, yes, knuckleballs, while wondering how much longer they would be asked to participate.

Daily, Tim Wakefield was among those who wondered.

He had little idea or understanding that the key to success was already in his possession, like the ability to play a guitar, and that it only needed to be unlocked, nurtured, and harvested.

Four

•

They say you don't want to have a knuckleballer pitching for
you or against you.

— *Longtime Los Angeles Dodgers manager Tommy Lasorda*

BACK IN MELBOURNE, often at dusk, Steve Wakefield
brought out the knuckleball with the intention of driving Tim
Wakefield back into the house. But in the Pittsburgh Pirates
organization during the late spring and summer of 1989, the knuckleball, as it turned out, was all that prevented Tim Wakefield from being
sent home.

Wakefield was among the Pirates lined up on the field before an
extended-spring game that year, playing catch with outfielder Jon
Martin, who had been selected in the 10th round, two rounds after
Wakefield, in the June 1988 draft. Like Wakefield, Martin had failed to
make a team out of spring training. The scene was hardly anything out
of the ordinary, just two struggling young players loosening up before
a game scheduled to be played within a matter of hours. Wakefield
tossed the occasional knuckleball to his teammate purely to alter the
routine, to have a little fun, to laugh at his slightly younger teammate — Martin was 20, Wakefield 22 — struggling to catch a pitch that
darted about like a butterfly.

Unbeknownst to either of them, Woody Huyke was stealthily standing by, watching with more than amusement, his curiosity piqued.
Huyke was then the manager of the Pirates team in extended spring

training, and he was still in the earlier stages of a career that would be spent almost exclusively in the player development operation of the Pittsburgh organization. Like Bill Lajoie, Huyke was open to most anything, but he knew the rules of player development, which included this one: *a guy with a good arm who plays a position and can't hit, you almost always try him as a pitcher before releasing him.* Tim Wakefield did not have the kind of arm strength that would have inspired such an experiment—his fastball, so to speak, was clocked at roughly 75 miles per hour during the prime of his career—but what he did possess was that knuckleball, the rarest of baseball offerings, and one that possessed potentially great value.

And so, as Tim Wakefield played what he thought was a relatively typical and uneventful game of catch with Jon Martin, and as sand trickled through the hourglass of his career, Woody Huyke cast the occasional glance their way and grew intrigued.

Was that thing for real? Could Wakefield throw it consistently? Was he even willing to try?

Casually, as if simply curious to learn the secret behind a card trick, Huyke wandered over to Wakefield and Martin. He watched the knuckler flutter yet again. The wheels in Huyke's mind then began to turn more rapidly, the evaluator intrigued by a discovery that might be worth a try given the player's dwindling prospects as a hitter.

"You think you can throw that for a strike?" Huyke asked nonchalantly.

Wakefield's reply: "Sure. I pitched some in high school. I don't see why not."

Wakefield threw the knuckler. Huyke watched. *Throw it again.* The pitch unsteadily floated toward Martin, the laces entirely visible, almost bouncing through the air as if it had been launched, without the slightest spin, from a slingshot. The young outfielder labored to catch the ball. *Do it again.* Once more, Wakefield threw the knuckler to his teammate, who struggled to catch the ball, and Huyke fixated on the pitch as if he were sitting in a 3-D movie, watching the ball tumble away from him with the kind of unpredictable, confounding movement that could cause a man's eyes to cross and his head to begin aching.

Huyke nodded and walked away, saying nothing more as Wakefield's mind began to race. *Why did he ask me that? What does he want me to do? Does he want me to throw batting practice? Does he want me to pitch?* The Pirates played their game, as scheduled. Wakefield did not remember the opponent or the outcome. What he did remember was that, after the game, Huyke sent him down to the bullpen to throw for Bruce Kison, a former major league pitcher who had won 115 games during a 15-year career with the Pirates, California Angels, and Red Sox. At the time, Kison was working as Pittsburgh's minor league pitching coordinator, a job he held until later becoming a major league pitching coach with both the Kansas City Royals and the Baltimore Orioles. Kison watched Wakefield throw, said relatively little, and, like Huyke, gave Wakefield absolutely no indication as to whether he had done well or poorly.

I still don't know if these guys like this thing or not.

Roughly a week later, Wakefield was promoted to Class A and joined the Pirates' South Atlantic League affiliate in Augusta, Georgia, which was a step up from the team's short-season affiliate in Watertown. By then, he was regarded as nothing more than a utility player. Wakefield played some at first base, some at third, and warmed up pitchers in the bullpen whenever there was a need. He did not pitch. Wakefield was desperate to remain in professional baseball, and he made it clear to anyone and everyone around the Augusta team that he was open to doing "whatever I could to stay there." No job was too small.

Late in the year, with roughly a month left in the season, the Pirates sent Wakefield back to the New York–Penn League, to the short-season, lower-level Class A team that he had played for only a year earlier. The only difference was that the team had moved from Watertown, New York, to Welland, Ontario, which hardly mattered to Wakefield. He didn't know why the Pirates were sending him there, or what it meant, but he was grateful to still have a job. Wakefield had yet to begin his career as a knuckleballer, but he was already being tugged from one location to the next, from Bradenton to Watertown to Augusta to Welland, a ride that was becoming increasingly bumpy. He was all over the place. Tim Wakefield needed a foundation, needed stability, and he was ready to cling to most anything in order to find it.

Upon reporting to Welland, Wakefield was introduced to manager

U. L. Washington, a former major league shortstop who hit .251 in 907 career games, most of them with the Kansas City Royals, the final 82 with the Pirates. At Welland, Washington used Wakefield exactly the way he had been employed at Augusta—as a utility infielder and bullpen catcher who would do whatever was asked of him. Wakefield was playing the infield one day when Washington came out of the dugout to make a pitching change. The manager summoned Wakefield into the game to pitch. Making no connection to the demonstrations he had given Huyke and Kison months earlier, Wakefield pitched exactly as he had done in high school—throwing fastballs and curveballs. He did not remember the results. After the game was over, Wakefield returned to the Pirates' locker room, where Washington approached him and delivered a very succinct message.

"No," said the skipper, who had long been renowned for chewing on a toothpick during games, even as a player. "We want you to throw *the knuckleball*."

Not long after, in another minor league game, Washington again brought Wakefield in to pitch, this time from second base. The walk to the mound was short, so Wakefield had little time to think. The series of events seemed so insignificant to him at the time, the games so much like any of the games he had played in high school or summer leagues, that he could not remember later how he performed, how the knuckler responded, what the Pirates were searching for. *Are they serious about this?* The entire event was relatively forgettable. But shortly thereafter, as the minor league season wound down, Wakefield had a conversation with Washington during which the manager told him that the Pirates wanted to make him a full-time pitcher. Wakefield bristled. He wanted to hit. He was drafted to hit. He knew he could hit. He resisted the idea until, like Don Vito Corleone in *The Godfather,* the Pirates made him an offer he could not refuse.

Not if he wanted to continue playing baseball.

"I was a little rebellious at first because I didn't want to give up hitting. I was disappointed they were giving up on me that quick," Wakefield said. "But then, they basically told me, 'You're going to pitch or you're going to go home.' So I said, 'Okay, I'll pitch.'"

That fall the Pirates sent Wakefield back to Bradenton, to the instructional league, which extended into November.

During the organizational meetings the team held near the end of the season — all minor league teams hold these meetings, which are the equivalent of performance or job reviews for the players — the Pirates had decided that Wakefield had no promise as a positional player. They were prepared to release him. Wakefield heard that Huyke had spoken up on his behalf: his manager in extended spring training believed Wakefield might have promise as a knuckleball pitcher. The cost of keeping Wakefield was minimal, so the Pirates rolled the dice. In the worst case, from the team's perspective, the Pirates could release Wakefield later. In the best case, they might hit the jackpot and develop an asset to be used in their own system, in a trade, or in any number of other ways.

During the fall of 1989, granted what many might have deemed a stay of execution, Wakefield made the conversion to full-time pitcher. He all but scrapped hitting. He worked out as a pitcher, trained as a pitcher, developed as a pitcher. Most of all, he tried to familiarize himself with a knuckleball that, to that point in his career, had been nothing more than something he used to amuse — and *be*muse — both himself and others.

"I knew I had a good knuckleball. I just had to learn how to control it," Wakefield said. "Basically, my first year, it was like, 'Go figure it out.'"

And so, with a new vision of what it would take to make it to the major leagues, Tim Wakefield set out to explore and investigate the whims of the knuckleball, regarded by many in baseball as a maddening, unpredictable, and entirely unreliable pitch.

And in this case, it was also the fine thread on which Tim Wakefield's career dangled.

Upon learning of his son's conversion from position player to knuckleballer, Steve Wakefield was, in a word, skeptical. He did not share those concerns with his son. Steve knew that the Pirates would not have asked his son to transform himself completely had he possessed the necessary skills to succeed as a hitter, and he had little reason to regard the knuckleball as anything but a deterrent for his son.

That was all he knew.

"I said to myself, 'Well, his career's going to be over now for sure,'" Steve Wakefield recalled.

Had Tim Wakefield understood that his odds for success at that stage were akin to the odds of winning the lottery, the young knuckle-baller might have harbored similar skepticism. Of course, he did not. Wakefield subsequently reported to spring training as a pitcher for the first time in his career and was assigned to Pittsburgh's affiliate in Salem, Virginia, of the Carolina League, one of the highest levels of Class A baseball and the league that features the Durham Bulls of *Bull Durham* fame. He was 23 now. Managed by Stan Cliburn, a former major league catcher who played all of 54 career games with the California Angels, the Salem Buccaneers were a positively dreadful lot who posted the worst record in the Carolina League that season, going 55–84 over a 139-game schedule.

Heaven knows how poorly the Buccaneers might have done had it not been for the slow and steady development of their experimenting knuckleballer.

By strict baseball standards, Wakefield's first year as a knuckleballer was relatively mediocre. By developmental standards, it was an indisputable success. Wakefield was frustrated at times by his inability to control the pitch consistently. At other times, he was awed by the power of a pitch that seemed near-mystical in nature as it transfixed hitters. When it worked, batters were confounded by it. When it failed, Wakefield issued walks (85) and allowed home runs (24) in bulk. The knuckler tugged him along by the collar, every which way but loose, and he often felt as if he was fighting the knuckleball himself as much as any hitter, catcher, or umpire.

If I could just get a tighter leash on this thing . . .

Steve and Judy Wakefield made the trip to Salem on more than one occasion during their son's first full year of minor league play — Salem was not a short-season affiliate, like Watertown or Welland — and they, like their son, did not really know what to think. They had no frame of reference. Steve Wakefield knew baseball well enough to know what the numbers meant, but what he did not know was that, at that level, the numbers lacked importance. The *experience* was what mattered more. Tim Wakefield needed time to learn the pitch, learn the game, and learn the routine at a new level of play. The knuckleball element complicated the development that any player would undergo, and so Wakefield and his parents had little way of knowing whether he was succeeding, failing, or just muddling along in between.

Salem, like many minor league cities and towns, had a core of season-ticket holders, fans who attended almost every game and had become organizational groupies, like Annie Savoy in *Bull Durham*. Steve and Judy Wakefield were in the stands one night watching their son pitch when they struck up a conversation with a couple of these loyalists. Judy Wakefield's description of them — "Two of the older gentlemen who went to the games" — conjures an image that cannot help but stir up comparisons to Statler and Waldorf, the disagreeable, elderly tandem that relentlessly heckles most everyone from the balcony of *The Muppet Show*. Indeed, the Statler and Waldorf of Salem had plenty to heckle at that summer, but their assessment of Tim Wakefield was beyond benign: the two fans assured the nervous parents that their son was excelling at his new job.

Their assessment?

"That he was going to make it to the big leagues," Judy Wakefield recalled.

Judy and Steve Wakefield still had their doubts as to whether their son had truly stumbled onto something special — with the knuckleball, after all, there are always doubts — but they certainly wanted to believe that he had. His performance only solidified their hopes as he led the team in victories (10), starts (28), and innings pitched (190⅓) during a season in which there had been relatively little else to root for. Tim Wakefield, too, regarded the season as a success, though he admitted later that he had no idea how to measure his own performance at that point.

In reality, of course, particularly given Wakefield's inexperience with the knuckleball, he had been just short of brilliant. Wakefield had allowed fewer hits (187) than he accumulated innings pitched, a ratio that is a goal for any pitcher, let alone a first-year knuckleballer. And while he had walked an average of four batters per nine innings, that ratio was quite good for a novice who had never pitched consistently at any level beyond high school.

Within the Pirates organization, team officials were thrilled. *We just might have something here.* Nonetheless, the Pirates were eager to see how Wakefield would perform the following year, in 1991, when they sent him to their affiliate in the Southern League, the Carolina Mudcats. The Mudcats were Class AA — more frequently referred to as Double A — a level at which the competition would stiffen considerably.

Double A is regarded as the level where true prospects distinguish themselves from the pretenders, where the weeding-out process intensifies. In the eyes of many scouts and evaluators, Double A is the level where pitchers effectively incorporate sliders into their repertoires, and sliders — let alone knuckleballs — are notoriously hard to hit.

One way or another, at the Double A level, organizational evaluators often get their answers. If a pitcher has an effective slider, he can handle Double A and advance to Triple A, one step below the majors. By contrast, if the hitter wins the battle, it is an indication that he is the one with major league material — not the pitcher.

Wakefield, of course, did not throw a slider — and never really would — though the same theory held true: Double A was his litmus test. He went out and pitched extremely well during the season, going 15–8 with a 2.90 ERA in 183 innings over 26 outings (25 starts). That performance ensured that Wakefield would open the 1992 season at Triple A, a proverbial heartbeat away from fulfilling his dream of playing in the major leagues.

Looking back later, Wakefield knew that he had lacked at least some measure of self-awareness during his minor league years, that he could not — and did not — appreciate or recognize the speed with which things were happening for him. He gripped the knuckler and threw it, and opposing hitters were flummoxed. It often seemed that simple. Opening the 1992 season at Buffalo, as expected, he picked up exactly where he had left off. In fact, as the competition improved, so did the knuckleballer. Wakefield made 20 starts that season for the Bisons and went 10–3 with a 3.06 ERA in 135⅓ innings — an average of nearly seven innings per start.

Through the summer of '92, Wakefield pitched well. He tried not to think too much about the majors, though he knew full well that the call to the big leagues could come at any time. Other members of the Bisons had been summoned to the major leagues during the season, and Wakefield knew that his opportunity would arrive if he could maintain a level of performance.

Just keep doing what you're doing and you'll be fine.

The Pirates had been to the National League Championship Series during each of the two previous seasons — 1990 and 1991 — and Pittsburgh was loaded with talent again. Wakefield rooted against no one, but all he needed was for a member of the Pirates pitching staff to be injured . . . or ineffective . . . or both.

Late in July, as the Bisons prepared for a game, Wakefield was summoned into the office of manager Marc Bombard, who delivered the news that Wakefield had been aching to hear from the time he was a boy toting a plastic bat and a plastic ball, hitting one home run after another over the roof of his parents' home in Melbourne. Wakefield was going to the major leagues. The Pirates wanted him to pitch for them on July 31, a day they would be hosting the St. Louis Cardinals at Three Rivers Stadium. Wakefield gathered his belongings and called his parents, relaying the news that Bombard had just given him before he set off to continue riding the knuckler as far as it would take him.

"I freaked out," he said. "The Pirates did a smart thing. They had me join the team in Chicago about three days before I was scheduled to start, just so I could get acclimated a little. I knew I was having a good year, and a couple of other guys had gone up before me, and I started to wonder if [I was bypassed] because of the knuckleball. But then I flew to Chicago and met the team there, and they took me back with them to Pittsburgh."

I started to wonder if I was bypassed because of the knuckleball.

Then I realized I was there because of it.

Of course, the major leagues can be overwhelming for any young man, particularly one who, less than three years earlier, had been on the verge of being released and who jumped at the chance to warm up pitchers in the bullpen or do whatever else it took to save his job. The Pirates knew this. Even if Wakefield was not aware of the meteoric nature of his rise — and he was not — the Pirates were. Upon arriving in Pittsburgh, Wakefield immediately fell under the care of pitching coach Ray Miller, a crusty, longtime baseball man who protected his impressionable young knuckleballer and nurtured him. Pirates center fielder Andy Van Slyke immediately took an interest in the young pitcher, inviting Wakefield to stay at his house. Van Slyke not only fed Wakefield but showed him how to act — "how to be a big leaguer." The two developed a strong friendship that would become lifelong. Wakefield received good mentoring and guidance from Van Slyke for which he would remain eternally grateful. That guidance made an indelible impression on him: he knew what he should be if he was ever afforded the luxury of a long major league career.

And his manager, of course, was none other than Jim Leyland, an accomplished skipper already regarded by many as one of the best managers in the game.

"I was young," said Wakefield, who had the impression when he arrived in the majors that Leyland was "a hard-ass." "I think I respect him more now knowing how he operated. At the time I didn't understand it."

Under the circumstances, Tim Wakefield now admitted that he was better off.

With what was about to happen next, after all, most anyone would have advised him to simply buckle up and enjoy the ride.

To Tim Wakefield, what stood out most at Three Rivers Stadium in Pittsburgh was the clarity of the entire picture, the crispness of the colors, the lighting. Everything was brighter. The details were sharper. High-definition television had yet to infiltrate American sports, but Wakefield felt as if he were stepping into an entirely new world. It was completely different from what he had experienced in the minor leagues. The baseballs were actually *white*. The light stanchions were bigger, the dozens of bulbs in each one illuminating every corner of the ballpark. Wakefield felt as if he had walked from the world of black-and-white television into a Hollywood production where the colors were suddenly as striking as those in *The Wizard of Oz*.

Welcome to the big leagues, kid.

In 1992, July 31 was a Friday. That meant a night game. Wakefield had slept relatively little the night before — "I was nervous," he said — and the day had dragged. He arrived at the ballpark in the early afternoon, changed into his uniform, and sought ways to pass the time. He found the wait excruciating. Although media members were allowed into every major league clubhouse three and a half hours before the scheduled start time, starting pitchers were off-limits to the press on the days they were scheduled to pitch. Ray Miller had given Wakefield some advice on what to expect in his dealings with the press, but Wakefield's greatest concerns were enduring the wait, getting to game time, and managing the energy he took with him to the mound.

Slow down. Stay focused. Don't rush.

Throwing the knuckleball, after all, was similar to most other athletic endeavors in at least one respect. Mechanically, everything had to be in sync. Wakefield's arm had to work with his legs, back, and hips. He had learned from playing golf that the timing had to be darned near perfect. The trick was to keep his mind from interfering, to not allow his arm to go too fast or his legs to drag because that would affect the movement and effectiveness of his pitches.

At the start, Wakefield felt rigid, tight, restricted. *Loosen up*, he thought. Just before he had been informed of his promotion to the major leagues, Wakefield had received advice from Bombard — or was it a coach? He could not remember now. He could only remember the message. *Don't pitch to the names.* The Cardinals had a roster of accomplished major leaguers, from shortstop Ozzie Smith to outfielder Ray Lankford to first baseman Andres Galarraga and others. Wakefield knew of them all. And yet he did not really know them, not in the real sense, not from any head-to-head competition. They were just *names*. The real Galarraga struck out 169 times in 1990. Lankford had struck out 147 times in 1991. Smith had not produced a home run all season and had managed just 22 in his entire career.

When the St. Louis hitters were announced for their respective turns at bat, Wakefield tried not to listen to the public-address announcer. He thought of something else. When he stepped onto the mound, he looked not at the batters but at the mitt of catcher Don Slaught. As a knuckleballer, Wakefield did not have to remember scouting reports and matchups or think about what pitch to throw, to whom, and in what situation. All he had to do was play catch with Slaught as if he were in the backyard of his home in Melbourne, tossing knuckleballs to his father, who had long since abandoned the chore of crouching behind an imaginary plate in favor of sitting on a capsized five-gallon bucket to minimize the stress on his back.

Against the Cardinals, Wakefield's initial goal was simple. *Survive the first inning.* Then his goal was to finish the second, then the third, then the fourth. Along the way, Pirates outfielder Barry Bonds and shortstop Jay Bell hit solo home runs to stake Wakefield to a 3–0 lead. His body loosened. *Don't pitch to the names.* He pitched more freely. *Throw to the bucket.* The Cardinals scored a pair of unearned runs in the fifth inning after Pirates third baseman Jeff King committed an error, but Wakefield minimized the damage and escaped the inning with a 3–2 advantage. After that, the Cardinals managed just one more hit the rest of the way—a leadoff single by Galarraga in the eighth inning, by which point Wakefield was in an unbreakable rhythm—and Leyland decided to leave his young knuckleballer in to record all 27 outs. Wakefield secured the final out on his 146th pitch of the game, a knuckleball that future Hall of Famer Smith dribbled out in front of the plate, where Slaught fielded it before throwing to first base.

Pirates 3, Cardinals 2.

And so began one of the more magical runs in recent baseball history.

For the Pirates and Wakefield both, what happened over the final three months of the 1992 baseball season in Pittsburgh was nothing short of what Leyland would one day term "a whirlwind" that made Wakefield, in the crusty manager's terms, "the [expletive] Elvis Presley of the National League." The log of innings from Wakefield's first seven starts resembled a string of scores on a 10-point scale — 9, 8, 8, 9, 6, 9, and 8.67 — and the Pirates went on the kind of hot streak that Leyland had been waiting for all season. Prior to Wakefield's arrival, the 1992 Pirates possessed a 3.56 team ERA and a 54–48 record, which was still good enough for first place in the National League East Division. Beginning on July 31, the Pirates went a sizzling 42–18 and lowered their *team* ERA by more than a half-run per contest, to 3.01. Even though the Pirates were a team stocked with good players — Bonds, King, Bell, and ace Doug Drabek were all well known by that point — most everyone connected their surge with Wakefield, the young knuckleballer who was turning the Pirates and all of baseball on its ear.

Bonds, in particular, awed Wakefield, and not solely with the raw ability that would make him a Hall of Fame–caliber talent long before his involvement in the steroids scandal that rocked the game years later. In 1992, Bonds was the consummate talent, a player who could hit for average (.311) and power (34 home runs, 103 RBI) while possessing game-changing speed (39 stolen bases, 109 runs scored). The one thing Bonds lacked was a strong throwing arm, but Wakefield marveled at how the outfielder masked that relative weakness by compensating in other ways.

"I only played with him for a few months, so I never really got to know him," Wakefield said. "But what I do remember is how strong he was, how quick he was. He never had a really strong throwing arm, but he knew how to get to the ball and get rid of it quickly. Teams couldn't run on him as much because of that. I remember times when there would be a guy on third, and someone would hit a fly to left field. [Bonds] would catch the ball, and the throw would be in the air so fast that the third-base coach had no choice but to hold the runner."

Wakefield's transition from the minors to the majors had been similarly fast and seamless, but even though that aided him in the short term, he believed that it hurt him in the long run. Consumed enough with just doing his job during his first months in the major leagues, he did not get caught up in the playoff race taking place around him. He did not know any better. By season's end, the Pirates had posted a

96–66 record to advance to the National League Championship Series for a third straight season, the previous two trips having resulted in losses to the Cincinnati Reds (by a 4–2 series count in 1990) and the Atlanta Braves (4–3 in 1991). Wakefield's presence and emergence was one of the main reasons the Pirates and their fans believed that the third time would be the charm. In his first run against major league competition, the Wakefield of 1992 had compiled an 8–1 record and a 2.15 ERA in 13 starts during which the Pirates had gone 9–4. He was such a force for Pittsburgh down the stretch that Leyland lined him up to pitch Game 3 of the playoffs, behind Drabek and veteran left-hander Danny Jackson.

Just before the start of the series with Atlanta, Wakefield joined the Pirates for their pregame workout in Atlanta and, in his terms, was "flabbergasted" by the scene around the batting cage at Fulton County Stadium. There were reporters everywhere, dozens of them, maybe hundreds. Wakefield all but had a panic attack. He had grown up in Melbourne, skipped around the minor leagues, and played for three months in Pittsburgh, where football reigned. He had never seen anything like this. Wakefield had traveled to New York, Los Angeles, Chicago, and Philadelphia after joining the major league club, but none of those stops prepared him for the virtual circus before him now.

Everyone's watching. This is bigger than I thought.

Matched against a formidable Atlanta team built around the pitching trio of right-hander John Smoltz and left-handers Steve Avery and Tom Glavine, the Pirates lost Games 1 and 2 in Atlanta, the latter by an unsightly 13–5 score while Jackson was unceremoniously rocked. Leyland had been hoping to avoid having his young knuckleballer pitch with the Pirates facing a 2–0 series deficit, but he had no choice. Wakefield's turn was up. The series moved to Pittsburgh on the designated travel day after Game 2, at which point Wakefield was asked to participate in a press conference featuring the managers and starting pitchers for Game 3. As he stepped onto the platform and took his seat behind a table, the size of the crowd stunned him. The room was jammed. Even during his regular-season success, Wakefield frequently was interviewed by no more than a small handful of reporters at a time. That was manageable. But this? This was a *crowd*. This was an *audience*. The size of the gathering intimidated him. He was anxious.

A day later, by the start of Game 3, Wakefield had done everything he could to treat his first career playoff start like the games he had pitched during the regular season. He was grateful that the game was being played in Pittsburgh. Though Drabek and Jackson lost in Games 1 and 2, Wakefield had watched them during the pregame hours, all but taking notes on how they prepared. *They're really not doing anything different than they did during the regular season.* Wakefield tried the same thing, tried to approach the game as he had any other during his brief time in the major leagues, tried to keep it simple. *Don't pitch to the names. Slow down. Breathe.*

The rest would take care of itself.

With the Pirates facing a virtual must-win situation — no team in baseball history had ever overcome a 3–0 series deficit at the time — Wakefield went out to the mound at Three Rivers Stadium and pitched a complete game, his fourth in 14 starts since joining the team. He threw just 109 pitches, including 77 strikes, an extremely high percentage for any pitcher, let alone a knuckleballer. The Pirates won by a 3–2 score, injecting life and drama into what had been a one-sided series up to that point and adding to the legend-in-the-making of Wakefield and his knuckleball.

Even Leyland admitted to having been caught up in the moment.

"I had no idea of what to expect," the veteran manager said. "I didn't really know who Tim Wakefield was. A lot of people didn't."

When the Pirates lost Game 4 to fall behind in the series, 3–1, Leyland grew desperate. He had little confidence in Jackson in the aftermath of the Game 2 debacle, so he called upon veteran Bob Walk, who would prove to be nothing short of masterful in a complete-game performance that anchored a 7–1 Pittsburgh victory. Walk's performance trimmed Atlanta's series lead to 3–2, but the Pirates still seemed destined to fail as the series shifted back to Atlanta for Game 6 and, if necessary, Game 7. Like most everyone in Pittsburgh, Leyland had developed a great deal of confidence in his knuckleballer, who continued to pitch in relative obliviousness as the Pirates continued their quest to reach the World Series.

Wakefield was not quite as dominating in Game 6 as he had been in Game 3 — but he was close. The Pirates scored eight times in the second inning against left-hander Glavine — who was matched against Wakefield for the second time in the series — and rolled to a 13–4 victory that forced a final, decisive seventh game. Wakefield allowed single runs in the fourth and seventh innings, the latter of which came after he had a 13–1 lead. After Leyland opted to let his knuckleballer finish what he started, Wakefield gave up another pair of meaningless runs in the ninth, which accounted for the 13–4 final. The knuckleballer had thrown a total of 141 pitches, an amazing 92 of them for strikes.

Had the 1992 National League Championship Series ended there — or following the eighth inning of Game 7 — Tim Wakefield, as a rookie, almost certainly would have been voted the most valuable player of the seven-game epic between Atlanta and Pittsburgh. Of course, it did not. Unavailable to pitch because of his 141-pitch masterpiece the night before, Wakefield watched from the dugout as the Pirates built a 2–0 lead behind a brilliant Drabek. The World Series was only outs away. Wakefield fully believed that the Pirates would win, that the World Series would come next, a belief that spoke not so much to his confidence as to his naïveté. Since the start of the 1991 campaign, Wakefield himself had accomplished everything he had set out to do. Combined, in the minor leagues and the majors and including the postseason, Wakefield had gone 35–13 over the span of two seasons. In 1992 alone — again including the playoffs and his time at Triple A — he had gone 20–4. Wakefield was borderline *unbeatable,* and he had the sense, the pure gut feeling, that things were playing out exactly as they were supposed to.

And yet, as Wakefield watched from the dugout, the Pirates began to teeter. Drabek, who had been brilliant all night, allowed a leadoff double to Terry Pendleton. *Okay, we're still up 2–0.* Then Braves outfielder David Justice reached on an untimely error by Pirates second baseman Jose Lind, putting runners at first and third, both potential tying runs now on base. *Damn.* Then Drabek walked heavy-legged first baseman Sid Bream on four pitches, loading the bases and further igniting an Atlanta crowd that already was smelling blood, that similarly had come to see victory as a birthright, that continued the unforgettable, rhythmic *tomahawk chop* that had become customary at Fulton County Stadium and felt to Wakefield, quite frankly, like a war cry.

Uh-oh. We're in trouble.

Thirteen pitches later, with the bases still loaded and the Pirates desperately clinging to a 2–1 lead by virtue of a sacrifice fly from Atlanta outfielder Ron Gant, Braves pinch-hitter Fernando Cabrera pulled a single through the hole between shortstop and third base. Wakefield all but gasped. Bonds fielded the ball and released the throw quickly — as usual — and Pirates catcher Mike LaValliere fielded the ball on a bounce. To Wakefield, as quickly as it all unfolded, the moment seemed suspended in time. Wearing a brace on his knee, a lumbering Bream then slid just beyond the tag of LaValliere as home plate umpire Randy Marsh made his decision — *Safe!* — and the Braves erupted into a celebration. For the Pirates, the ride was over. Wakefield was left to examine the fast and final events of a season that had felt just as furious, right up until the moment it crashed to a halt.

"At the time, that was probably the biggest impact of anybody that's ever come to the big leagues," Leyland said, recalling the effect that Wakefield had on the Pirates and, for that matter, the entire 1992 baseball season. "That kind of stuff just doesn't happen. That's a fairy tale."

Tim Wakefield, for his part, found it to be very real. To that point in his major league career, he had known nothing else. He believed that the 1992 season was just the start of a career that would be filled with winning, that he would soon get another chance at the World Series, that a return trip to October would be as simple as showing up and pitching.

But all too soon, Tim Wakefield would discover that baseball is as fickle as the pitch that had brought him to the major leagues in the first place.

• • •

Between the end of the 1992 season and the start of spring training in 1993, the Pittsburgh Pirates underwent massive changes, many of them triggered by a baseball landscape that, in need of major reform, was undergoing major renovations. Teams like the Pirates that played in small markets did not have the revenue to compete with larger clubs on an open market, which benefited the big spenders. Baseball was built on capitalism, not socialism, and so while teams like the New York Yankees and Boston Red Sox annually earned millions of dollars in local broadcast fees, teams like the Pirates earned relative pennies on the dollar. There was no sharing of wealth then. And so, when it came time for teams to bid on players, the big-market clubs had an enormous advantage over the smaller-market clubs, which more often than not had to restock their shelves with younger, less proven, less effective talent.

Following the 1992 season, the Pirates faced economic crisis. The team had drawn 1.8 million fans in 1992, but escalating player costs required the Pirates to slash payroll from $33 million in 1992 to $23 million in 1993, a 20 percent cut. For a club like Pittsburgh, that was an enormous downsizing, and it would turn the Pirates from a perennial championship contender (as they were in 1990, 1991, and 1992) into a club that would conclude the 2010 campaign with an incredible 18 straight losing seasons. During that period, the Pirates would lose the most games and post the worst winning percentage (including expansion franchises) of any club in baseball.

But while the Pirates bade farewell to, among others, Bonds and Drabek during the winter of 1992–93, Tim Wakefield did not seem especially concerned. He was too caught up in his own success. Wakefield reported to spring training as a star following his improbable ascension in 1992, and as most any 25-year-old would, he reveled in it. *We'll still win because we still have me.* What Wakefield neglected to acknowledge, of course, was that his performance had been a wild aberration, that the Pirates had succeeded because they had been a team, and that baseball is a game where the absence of one player can adversely affect another by changing the distribution of labor, workload, and demands.

"At the time, I didn't realize it. I just wanted to be *the man*," Wakefield said. "I went from having two months in the big leagues to being the opening day starter."

The results were predictable, if not downright awakening. Wakefield opened the season with a 9–4 victory over the San Diego Padres, a game in which he had nine strikeouts to go along with nine walks. Four starts later, he walked 10 and threw 172 pitches, albeit in a 10-inning victory over a Braves team he was facing for the first time since the previous October. Wakefield subsequently went 11 outings without a victory — partly as the result of bad luck, partly as the result of relative ineffectiveness — and ended up in the bullpen for a time, his ERA ballooning to such heights (6.35) that the Pirates did what any team would do with a young player who was struggling: they sent him back to the minor leagues.

Wakefield did not know what hit him. The game that had seemed so easy to him only a year earlier was now impossibly difficult, and he was left to sort through the rubble with the Double A Carolina Mudcats, a team for which he had gone 15–8 in 1991 and one for which he never really wanted to play again. The Pirates, in fact, were sending Wakefield all the way back to Double A, leapfrogging Triple A Buffalo entirely, a decision that was both symbolic and, to Wakefield, crippling. Wakefield understood the significance as well as anyone. Triple A teams *flew* to road games, traveled more comfortably, and were treated relatively well. The Double A leagues meant bus trips, long days, and a bigger and longer uphill climb back to the big leagues. Wakefield's confidence was destroyed. He was devastated. He sulked.

Unsurprisingly, his season further deteriorated. Wakefield went 3–5 with a 6.99 ERA in nine starts, at which point even Mudcats loyalists began to question whether he belonged there. Wakefield was on the mound pitching one night when the public-address announcer revealed that Pirates general manager Cam Bonifay was in attendance to scout some of the younger players in the Pittsburgh organization, and some fans regarded that as an opportunity to express their feelings about the struggling young knuckleballer.

"Hey, Cam!" one spectator yelled loud enough for the whole stadium to hear. "Why don't you take Wakefield back to Pittsburgh with you and throw him in one of the three rivers? We're trying to win a pennant down here."

Wakefield would have chuckled had he not been embarrassed.

In hopes of boosting Wakefield's confidence, the Pirates recalled him after rosters expanded on September 1, but Wakefield still felt "lost." He felt as if he were "searching." Still, he concluded the 1993 season with a pair of brilliant, complete-game shutouts against the Chicago Cubs and Philadelphia Phillies that allowed him to finish the year with a 6–11 record and 5.61 ERA, numbers that were an enormous disappointment given his contributions to the Pirates a year earlier. Nonetheless, the final two outings were an extremely encouraging sign, a suggestion to Wakefield and everyone else that he had reclaimed his grip.

I've got it back.

I can't wait until next year.

As it turned out, next year never came. In the aftermath of minor elbow surgery to remove a bone chip that had troubled him throughout the 1993 season, Wakefield had difficulty getting a feel for the knuckler throughout spring training. When camp broke, he wasn't even on the big league team, the Pirates having opted instead to send him to Triple A Buffalo with the hope of bringing him back to the majors within weeks.

It wasn't Double A, but still, Wakefield was overcome with the frustration of traveling *down* through the system, not *up*. He took the mound and constantly tinkered. He tried anything and everything to harness his knuckleball. He got little or no help from coaches to whom the knuckleball was foreign, and he crumbled beneath the weight of his own expectations and his prior success.

Wakefield spent the entire 1994 season pitching for the Bisons, going 5–15 with a 5.84 ERA in 30 outings (29 starts, one relief appearance). While he led the Bisons in starts (29), innings (175⅔), strikeouts (83), and complete games (4) and finished second in wins (5), he led the entire minor leagues — all teams at all levels — in virtually every negative pitching statistic, from hits (197) to runs (127) to walks (98) to home runs (27). In his mind, the games all ran together, one bad start followed by another, then another, then another. Whatever control Wakefield had over his emotions disappeared as quickly as his command of the knuckler. He found himself incapable of the focus he had brought to the 1992 season or, for that matter, the end of 1993. He tried *everything*. He altered his grip. He tinkered with his delivery. Obsessing on regaining control of the pitch, maybe he tried too much. Like Kevin Costner at the driving range in *Tin Cup*, Wakefield felt like a golfer with a case of the shanks. He was willing to stand on one leg, with his hat on inside out and his pocket linings pulled out, if that posture would have brought back the effectiveness of his knuckleball. Like "Nuke" Laloosh in *Bull Durham*, he would have even tried breathing through his eyelids.

But nothing worked.

Ultimately, the Pirates reached their end with him, though that did not come until the spring of 1995, following a work stoppage that had cut short the 1994 major league season and canceled the World Series while simultaneously cutting into the start of the 1995 campaign. (At Triple A in 1994, however, Wakefield had no such luxury. He continued to pitch, continued to lose, continued to search, because the work stoppage did not affect minor league players.) By the time the work stoppage was settled and baseball was set to begin anew, the Pirates had decided that it was time to cut bait. Huyke could not pass Wakefield at the team's training site in Bradenton, Florida, without looking away. Leyland, to the present day, regarded it as one of the most difficult conversations he had ever taken part in, partly because of what Wakefield did for the Pirates in 1992, partly because he liked the pitcher personally.

"I really don't have the answer to that question. That's also kind of a mystery [like the knuckleball]," Leyland said when asked about the end of Wakefield's career in Pittsburgh. "The success came so fast. I don't know if the expectations mounted on Tim or not. He's one of the best people you'll ever meet and a wonderful human being. I always suspected that stuff just happened too fast. Everybody liked him. Everybody wanted a piece of him. He was the talk of the whole country.

"It was very difficult," Leyland continued. "I kind of remember sitting there with Cam Bonifay [the Pirates general manager], and it was just a very difficult thing. I think we felt that if he was ever going to get it back, it wasn't going to be with us. That was such heartbreak. In the long run, that was probably good for him, because I think it did kind of resurrect and resuscitate him, but it was hard at the time."

Wakefield, for his part, was all but destroyed as he packed up his belongings and began the drive back home to Melbourne, to his previous life. *It's over,* he thought. *I'm done.* He was convinced of that. He was already planning for life without baseball. He was considering going back to school. Both the rise and the fall had occurred with astonishing speed, and years later Wakefield could still feel the turbulence when he recounted the early years of his career. From 1990 to 1992, he had gone from being a struggling positional player on the verge of release to a fluky knuckleballer who came within a whisker of being the MVP of the 1992 National Championship Series. From 1992 to 1994, he tumbled uncontrollably to such depths that the Pirates released him in the spring of 1995. This was the kind of journey that left onlookers with their heads spinning.

"Now imagine how *I* felt at the time," Wakefield said.

Although, at the time, he wasn't sure how he felt.

It hurt too much just to think about it.

Five

●

Tim was so successful early, and then he just lost it. That's when
it becomes very tough mentally to throw a pitch that everybody
knows is coming. I've told him that he's got to keep learning,
he's got to eat, sleep, walk, and talk the knuckleball until it floats
in his bloodstream like a spirit inside of him.

— Phil Niekro

IN ALMOST EVERY baseball player's career, there comes a season in which everything neatly and predictably falls into place.
For Tim Wakefield, that time came in the summer of 1995.

Released by the Pittsburgh Pirates during spring training, a desperate Wakefield searched for any way he could find to extend his baseball
career, be it in Boston or Baja. He wasn't ready to quit yet. He didn't
want to quit. He and agent Bill Moore immediately began looking for
new places of employment, a task that was infinitely easier than in
many other professions because Wakefield was, after all, a pitcher. In all
of baseball, at any level, there is no scarcer resource. Almost everyone
almost always needs at least some pitching, and the Pirates had given
him a small measure of hope by emphasizing that, at the very least, he
needed "a change of scenery." Wakefield remembered that part specifically. Leyland had said that the Pirates didn't think Wakefield was still
capable of succeeding *here* — in *Pittsburgh* — where the expectations
for him had been blown wildly out of proportion. Wakefield began to
believe that he simply needed a new start. He *wanted* to believe that.
He clung to whatever logic he could.

Indeed, in many ways, Wakefield's success with the Pirates during the 1992 playoffs gave him all the evidence he would need in convincing teams that he was capable of being a big league winner. Major league history is littered with players who failed with one team and succeeded with another—borderline Hall of Fame pitcher Luis Tiant was released *twice,* for goodness' sake—and the explanation for this has never become fully clear. Maybe it's a matter of timing, or maybe it's a matter of maturity. Wakefield's knuckleball fed into this kind of thinking—if it worked once, couldn't it work again?—and his 1992 performance was the ultimate lure, something both he and his agent could hold out in front of teams as if trying to sell them a time share in the Bahamas.

See? This is what you could end up with. All we need is a little of your time. The payoff could be huge.

In many ways, there were truly no strings attached. For the major league teams that operated with multimillion-dollar payrolls, Wakefield could be had for something close to the minimum major league salary—$109,000 per year in 1995—making the risk of such a signing minimal or virtually nonexistent. That financial reality could make the interest in someone like Wakefield greater than the interest in a higher-profiled star, if only for the simple reason that everyone could afford a pitcher like Wakefield. Most every team in baseball was willing to spend a dollar for a lottery ticket in exchange for the chance to strike it rich.

As it turned out, the Boston Red Sox were the ones to hit the jackpot.

Hired by the Red Sox slightly more than a year earlier, in January 1994, Boston general manager Dan Duquette, having inherited a Boston baseball operation that had deteriorated badly during the early 1990s under aging general manager Lou Gorman, had set about the business of rebuilding the Red Sox from the inside out. Although the Sox had played in one World Series and three postseasons under Gorman from 1986 to 1990, they hit rock bottom under overmatched manager Butch Hobson in 1992 and 1993, at which point de facto owner John Harrington opted for a shake-up. With the economic landscape of baseball changing, Harrington bumped a willing Gorman into a ceremonial front-office position and handed the operation over to the younger, more corporate Duquette in January 1994. As baseball headed into the labor war that led to the 1994 work stoppage (and cancelation of the World Series) and dragged on into the start of the 1995 campaign, Harrington wanted someone in charge of his baseball team who could squeeze more from less, someone who could find and develop cheap, young talent to restore his club to competitive levels while minimizing costs.

A New England native who grew up in Dalton, Massachusetts, Duquette seemed the perfect fit for the provincial Red Sox following.

Except for a collective bargaining agreement between the owners and players, Major League Baseball had no real governing rules during the historic work stoppage, no system under which to operate. In retrospect, the chaotic state of the game helped Duquette greatly during the winter of 1994–95, if only because competing organizations were thrown into a similar state of upheaval. *Nobody* in the game knew exactly what was going on. When parameters were finally put in place, an inordinate number of players were left without contracts in what had become a very condensed off-season, and so Dan Duquette was able to rebuild the Red Sox quickly with an assortment of bargain outlet purchases that included, among others, pitchers Erik Hanson and Zane Smith.

"That was a season unlike any other," Duquette said. "The players left [on strike] in August [1994], and spring training didn't even start until late March or April [1995]. . . . There were a number of veteran pitchers [available], so we signed a couple of 'em. They hadn't done as well of late, but they had pitched well in the past, so we signed them."

Of course, that description applied to Tim Wakefield.

He hadn't done too well of late, but he had pitched well in the past.

Nonetheless, for as much as a team like the Red Sox benefited from the work stoppage, the Sox, like other clubs, incurred some penalties, too. Amid the protracted and fruitless discussions between the owners and representatives of the players' union, many players put off conditioning during the winter months and allowed themselves to get woefully out of shape. Some reported to camp in laughable physical condition. And when spring training was condensed to three weeks because of the time already lost, a worst-case scenario developed for those who had made poor use of the winter months. Out-of-shape players needed more time, not less, and the result was predictable, particularly for pitchers: during spring training and the early stages of the regular season, there seemed to be an inordinate number of injuries to players who had tried to do too much, too quickly. The injuries threw off the competitive balance of the major leagues and created a new set of problems.

Because of the attrition rate, teams needed even *more* pitching than usual.

And Duquette was running an organization that had relatively little to begin with. Things reached the crisis stage for the Red Sox when an injury befell ace pitcher Roger Clemens, then a three-time Cy Young Award winner and easily the club's biggest star and most marketable commodity. Clemens had slipped some in the 1993 and 1994 seasons, going a combined 20–21 for a dreadful Red Sox team, but there was some renewed hope for him and for the team entering 1995 thanks largely to the overhaul in the Red Sox organization. During the work stoppage, Duquette had fired the underwhelming Hobson and replaced him with Kevin Kennedy, who had recently managed the Texas Rangers. (Hobson had had no prior major league managerial experience when the Red Sox promoted him from the minor leagues.) Duquette also had acquired rock star slugger Jose Canseco (a Kennedy favorite) from the Texas Rangers in an off-season trade, giving the Red Sox, if nothing else, another gate attraction (along with Clemens and budding slugger Mo Vaughn) that would help keep the Sox interesting should the team prove to be mediocre on the field. What the Red Sox lacked most was pitching, and that deficit explained why Duquette had been bargain-hunting — and buying in relative bulk — during the early spring. So it only added to Duquette's frustration when Clemens's right shoulder flared up during the early stages of camp, largely because Clemens, like many players, had taken a passive approach to conditioning during the work stoppage and shown up for camp out of shape.

Duquette therefore was looking for any pitcher who could give them, above all else, *innings*. He needed outs. Opening day was less than a week away when Duquette noticed that the Pirates had released Wakefield. Duquette was quite familiar with the knuckleballer from his time as an executive with the Montreal Expos, a team that was in the same division with the Pirates, the National League East, before baseball underwent realignment in 1994. Wakefield's availability immediately piqued Duquette's interest.

"I had seen him pitch late in '92, and he pitched the Pirates to the East Division championship over the Expos," Duquette recalled. "He provided the boost and the innings the Pirates needed to win the division, and that's when I became aware of him. So having seen him pitch brilliantly down the stretch for Pittsburgh, I knew he was the kind of pitcher who could pitch innings, but could also pitch when it counted because I saw him do it."

Naturally, Duquette was not the only baseball executive interested in Wakefield, particularly at a time when the game was in a state of flux and teams were scrambling. The Baltimore Orioles also expressed interest in Wakefield, the knuckleballer remembered, and Duquette recalled that the Florida Marlins had an eye on him. The Marlins' general manager at the time was Dave Dombrowski, who preceded Duquette as general manager of the Montreal Expos and had also seen Wakefield excel against the Expos as a member of the Pirates in 1992. Duquette knew how Dombrowski thought; if Dombrowski valued Wakefield, Duquette knew that the Marlins would make a push. Duquette believed that in order to acquire Wakefield the Red Sox would need to tap every available resource and make Boston the most appealing of any destination. Because all of the teams interested in Wakefield were likely to offer the pitcher similar financial deals — something close to the major league minimum salary — Duquette believed that other factors would determine where Wakefield landed.

Duquette had several advantages over Dombrowski and the Marlins as well as the Orioles, a division rival of the Red Sox and an organization in a state of flux. For starters, Duquette had a strong relationship with Bill Moore, the Arizona-based agent who operated almost exclusively with Wakefield's long-term interests, not the bottom line, in mind. Beyond that, Duquette's right-hand man and chief adviser was a man named Eddie Haas, a longtime baseball evaluator who embodied the cliché of the "crusty old baseball man." During many spring trainings, the white-haired Haas rode next to Duquette in a golf cart as the pair made their way from field to field around the Red Sox minor league complex, the older adviser gnawing on a cigar beneath the brim of a large straw hat. That Haas rarely spoke to anyone and hardly even exchanged pleasantries with anyone other than Duquette only added to the mystery of a man who always seemed shrouded in a puff of smoke.

The fact that Haas's full name was G. Edwin Haas prompted chuckles among the Red Sox beat reporters, who saw him as the "J. Edgar Hoover" of the Red Sox. (For what it's worth, the G stood for George.) The analogy was loose, at best, but Haas was nonetheless seen as Duquette's director of black ops — which was a colorful way to think of a man who had spent a lifetime in baseball and knew, well, just about everyone. A native of Paducah, Kentucky, Haas was then approaching his 60th birthday and had spent more than 40 years in professional baseball as a player, a coach, a manager, and a scout — a range of responsibilities and experiences that made him one of Duquette's most trustworthy evaluators of talent. Haas had spent many of those years in the organization of the Atlanta Braves, a stint during which he had encountered some of the game's most accomplished and unique talents, ranging from A (Aaron, Hank) to Z (Smith, Zane).

In Atlanta, too, Haas had learned about the value and whims of the knuckleball through the career of Phil Niekro, a career 318-game winner who thrice won 20 games in a season, twice lost 20 games in a season, and was regarded, quite simply, as perhaps the greatest knuckleball pitcher of all time.

"Eddie Haas was with the Braves when Niekro was with the Braves, and he extolled the virtues of the knuckleball," Duquette said. "He said the project was worth pursuing. He said, 'If we can stabilize the knuckleball, [Wakefield] could pitch for a long time.' I distinctly remember Eddie saying that [Wakefield] could pitch into his 40s."

Through conversations with Moore, Duquette learned that Wakefield's confidence had been badly shaken during his time with the Pirates, news that came as no surprise to the Red Sox general manager given the "whirlwind" existence that Jim Leyland had once described. During the six-year period from 1988 to 1994, Wakefield had been drafted as a positional player, nearly released, and converted to a knuckleballer, after which he experienced a dazzling and meteoric ascent to national prominence and then nosedived like a heavily weighted lawn dart. More than anything, Moore wanted stability for his client, something Duquette and Haas moved quickly to provide.

Through Haas, the Red Sox reached out to both Phil and Joe Niekro, who were then coaching the Colorado Silver Bullets, an all-women's baseball team sponsored by the Coors Brewing Company. As luck would have it, the Silver Bullets trained at City of Palms Park, Florida, the spring training home of the Red Sox. The idea of pairing Wakefield with Niekro was far too sensible on many levels for anyone to overlook.

Not only could Haas and the Red Sox provide Wakefield with access to one of the greatest knuckleballers of all time, but the Red Sox could do it while offering Wakefield (and the Niekros) nothing more than a five-minute commute from their minor league training facility to their spring training stadium.

For all parties, the deal was too good to pass up.

"Bill Moore said to me, '[Wakefield] just needs another opportunity. He's just lost his confidence, and he's lost command of his knuckleball,'" Duquette recalled. "So we put together a program for [Wakefield] that included the Niekros. We brought Phil in, and I hired him as a consultant. Joe came to the first session, too. The knuckleballers are a small fraternity in baseball, and the Niekros are the head of the fraternity."

Indeed, the Red Sox were pressed for time.

In more ways than one, Tim Wakefield was about to begin rush week.

For Wakefield, working with the Niekros—particularly Phil—was an invaluable opportunity that, incredibly, no one had yet afforded him.

Wakefield had briefly spoken over the phone with knuckleballers Charlie Hough and Tom Candiotti in recent years, but Niekro was different. Just as Wilbur Wood had seen Hoyt Wilhelm as "the king of the knuckleball," so Wakefield regarded Niekro as "the master" of the pitch. While the Red Sox had also offered him the opportunity to pitch at Triple A rather than Double A — the Orioles offered only the lower level, something Wakefield wanted no part of — the idea of working with Niekro was an obvious lure. Wakefield had completely lost his feel for the pitch during most of his final two years with the Pirates, and the worst part was that he often felt as if there was no one capable of helping him. He felt isolated and abandoned. Accomplished and respected pitching coaches like Ray Miller could not help him. Conventional baseball knowledge and wisdom were often useless in understanding the knuckler, and Wakefield sometimes joked that his association with the pitch made him feel like "a freak." At that stage of his career, what Wakefield needed to know more than anything else was that the knuckleball could indeed work again, that there were others who understood it, and that he was anything but alone.

In Phil Niekro, Wakefield found a knuckleball Yoda who had ridden the pitch to more than 300 career victories and whose accomplishments would land him, two years later, in the Baseball Hall of Fame in Cooperstown, New York.

Quite simply, there was no one better for the job.

Immediately, Wakefield was captivated. He felt as if he were in the presence of royalty. The gray-haired Niekro had the distinguished look of a college professor, minus the tweed jacket, and he spoke clearly, slowly, definitively. He did not raise his voice. Wakefield found Niekro's manner to be "easygoing," and he would later speak of Niekro as having an "aura" and the reassuring presence of a "Zen master." Niekro was, above all else, *calm* and *controlled,* qualities that Wakefield was sorely lacking during a period of his career when everything seemed to be coming apart.

"I don't remember who said it, but someone told me a knuckleballer had to have the fingers of a safecracker and the mind of a Zen Buddhist," Wakefield said. In fact, this remark came from former major league pitcher Jim Bouton, who adopted the knuckleball late in his career.

That description perfectly fit Niekro.

Phil Niekro took one look at Tim Wakefield and instantly knew that the knuckleballer's mind needed as much fixing as his arm, his fingers, or his grip. In fact, Wakefield's mind needed the most help. The young pitcher's career of extremes — great success and colossal failure — made it Niekro's challenge to convince him that there was a happy medium, a middle ground, a place that would make the knuckleball pitcher no more or less vulnerable than anyone else to the whims of a game designed to bring all players as many defeats as victories. *Baseball is a game where success is measured first by playing .500.* For certain, Niekro believed that the knuckleball had a mystical nature to it, that the pitch could be thrown with the same mechanics, over and over again, and "never do the same thing twice." But in order for it to work at all, Niekro preached, you had to *believe* in it, to trust it, to accept the bad with the good and live with the consequences, the way any pitcher would.

And so, during an introductory session in Fort Myers that included Wakefield, both Niekro brothers, and Duquette, Wakefield began rebuilding his psyche, his career, and, quite simply, his faith.

For Wakefield, Niekro's logic required an enormous shift in thought, if only because nobody had ever presented the knuckler to him in quite the same light; on the contrary, he had been all but taught that the pitch was unreliable. In that regard, especially, Niekro was different. Wakefield saw a man who had thrown the knuckler for 24 years and pitched in 864 career games, who had amassed 318 victories to go along with 274 losses. He saw a man whose mere ability to take the ball and pitch brought enormous benefits to his team. He saw a man who understood that winning comes from being in the game at all, from having worked for the *chance* to win or to lose. He saw a man whose career proved that the final outcome is often beyond one's control and who emphasized the simple things over the complex.

He saw a man, too, who recognized things in the knuckleball that others did not.

Indeed, where conventional baseball thinkers saw the knuckler as frighteningly unreliable, Niekro saw it as wonderfully unpredictable. *Use the uncertainty to your advantage.* Where conventional baseball thinkers saw walks and passed balls, Niekro saw abandoned base runners and wild swings. *It's the only pitch in baseball where, every time you throw it, it can be an out pitch.* Where conventional baseball thinkers saw an unclear role for the knuckleballer, Niekro saw a versatile pitcher who could start games or finish them, an adaptability that would lend itself to a long and fruitful career. *If you learn to command this pitch, you can pitch until you're 45.*

From the outset, Niekro could see that Wakefield's mechanics were good and that his knuckler was, in a word, *special.* Wakefield's implementation of it was something altogether different. During the week they worked together, Wakefield and Niekro traveled to the Red Sox minor league complex, where he pitched simulated games against an assortment of minor league players and hopefuls, participants in the same kind of extended spring program in which Wakefield had been participating when Woody Huyke first saw him throw the knuckler. *These kids are just like me.* During the sessions, Niekro would stand behind Wakefield, *on the field,* delivering instructions to a student who was all too eager to follow them. *Take a little off this pitch.* Wakefield would take a little off the next pitch. *Good, now throw this one as hard as you can.* Wakefield would throw with everything he had.

Wakefield learned to pitch with the knuckler the way a conventional pitcher would learn to manage an array of pitches, with one obvious exception: where a conventional pitcher could change from a fastball to a curveball to a changeup, Wakefield had to mix it up by changing speeds and elevations with the knuckleball.

If Wakefield could do that while keeping his delivery sound and consistent — and the events of 1992 had proven to Niekro, among others, that Wakefield could do that — he could be every bit as effective as a conventional pitcher, Niekro stressed, and no more vulnerable to slumps. After all, short of velocity, wasn't *movement* something that all baseball evaluators coveted? Wasn't that the objective? Niekro believed that conventional baseball thinkers contradicted themselves in this regard: on the one hand, they wanted movement, but on the other hand, they claimed that the knuckleball moved so much that it created problems. Well, which one was it? What Niekro told Wakefield, in the end, was that he was a pitcher like any other pitcher, and that the knuckleball actually gave him more weaponry than was available to the conventional right-hander or left-hander who took the mound every five days.

The message was striking.

They don't understand you.

But I do.

Trust me.

"Before we started working, I told Tim, 'If you have confidence in it, you won't care who's hitting. There are going to be days when it's going to be there for you and days when it's not, but no matter what, the next day, you take your glove and your spikes with you because you can pitch,'" Niekro recalled. "That's the advantage a knuckleball pitcher has. It's in our heads and in our arms. If we pitched nine innings, we were as tired mentally and physically as other pitchers, but we didn't get sore arms. If you can get the pitch over the plate, it'll keep you in the big leagues for a long time — that's for sure.

"Managers and pitching coaches, they can't help you much with the knuckleball," Niekro said. "You're basically your own coach."

In Fort Myers, then, the ultimate goal for Phil and Joe Niekro was obvious. In connecting with Wakefield, the knuckleballing brothers sought to repair the pitcher's confidence and rebuild his self-esteem, to rehabilitate him. To convince him that he was not alone. To assure him that being a little different was a *strength*. To remind him that he belonged in the major leagues, that he had the mind and arm to succeed, that he could handle failure just as well as he could embrace success.

What they sought, in short, was to make Tim Wakefield his own coach.

The return to glory came far sooner than anyone expected or could have reasonably imagined. Tim Wakefield spent roughly 10 days in

Fort Myers before the Red Sox assigned him to their Triple A affiliate in Pawtucket, Rhode Island, as promised. Wakefield made four starts with the Pawtucket Red Sox, for whom he went 2–1 with a 2.52 ERA in a stretch far more reminiscent of the fall of 1992 than the summer of 1994. Wakefield had pitched a mere 25 innings for the PawSox when the Red Sox quickly summoned him to the major leagues in the midst of what was a deteriorating crisis.

Following an abbreviated spring training as a result of the work stoppage, the early stages of the 1995 baseball season had the feel of a fire drill. The Red Sox took advantage. The Red Sox rumbled to a 14–5 start over their first 19 games, a stretch that was seen by most critics as the baseball equivalent to Andy Warhol's prescribed 15 minutes of fame. In baseball, almost anyone — or any *team* — could have a good day, week, or month. Many could have even one good year. But only the good players and teams could repeat the performance time after time, year after year, a reality that tended to weed out the weak and reaffirmed one of Phil Niekro's fundamental beliefs.

The hard part is to always be in the game.

By late May, the 1995 Red Sox certainly seemed like a team destined for some counterbalancing. After its eye-opening start, the team lost five of six to the Cleveland Indians and Seattle Mariners, two of the more highly regarded teams in the American League. With Clemens already sidelined, the Sox subsequently lost slugger Jose Canseco as well as pitchers Aaron Sele and Vaughn Eshelman to injury. Because Boston's start had been seen as an aberration — remember that, before the work stoppage that wiped out parts of the 1994 and 1995 seasons, the Red Sox had posted three straight losing seasons — the general feeling throughout New England (and all of baseball) was that the Red Sox were plummeting back to reality. The Red Sox had remaining road series in Anaheim (against the then-California Angels) and Oakland (against the A's) before heading home, and there was some concern that the club would be back playing at C level by the time they returned to Boston.

Tim Wakefield flew to Seattle to join his new teammates just as Canseco, Sele, and Eshelman were all flying back to Boston to be examined by team medical personnel. Their fortunes having passed in the airspace above the continental United States, the Red Sox were in the late stages of a 4–3 loss to the Mariners on May 25 when Tim Wakefield arrived in the visiting clubhouse at the cavernous Kingdome in Seattle. He was not sure what he should say, where he should sit, who he should speak with. The entire situation was foreign and awkward. To that point, Wakefield had spent his entire career in baseball in the Pirates organization, and so there was always that link, that connection, whenever he arrived at a new level of the minor leagues, even when he arrived in the majors. *We're on the same side.* But the feeling in Seattle — he felt like a midwesterner who had just stepped off a train in Grand Central Station — was entirely different, and the reality of a new beginning now started to dawn on him.

Now what?

In the wake of the loss, the Red Sox clubhouse was relatively quiet. Equipment bags were scattered about the room and stationed before the players' lockers as they prepared for a flight to Anaheim later that day. The routine of such afternoons, which the players referred to as *getaway days,* was a succession of annoying tasks. In this case, following a night game on Wednesday, the Red Sox had had a Thursday day game that, with a starting time of 12:26 PM, had required an unusually early wake-up call. They had already packed up and checked out of their hotel. After going to the ballpark, they had unpacked, played the game, then returned to the clubhouse to pack up again, all in anticipation of a flight later that night. Then they would arrive at a new hotel in the Anaheim area and unpack again, relieved at the prospect of being able to stay in one place, without packing or unpacking, for at least two days.

Wakefield, whose day began with an early wake-up call on the East Coast, had spent enough time in the major leagues to know this routine by the time he arrived out west at the Kingdome. He wondered why he had not simply flown to Anaheim and met the team there. He learned the answer when the coaches told him to put on workout clothes and head out to the bullpen, where he would have his inaugural throwing session with his new catcher, Mike Macfarlane. Wakefield felt bad about this. Macfarlane had come into the clubhouse after being behind the plate for the entire loss, and now he was being asked to put his equipment on again to catch Wakefield in the bullpen. Wakefield felt this was a terrible way to meet his new batterymate and, for that matter, his new team.

What a first impression.

Two days later, he gave what he felt was a far better representation of himself.

The day after the Seattle finale, the Red Sox began a three-game set against the Angels with an 8–3 victory behind right-hander Hanson that at least temporarily stopped the bleeding. Nonetheless, like Sox officials, Wakefield knew that the injuries to the pitching staff were likely to begin having an erosive effect, if for no other reason than the fact that the staff's depth had been whittled away. *This is my chance to help.* More than anything, Wakefield hoped to give the Red Sox innings and to provide some stability to a staff that badly needed it, but the simple truth was that no one—from Sox officials and players to Wakefield himself—had the slightest clue of what to expect when he made his Red Sox debut on May 27, 1995.

Staked to a 2–0 lead in the top of the first inning, and 20 months removed from his last major league experience, Wakefield took the mound for the bottom of the first inning feeling almost exactly as he had on July 31, 1992, when he made his major league debut for the Pirates. *Just get through the first inning.* Wakefield was nervous and tight. He immediately walked the leadoff man, Tony Phillips, who promptly advanced to second base on a passed ball. Then Wakefield walked another. *Here we go again.* The Angels trimmed Boston's lead to 2–1 on a run-scoring single by first baseman J. T. Snow before a laboring Wakefield retired third baseman Eduardo Perez on a fly to right field, ending an inning during which he required 26 pitches to record three outs.

Whew.

And then, as if he had merely needed to exhale, Tim Wakefield got his groove back.

As the Red Sox slowly opened up their lead—to 4–1, 10–1, and, ultimately, 12–1 — Wakefield rhythmically carved up the Angels with one knuckler after another, his concentration rising with every pitch. This was a dramatic change from the last time he had pitched in the major leagues. When he had pitched well in Pittsburgh, Wakefield often had felt so "locked in," as he put it, that he didn't remember thinking about *anything*. He just pitched. The process became second nature. *Grip, kick, throw*. But when things had unraveled, Wakefield's mind would begin to race and he would lose focus, discipline, patience. *Why was that last knuckleball flat? How do I fix it?* He would start tinkering and changing things, as he had done throughout the miserable summer of 1994, triggering a counterproductive chain reaction that made him worse, not better.

Over his final six innings against the Angels, Wakefield threw just 64 pitches and allowed only four hits while failing to issue another walk. The Angels looked downright befuddled. By the time manager Kevin Kennedy pulled Wakefield from the game after the seventh inning — Kennedy was already looking ahead — the Red Sox were en route to a resounding 12–1 victory that built on Hanson's performance from the previous night. Wakefield left the mound feeling rejuvenated, *restored,* as if the failure in Pittsburgh and the subsequent sessions with Niekro had taken him to where he had been at the beginning.

"I think my concentration level got back to where it needed to be," he said.

Three days later, with Boston's pitching staff still in a decrepit state and Wakefield coming off a comfortable 90-pitch outing, Kennedy made a most unusual request of his new knuckleballer: the manager asked him to pitch on just two days of rest. In fact, during the game in Anaheim, Kennedy had asked Wakefield about the possibility of coming back to pitch on preposterously short rest if needed; the knuckleballer was all too eager to do it if it would help his new team. Once the affair with the Angels was fully in hand, Kennedy yanked Wakefield from the game with the idea of using him again almost immediately, this time against the A's and crafty right-hander Ron Darling on Tuesday, May 30, in Oakland. Kennedy's hope was that Wakefield would be able to pitch approximately five innings, absorbing an ample part of the workload left behind by Sele and Eshelman. Four days into Wakefield's career as a member of the Red Sox, the team already was asking him to do the work of two men.

Picking up precisely where he left off against the Angels, and looking like a young Luke Skywalker who had just discovered the secret to mastering the Force, Wakefield systematically dissected the Athletics as if on autopilot. On a night when Kennedy hoped that Wakefield would be able to last through the fifth inning—and against the equally efficient Darling—Wakefield pitched into the eighth. All in all, Wakefield recorded 22 more outs—he pitched 7⅓ innings—and allowed only a single through the first seven innings, making great use of a fifth-inning sacrifice fly by teammate Tim Naehring that produced the game's only run and gave the Red Sox a stirring 1–0 victory.

With Wakefield and Darling matching one another in a duel of pitching proficiency, the game lasted a mere two hours, seven minutes.

Just like that, the Red Sox felt as if they had unearthed a treasure.

"That's what you call complete command of the ball game," a gushing Kennedy said of Wakefield's performance.

Of course, even assessment that missed the point.

In actuality, Wakefield had been in complete command of *two* ball games.

Wakefield's performances in Anaheim and Oakland were merely the beginning of a run that would alter the 1995 baseball season in Boston and, for that matter, the entire course of Wakefield's career. Five days after beating the A's and Darling—this time on the far more traditional four days of rest—Wakefield made his home debut at Fenway Park as a member of the Red Sox and pitched Boston to a 2–1, complete-game, 10-inning victory over the Seattle Mariners. Five days later, on June 9, he faced the A's a second time and threw another complete game, this one a 4–1 victory. By the time the run was complete, the Red Sox had gone from 16–10 to 26–13—from being a team headed back to earth to one indisputably shooting for the moon.

In a span of just 13 days, Wakefield won four games and pitched 33⅓ innings, an *average* of 8⅓ innings per start. He allowed just two earned runs. The Red Sox, like their resurrected pitcher, were believing fully in the wonders of the knuckleball, from the man throwing it to the man catching it to the thousands of fans in Fenway Park watching it. As the excitement built in Boston, Wakefield remained true.

Grip, kick, throw.

"I didn't know I'd have this much fun with a knuckleballer out there," catcher Mike Macfarlane said after one of the pitcher's early starts. "It was fun as hell."

Still, through it all, there was a sense that the other shoe would inevitably drop.

And it would.

Paired with the effervescent, likable, and chronically positive Macfarlane, Wakefield's improbable, career-resuscitating run with the Red Sox endured throughout much of the New England summer of 1995. Though Wakefield went three straight starts without a victory from mid to late June, he took the mound against the Detroit Tigers on June 29 with a 4–1 record and 1.72 ERA. By then, Wakefield had been all but assured a regular place in Boston's five-man rotation for the foreseeable future, and the Red Sox had fully begun to believe that they, like their riches-to-rags-to-riches knuckleballer, could ride baseball's most mystical pitch like a hot, high roller at the craps table. Their focused knuckleballer seemed to possess persuasive powers that bordered on the evangelical. Wakefield's mantra was their mantra.

Blessed are those who do not question.

Have faith.

Believe.

From June 29 through August 13, 1995, Wakefield made 10 starts for the Red Sox and won them all, a streak of truly historic proportion. Since 1936, no starting pitcher in baseball had won more than 13 starts in a row during any season; since 1960, only 14 had won more than 10. Wakefield's streak would remain the third-longest in club history and the longest since 1950, when left-hander Mel Parnell won 11 straight starts.

"He pitched absolutely lights out," Duquette said of a period during which Wakefield posted a 1.60 ERA and became one of only 23 pitchers in history ever to start a season 14–1. "Make no mistake, he pitched us to the East Division championship. Unbelievable run and debut. It was like magic."

Indeed, the 1995 Red Sox rumbled to the American League East Division championship and an appearance in the postseason, defying all expectations and logic.

Their story, in many ways, was truly the stuff of lore.

And yet, throughout it all, there was always the sense that things eventually would go *poof.*

To this day, Tim Wakefield regards the summer of 1995 as Nirvana, that time and place where mind, body, spirit, and knuckler were in complete harmony. Even compared to his meteoric rise with the Pittsburgh Pirates in 1992, he regards the 1995 season as the most successful stretch of his career—a period when the game was absurdly simple for him, when pitching was a matter of *grip, kick, and throw.*

And yet, baseball being baseball, there was always the knowledge that the streak would not and could not continue, and that reality had nothing to do with Wakefield or his trademark pitch.

In the wake of his performance with the Pirates in 1992, Wakefield had been permanently scarred by his success when he set a standard for himself that no pitcher could have possibly lived up to. When the Pirates overhauled their organization following the 1992 season, Wakefield had been placed in an impossible position. He was a young man still trying to adjust to unprecedented success and attention, but with no real understanding of why he was succeeding at all. The game and the world sped up on Wakefield to the point where he simply could not keep up, and his legacy in Pittsburgh eventually came crashing down around him, his career smashed in the process. *A million little pieces.*

With the Red Sox in 1995, Wakefield, infused with confidence by the brothers Niekro, tried to take a far more deliberate approach by adopting the oldest baseball cliché and embracing it to the fullest: he tried to take one game at a time. Instead of focusing on the next game or the next batter, he tried to focus only on the next pitch. He would dig his fingernails into the leather cover of the baseball, rock back, release. What happened after that, he reasoned, was beyond his control. Sometimes, standing on the mound, Wakefield could hear Niekro's voice, as if Niekro were still hovering behind him on the practice fields of Florida like a holographic Obi-Wan Kenobi, instructing Wakefield in what to do next. *Take a little off this one. Throw the next one as hard as you can.* Wakefield often seemed to be engrossed in a conversation with himself and could come off as abrupt or uncooperative. He shrugged off questions about his success, dismissed any and all talk of a winning streak, and deflected all requests for commentary to his manager, teammates, and coaches. *I just want to pitch.* The more he won, the more he simplified, the more he focused, and the more he won. Anticipating the fall that would inevitably come, he desperately tried to keep everything on even ground and prepare himself for the kind of failure that had so devastated him in Pittsburgh and beyond, so as not to experience the same unforgettable pain.

At times, it seemed, all the winning seemed to have a paradoxical effect.

The fall is only going to be that much greater.

Macfarlane was a perfect complement and mate for Wakefield, the outgoing and infectiously good-natured catcher's personality serving as the pitcher's perfect alter ego and inner child. Armed with an oversized catcher's mitt that now had become far more common for catchers working with knuckleballers, Macfarlane thoroughly embraced a challenge that many catchers ran from. Despite having never caught a knuckleball, the boyish-looking catcher welcomed the chance with unbridled enthusiasm. He said the things that Wakefield did not. Known for passionately and outwardly expressing his passions and his feelings, Macfarlane would announce every one of Wakefield's starts as if he were the ringmaster at a circus — "Freak show!" the catcher would shout throughout the Boston clubhouse — and he did so with a gleeful disposition so genuine that his teammates, particularly Wakefield, could not help but chuckle.

And Macfarlane did it all during a season in which he amassed a whopping 26 passed balls, a total that might have been embarrassing had Macfarlane allowed it to be. That passed-ball total was the most in baseball by any catcher since 1987, when Texas Rangers catcher Geno Petralli amassed the ungodly total of 35 passed balls while catching — you guessed it — knuckleballer Charlie Hough.

When the winning streak ended in the final weeks of the 1995 regular season, Wakefield was not pitching poorly as much as he was pitching mediocre. Though he went 2–7 with a 5.60 ERA over his final 10 starts, those statistics were slightly skewed by one especially poor outing. In his final nine starts, Wakefield's ERA of 4.84 was only slightly above the league average of 4.71, but the absurd success that had defined his midsummer stretch was indisputably gone. Wakefield knew this would happen at some point because the game demanded it. He had learned that much.

For pitchers, winning requires a great deal — decent run support, good defense, more than a little luck — and Wakefield went from experiencing virtually all of it to experiencing relatively little.

Still, his performance had sufficiently ebbed that the Red Sox pushed him back to Game 3 of the playoffs — Clemens had long since returned by that point and would start Game 1 while Hanson started Game 2. Ultimately, his position in the rotation was of little consequence. Matched against a Cleveland team that was by far the best in the American League, the Red Sox were unceremoniously swept out of the first round, losing the first three games in a best-of-five series. As disappointing as the conclusion of the 1995 baseball season in Boston should have been, the Red Sox braced for winter with an undeniable sense of optimism, the team having discovered an unexpected and newfound hope following a series of seasons in which it had enjoyed relatively none.

As for Wakefield, he finished 1995 with a 16–8 record and 2.95 ERA that placed him among the American League leaders in an array of categories and earned him a third-place finish in the American League Cy Young Award balloting, as well as a 13th-place finish in the American League Most Valuable Player Award balloting. And yet, despite all his success that year, Wakefield found himself unwilling to celebrate too much, unable to feel too safe, and incapable of looking too far ahead.

"I was in survival mode," he said.

Though he didn't know it at the time, he already had survived.

The worst was over.

He would never see the minor leagues again.

Six

●

"Do you ever know which way it's going to move?"
"Not really. I mean, no."

— Exchange between a reporter and catcher Kevin
Cash about Tim Wakefield's knuckleball

FOR THE RED SOX, following a 1995 season that unexpectedly produced a trip to the postseason, the bill came due in 1996. With labor peace between baseball players and owners finally established, there were no unsettling distractions. With the game back on track, the variables that had helped the Red Sox rumble to the 1995 American League East Division championship had been eliminated. Nonetheless, expectations in Boston were high, and the Red Sox were not especially well equipped to deal with them.

Tim Wakefield knew the problem quite well.

Four years after his meteoric rise with the Pittsburgh Pirates, Wakefield suddenly found himself in almost exactly the same place again, albeit this time with a Red Sox team that had not undergone the massive changes that reshaped the Pittsburgh team of 1992–93. The Red Sox were under no orders to trim payroll and cut costs. General manager Dan Duquette had made changes and additions to the Red Sox roster — in the modern, free-agency age of baseball, every team had a fair amount of turnover every year — but the Boston nucleus had generally remained intact. Though he was entering the final year of his contract, longtime Red Sox ace Roger Clemens was still with the club.

Reigning American League Most Valuable Player Mo Vaughn also returned. Jose Canseco, too, was back. And though the Red Sox had lost right-hander Erik Hanson to free agency, Duquette had replaced him with Tom Gordon, a durable young right-hander who had begun his career with the Kansas City Royals. The Red Sox were not expecting Wakefield to carry them so much as they were expecting him to give them precisely what he was capable of giving them — innings. Still, Wakefield's historic run in 1995 certainly sat in the back of most everyone's mind, especially Wakefield's.

I hope they're not expecting me to do that again.

Beyond the baseball, Wakefield also had other things on his mind. Given the turmoil of his first four years in the major leagues, it was understandable that Wakefield was especially concerned about his contract. He had gone from major league star to minor league laughingstock back to major league star again, and a guaranteed contract was the closest he could get to a tangible measure of security. A contract meant something to him. It would be an indication that the team was as bound to him as he was to them. Major league rules generally prohibited a player from earning big dollars — at least in baseball terms — until he had three full seasons of major league experience to his credit. At that point, the player would at least qualify for salary arbitration — which generally required the team to pay him at a level commensurate with his peers in terms of performance and experience. Once a player accrued six full years of major league service, he was eligible for free agency, under which he could peddle his services to the highest bidder. This was the kind of leverage that was fervently sought by every player.

In the spring of 1996, Wakefield was still a year short of qualifying for salary arbitration. He knew this. He also knew that he had given the Red Sox 16 victories and nearly 200 innings in a season shortened by a work stoppage, a reality that made him one of the most underpaid players in the game. Wakefield discussed the issue at length with his agent, Bill Moore, who advised him to report to camp as usual, to do his work, to be patient. Wakefield considered holding out and at one point declined to pitch in an intrasquad scrimmage because his contract issue was still unsettled, though a resolution to the matter really was just a matter of time. Ultimately, Wakefield agreed to a salary of $450,000 with bonus clauses that could earn him even more. These were extremely fair terms for a pitcher with his track record and a sign, on some small level, that the Red Sox regarded him as a part of their future.

Almost any other pitcher with relatively little experience and an inconsistent history would have had no leverage at all. As allowed by major league rules governing the early part of players' careers, the team might have unilaterally renewed his contract without earnestly negotiating at all. Teams had the hammer in the early years and were frequently willing to use it, but the Red Sox took a far more diplomatic approach with Wakefield, whom they wanted to keep happy, focused, and productive.

We're not going to mess with this guy.

Still just 29, Wakefield was eager to put the entire process behind him, if for no other reason than that his Pittsburgh experience had literally been traumatic. *They can still release me at any time.* Despite his performance in 1995, he began the 1996 season, even as he said and did all the right things, still feeling like his job was at stake. The Red Sox earmarked a spot for Wakefield in their rotation along with Clemens, Gordon, Aaron Sele, and soft-throwing lefty Jamie Moyer, only the last of whom had to earn his way into the group. Wakefield was all but assured a spot from the moment he arrived in camp, but his experience in Pittsburgh had long since taught the knuckleballer that he could take nothing for granted, that he was never safe, that his fortunes could dip as quickly and unexpectedly as the pitch that had delivered him to Boston in the first place.

If you pitch poorly, you're gone.

Following a 1995 season that had been aberrational throughout the major leagues — again, the work stoppage had created a muddle from which teams would emerge slowly — the 1996 Red Sox were well positioned to disappoint. A number of unpredictable variables had contributed to the team's success in 1995, most notably the acquisitions of Erik Hanson and Wakefield. Hanson, who won 17 games, had been signed *during spring training*. Wakefield, who nearly won the Cy Young Award, had been *released* by another team at roughly the same time. Although this conjunction of events was highly out of the ordinary—a classic case of the right players being in the right place at the right time—now that Hanson was gone entirely and Wakefield had ended 1995 pitching at something far closer to a realistic level, baseball overall had *equalized*. Now the Red Sox were among the teams that had come back to the pack while others rose.

Even so, the 1996 Red Sox badly stumbled out of the gate. The team lost their first five games of the season, 12 of their first 14, and 15 of their first 18. In hindsight it would become clear that they were crumbling beneath the weight and pressure of their own unreasonable expectations. After a poor spring, Wakefield began the regular season with a horrific outing against the Texas Rangers that produced a 13–2 Red Sox defeat. The next time out, 11 days later, he allowed nine hits and eight runs in an 8–0 loss to the Cleveland Indians, a performance that left him with more losses (two) than he had suffered during his first 17 starts in 1995. The 11-day gap between his first two outings was partly the result of a rainout and partly a response to Wakefield's poor spring performance—because he had been pitching poorly, the Red Sox skipped Wakefield when his turn came to pitch rather than skip someone else. This decision disrupted Wakefield's timing and confidence at an indisputably delicate time, triggering a chain reaction.

And so, two weeks into a 1996 season that Wakefield and the Red Sox had entered with great anticipation, the knuckleballer and his team were both in a tailspin.

The Red Sox wasted no time and sent Wakefield to Fort Myers for a remedial session with Phil Niekro, whom Wakefield was all too eager to see. Again, Niekro eased Wakefield's mind, stabilized his mechanics, set him back on track. They spent a mere two days together, Niekro again standing behind Wakefield as he threw, all but planting his voice between Wakefield's ears as if he were the Hardball Whisperer. Wakefield felt as if he had been reprogrammed. After returning to the Red Sox, he looked like a different man as he pitched seven strong innings in a 2–1 victory over a Cleveland team that had battered him only five days earlier. In his next outing, he backboned an 8–3 win over the Texas Rangers. Wakefield and the Red Sox then concluded the first month of the 1996 season with a lopsided 13–4 win over Texas, a victory that left Boston with a miserable 7–19 record. Two of the Boston victories in April had come in games started by Wakefield.

He was better, to be sure, but Wakefield at times still felt as if he were fighting himself and the knuckleball. Maybe those struggles were one and the same. Wakefield tried desperately to apply what Niekro had taught him, but the process was less natural, more forced. Part of him feared the worst. He was still learning to deal with failure. Few players in history have had the kind of success Wakefield enjoyed as a rookie in 1992. And then, three years later, Wakefield went on a similar run in his first weeks with the Red Sox, during his first year in Boston, this time going 14–1. In baseball, those kinds of streaks are the exception rather than the rule, and the game is built on failure far more than success.

And so, this time, Wakefield did everything in his power to remain composed. Like the 1993 Pirates, the 1996 Red Sox were stumbling amid expectations, prompting most every member of the Boston team to try a little too hard and squeeze a little too tightly—particularly a maturing knuckleballer trying to apply the counterintuitive logic to a pitch that had failed him once before, leading to a destructive fall.

Tim Wakefield, like the Red Sox, was in inner turmoil, his mind and emotions sparring with one another as Niekro's lessons echoed in his head.

Use the uncertainty to your advantage.

But what if I'm unsure of it myself?

It's the only pitch in baseball where, every time you throw it, it can be an out pitch.

But what if I can't control it?

If you learn to command this pitch, you can pitch until you're 45.

But if I can't, I could be out of baseball at 29.

Tim Wakefield dug in defiantly and braced himself. He had gone from success to failure to success again, and the early pattern of his career suggested that failure was coming next. The ride was getting as turbulent as the track of the pitch itself. Wakefield loved the highs but dreaded the lows. What he wanted most of all was a more stable existence somewhere in the middle that would make him feel safe and less vulnerable, a place he could trust, a place somewhere between 1994 and 1995.

But then, even at 29, Wakefield's life as a knuckleballer was just beginning.

He was learning about the pitch as much as he was about himself.

If charted on a graph, the early stages of Tim Wakefield's career would look something like this: long, high spikes followed by steep, precipitous drops. The knuckleball had given Wakefield extended bursts of success and failure as he harnessed the pitch for good chunks of time and then completely lost control of it for others.

On May 5, 1996, Wakefield learned that the knuckler could also blow in and out with the force and unpredictability of a midwestern thunderstorm, causing enough damage in an extremely short period of time to leave onlookers wondering precisely what had happened.

Wakefield and the Red Sox seemed well on their way to a victory, with a 3–0 lead entering the fourth inning, when a game that had seemed under complete control spontaneously combusted into a raging ball of fire. There was little or no warning. While athletes routinely speak of the fine line between winning and losing — in any sport — often overlooked is the reality that, over time, talent and execution generally win out. This is especially true in baseball, where, over the course of a 162-game season, luck tends to even out and talent most often separates the good teams from the bad ones. The gap between success and failure, as it turns out, is not nearly as great in the major leagues as it might be in some other arenas, if for no other reason than the fact that the game is a marathon and not a sprint.

As a result, small missteps can be overcome, mistakes can be erased, and transgressions frequently can be overlooked.

But for Wakefield, the line between success and failure that spring was microscopically thin. His confidence was brittle. Knuckleballers had less margin for error to begin with, to be sure, but Wakefield, the

Red Sox, and the entire six-state region of New England were about to learn about the whims of the knuckleball through a trial by fire. Whether Wakefield and Boston liked it or not, there were going to be growing pains. And that never was more apparent than in the middle innings of what would become a historic game for the knuckleballing member of the Red Sox, even if for all the wrong reasons.

Having allowed only two hits and a walk through the first three innings, Wakefield opened the fourth by allowing a single to Joe Carter, the likable Toronto outfielder and first baseman who had made a career of torturing the Red Sox. Carter was running with the pitch when teammate Ed Sprague followed with a line drive to third baseman Tim Naehring, a sure-handed fielder who would end his major league career with 77 consecutive errorless games, all at third base. Naehring merely had to catch the ball and throw to first base for an easy double play, a relatively routine play that the gritty third baseman could virtually make in his sleep.

Of course, Naehring missed the ball. And so, instead of having two outs with nobody on base, the Jays had runners on first and third with nobody out.

When Wakefield followed up that gaffe by striking out John Olerud, all of Fenway Park, from the deepest rows of the center-field bleachers to the first row of the box seats behind home plate, shared the same observation: *He should be out of the inning already.* Wakefield, too, briefly processed the thought. Still eight years away from the world championship that would end an epic 86-year drought, the Red Sox organization and its followers were still weighed down by a doomsday mentality that usually played out like a self-fulfilling prophecy and almost always reaffirmed one of Murphy's Laws: *Anything that can go wrong will.*

Understandably, given the early track of his career, Wakefield was not immune to this line of thinking. To that point, any string of success for Wakefield had usually meant that disaster was waiting around the corner. The failure had been difficult to handle. And so, after throwing a passed ball that scored Carter from third and moved Sprague to second, Wakefield allowed six of the next seven Jays to reach base on a walk, three singles, a double, and a home run, the final and most destructive blow delivered by Carter. The final four of those hits came with two outs. Just like that, a 3–0 Red Sox lead had turned into an 8–3 deficit, an avalanche triggered by a simple fielding miscue by the third baseman.

Or was it?

After Naehring's error, Wakefield had many opportunities to reclaim control. Instead, as baseball people often put it, he *caved in* under the weight of a crisis spiraling badly out of control. Deep down, Wakefield knew this. If he didn't want to admit it to himself then, he certainly would later in his career. But Wakefield in the spring of 1996 was still unsure of himself and of the knuckleball, and he was in little position to assume the weight of a Red Sox team that simply could not get out of its own way. During and after the inning, Wakefield was conflicted. On the one hand, as he sat in the home dugout at Fenway Park, he had been victimized by the misplay. *They failed me.* On the other, he knew that Naehring was an exceptional fielder and that part of being a team was to minimize the mistakes of others. *No, I failed them.* The entire, sudden series of events had left him confused and frustrated, the knuckleball confounding the pitcher as much as it could the hitters.

Recognizing not only the volatility of the knuckleball but the fact that Wakefield could reclaim his touch as quickly as he had lost it, manager Kevin Kennedy left him in the game. With the Red Sox now facing a five-run deficit, Wakefield pitched a scoreless fourth and fifth before the Jays rallied in the sixth — thanks again, in part, to the Boston defense. The Red Sox made two more errors in the inning — one by all-thumbs second baseman Wilfredo Cordero, the other by typically slick-fielding outfielder Milt Cuyler — and triggered a three-run Jays rally that made the score 11–3. Wakefield ultimately left the game after throwing 133 pitches and facing 33 batters, producing a pitching line that remains among the most unique and peculiar in both his career and the history of the game:

In 5⅔ innings, he was responsible for 10 hits, 11 runs, one earned run, five walks, and six strikeouts.

As much as anyone, Wakefield recognized the irony of the performance, if for no other reason than the fact that baseball protects pitchers from mistakes committed by teammates. That is why the ERA (earned run average) was created in the first place. In any game, all runs are classified as either earned (meaning they are the pitcher's responsibility) or unearned (meaning they are not), and ERA has thus become a standard by which all pitchers are measured. ERAs have fluctuated over time — the average ERA in the American League was 4.71 in 1995 and 4.99 in 1996 — but the statistic has been heavily weighted since its inception in the early 20th century, a fascinating fact given the manner in which statistical analysis has exploded in the modern game.

There was an obvious catch to Wakefield's performance against the Jays: of the 11 runs that Toronto scored, 10 were *unearned* as a result of Boston's defensive ineptitude. It would have been easy to blame his teammates Naehring, Cordero, and Cuyler for that fact, but Wakefield also knew that he had hardly done his own job to the best of his ability. Wakefield believed in the code that prevails in any major league clubhouse — *you watch my back and I'll watch yours* — and he knew, too, that statistics can be very misleading. During the loss to the Jays, Wakefield's ERA *decreased* from 5.97 to 5.24, though that was of little solace to him or the Red Sox, who ultimately suffered one more defeat — this one 11–4 — in a season that had them all frustrated.

Still, from a record-keeping perspective, Wakefield's performance was truly historic. Since 1920, in all of baseball, a pitcher had allowed as many as 10 unearned runs in a game only six times. Of those six games, only one had occurred after 1930 (a 13–6 loss to the Baltimore Orioles by New York Yankees right-hander Andy Hawkins in which all 10 runs he allowed were unearned). Wakefield would remain the only other pitcher to be credited with such a dubious distinction in the last 80 years, the kind of oddity that Wakefield, the Red Sox, and their followers would chalk up to one very obvious explanation: the knuckleball.

But soon Wakefield and the Sox would learn that the quirks of the pitch brought certain advantages, too.

When the Red Sox arrived at Comiskey Park on June 10, 1996, for the opener of a three-game series with the Chicago White Sox, their hopes for a successful season were continuing to dwindle. The leaders of the team were getting visibly frustrated. The Sox were just 24–36, 12 games under .500, the second-worst record in the American League. One of their recent defeats had come via a 3–2 decision in which ace Clemens had departed with a 2–1 lead over the Milwaukee Brewers. The win was the first of two consecutive extra-inning losses to the Brewers, defeats that had not only demoralized the Red Sox but also drained them physically.

Simply put, the Red Sox were running out of pitchers. Starters were getting knocked out of games early, and relievers were repeatedly blowing late leads, increasing the strain and workload for a pitching staff that had relatively little depth to begin with.

Wakefield knew this as the Sox prepared to face the White Sox, but any doubt he might have had was eliminated when manager Kevin Kennedy delivered a message to him on the flight to Chicago. Because scheduled starter Aaron Sele was sick, the Red Sox needed a pitcher immediately. Kennedy naturally turned to Wakefield, who could serve as both his starter and his bullpen on the same night. *No matter what, I need innings from you tonight.* Wakefield had pitched better since the Toronto game, but his previous outing had been a brief, 3⅔-inning affair during which he threw just 77 pitches of an eventual 10–7 Red Sox victory. As always, Wakefield took great satisfaction in knowing that at least the team had won the game. Given the manner in which Kennedy had been compelled to aggressively employ his bullpen in the Milwaukee series and the overall sorry state of the Boston pitching staff, Wakefield had already been scheduled to take the mound on only three days of rest. Now he was being asked to make the kind of contribution that he knew he could deliver and that Niekro had foretold.

There are going to be days when it's going to be there for you and days when it's not, but no matter what, the next day, you take your glove and your spikes with you because you can pitch. That's the advantage a knuckleball pitcher has. It's in our heads and in our arms.

In fact, even at that stage of his career, Wakefield relished opportunities like this one when the Red Sox were in need and a manager, coach, or teammate would come to him and make it clear that he was needed more than usual. *They're asking for my help.* These were the moments when Wakefield most felt a part of the team, felt appreciated, and felt that he belonged. They were all in it *together*. Wakefield found a great deal of satisfaction in these moments partly because he was making a contribution and partly because his kind of contribution highlighted the communal approach. Nobody was pointing any fingers and nobody was issuing any blame. Rather, the Red Sox were interested in finding solutions. In the middle of the 1996 run, when the Red Sox were at the nadir of their season, Wakefield took a great measure of pride in the fact that he was the one — not Clemens, not Gordon, not Sele, not anyone else — who was called into the manager's office.

They needed *him*.

What transpired on the field that night was not unpredictable so much as it was eye-opening, bringing into focus just how desperate the Red Sox had become. Wakefield allowed two runs in the first inning, another in the second, two more in the third, and another in the fourth. The White Sox had at least one base runner in each of their eight team at-bats, eliminating any need to bat in the bottom of the ninth inning as they rumbled to an easy 8–2 victory. The most noteworthy part of the game was not that Wakefield pitched all eight innings for Boston, but that he was never even in danger of being lifted from an affair in which he allowed an absurd 16 hits, eight runs, three walks, and 19 base runners while throwing an insane 158 pitches. During the game, in fact, Kennedy took it upon himself to make the kind of conversational visit to the mound normally conducted by the pitching coach — just to reaffirm to Wakefield that his performance was appreciated, that he was helping the team, that his efforts were for the greater good.

On that night, quite simply, Tim Wakefield was being made a sacrificial lamb. The Red Sox were in such a battered state that they needed someone to give their pitching staff a reprieve.

Who better than the team knuckleballer?

Had he been wired differently, Wakefield might have bristled at such a request. Future Sox great Pedro Martinez, for instance, sacrificed a start and prematurely pulled the plug on his 2002 season because the Sox were out of contention. Wakefield took the opposite approach.

I can do something for the team that other guys can't and won't. The knuckleballer offered no complaints and no excuses for the outing, which once again landed him in the history books.

Over a 50-year span since 1960, only seven pitchers in baseball have pitched a complete game while allowing as many as 16 hits and 19 base runners; no one has done it since Wakefield in 1996. The feat, in fact, has been accomplished only 16 times since 1920; six of those performances came in games in which the starting pitcher received at least 10 runs from his offense, and three came in games that featured 18 or more runs of support for the pitcher. Indeed, modern pitchers are almost never asked to do what Wakefield did for the Red Sox that night, which was to completely swallow his pride and sacrifice his own personal statistics—Wakefield's ERA climbed from 5.70 to 5.80—while the rest of the pitching staff licked its wounds.

At the lowest point of the 1996 Red Sox season, Tim Wakefield did the dirty work.

Truth be told, Wakefield's sacrifices went beyond one start, a fact that was sorely overlooked at a time when the Red Sox were struggling and team followers had no frame of reference with regard to Wakefield's value. Kennedy, in fact, had moved Wakefield up a day, pitching him on three days of rest, for a very specific reason: doing so effectively would give Red Sox relievers and pitchers three full days of rest, an unheard-of break during the course of the season. On Sunday, Sox pitchers had labored through a day game against Milwaukee. On Monday, they had the day off. On Tuesday, Wakefield gave everyone a break. By the time starter Vaughn Eshelman took the mound for the second game of the Chicago series, nearly 72 hours had passed since someone other than Wakefield had thrown a pitch in a game.

With their arms at least temporarily recharged, the Red Sox went on their longest winning streak of the season, claiming four straight victories and five in six games. Wakefield suffered the only loss, a development that was unsurprising. Coming off his sacrificial 158-pitch outing against the White Sox, Wakefield took the mound for the third time in nine days and allowed five runs in the first inning of an eventual 13–3 loss to the Texas Rangers. Overall, the Red Sox certainly were playing better, but their short-term improvement had come at the expense of their knuckleballer, whose first half had consisted of starts on short rest and abnormally long rest, as well as outings in which he allowed 16 hits and 10 unearned runs.

As the Red Sox were stabilizing, Tim Wakefield was being jerked all over the place.

Part of him wondered if anybody noticed.

Part of him didn't care.

He was simply happy to have a job.

For whatever reason — the law of averages, the actions of management, or the resiliency of their players — the Red Sox made a complete turnaround at the midpoint of their 1996 season. Frustrated with the team's defensive play, particularly in the middle of the diamond, general manager Dan Duquette acquired second baseman Jeff Frye from the Texas Rangers and, later, outfielder Darren Bragg from the Seattle Mariners. Frye and Bragg were both gritty, competitive players who infused the Red Sox with the kind of fight they had lacked during the first three months of the season.

As soon as the Red Sox stabilized, Wakefield, too, found a comfort zone, offering further evidence of the symbiotic relationship that could exist between a knuckleballer and the team for which he pitched.

When the Red Sox needed help returning to an even keel, Wakefield was willing to make the necessary sacrifices to promote stability. And when the team found that balance, Wakefield could settle into a more proper role in the middle of the rotation, where he could more freely endure the bumps and turns of the knuckler to give the Red Sox what they needed most from him: innings.

Though Wakefield did not realize it at the time, his performance through the first half of the 1996 season helped solidify his place in the Boston clubhouse, where he was becoming a fixture. Wakefield generally went about his work and kept quiet, and his attitude, particularly during times of crisis, was endearing him to teammates and management alike. *This guy isn't afraid to take a bullet.* The man who was still happy to have a job was planting roots in Boston, his place in the major leagues growing steadier, more secure, more certain. Teammates respected his team-first attitude. Management recognized his willingness to help. Privately, Wakefield hoped that people would take notice of his sacrifices, but he also knew, and had learned, that baseball was a results-oriented business.

Even in victory, Wakefield labored. Though credited with the win in an 8–6 victory over the New York Yankees, Wakefield allowed 13 hits and six runs in five innings. His ERA climbed to a disturbing 6.45, still well above the league average and exactly 3.5 runs per game higher than the 2.95 ERA he had posted during the 1995 campaign. He still wasn't pitching well and had yet to find a rhythm. Wakefield found those moments particularly isolating, Phil Niekro's words once again reverberating in his mind.

Managers and pitching coaches, they can't help you much with the knuckleball. You're basically your own coach.

As it turned out, Wakefield was not as isolated as he thought.

The Red Sox had a handful of leaders in Wakefield's first years with the team, none of them more noticeable than gregarious left fielder Mike Greenwell, whose mouth seemed to move nonstop. Greenwell, who was in the midst of his last major league season, spent much of the 1996 season on the disabled list and in the minor leagues on a rehabilitation assignment, but he returned to the team in July. Greenwell was just 33 — only a few years older than Wakefield — but he had suffered an elbow injury earlier in his career that damaged what was already a weak throwing arm. As he crept toward his mid-30s, Greenwell was becoming more of a defensive liability and less of a threat at the plate, where an absence of power was contributing to his decrease in value. On the one hand, Greenwell wasn't a good enough outfielder to play in the field anymore. On the other, he didn't hit for enough power to be a designated hitter.

Mike Greenwell was on the way out, the classic in-betweener caught between youth and old age, a holdover from a previous Red Sox regime who was about to be swept out in the transition to a new general manager.

Wakefield respected players like Greenwell, who was playing in his

12th major league season and had played in a pair of All-Star Games while finishing as high as second in the Most Valuable Player Award balloting (1988). Wakefield also personally liked Greenwell, a live wire who injected a great deal of personality into the Red Sox clubhouse but also played hard, played hurt, performed. He got the most of his ability. Wakefield believed that players like Greenwell were to be respected. Greenwell's antics and outspoken nature often made him an easy target for fans and media — players, too, often liked to needle him — but he was generally quite well liked. And in a city like Boston, where the Red Sox had built a long tradition, a 12-year career was nothing to sneeze at, particularly for a left fielder who followed the line of kings that had run from one Hall of Fame player to the next — Ted Williams (1939–60), Carl Yastrzemski (1961–83), and Jim Rice (1974–89). Greenwell fancied himself an extension of that reign — and in many ways he was — and Wakefield saw him as the rare player who was a representative and ambassador for his team. *Mike Greenwell, Red Sox.* As much as baseball followers identified the Red Sox through players like Roger Clemens, Greenwell's name deserved to be right there on the masthead, whatever his title.

But in 1996 Wakefield didn't necessarily recognize that Greenwell was much nearer the end of his Red Sox career than the beginning. *I was just happy to have a job.* The knuckleballer was far more concerned with his own seemingly never-ending struggles. On the night of July 20, Greenwell had finally returned from hand surgery and watched from the dugout bench as Wakefield took the mound against the Baltimore Orioles. While Wakefield was setting down the Orioles, Greenwell talked with teammates about the knuckleballer's effort to reclaim the magic he had unlocked during the 1995 season and offered a rather simple, succinct observation.

During the game, Greenwell approached catcher Bill Haselman and told him he had noticed that Wakefield seemed to be throwing the knuckleball harder than he had in 1995. The outfielder then waited for the right opportunity to relay the same message to the pitcher — a veteran player sidling up to a younger one in as nonthreatening a manner as possible.

Hey, Wake, got a minute?

Sure.

It looks to me like you're throwing that thing harder this year.

It does?

Then came the words that might as well have come from Phil Niekro.

Try taking a little off.

And just like that, as if keyhole tumblers were falling into place, Tim Wakefield found his groove again.

For Wakefield, of course, the entire story served a rather fitting purpose, touching on many of the pressure points that would exist throughout his career with the Red Sox. Greenwell was precisely the kind of player Wakefield wanted to be: a fixture. Someone like Clemens, who had Hall of Fame talent, was not a fair comparison. And what Greenwell told Wakefield was a terribly appropriate message for a player who was throwing every pitch as if his career depended on it, who was holding on too tight. Greenwell had seen that Wakefield's problems, ironically, came not from throwing the ball too soft but from throwing it too hard, which could be particularly counterproductive with a pitch like the knuckleball.

Ease up a little.

Don't put so much pressure on yourself.

You're trying too hard.

Whatever the reason — Greenwell's advice, Wakefield's natural ability, a little of each — Wakefield began pitching better instantly. Against the Orioles that night, Wakefield pitched 8⅓ innings without allowing a run in a 2–0 Red Sox victory. Two starts later, against the Kansas City Royals, he again went 8⅓ innings. From that point forward, Wakefield pitched at least seven innings in all but two of his final 11 starts — and in those two games he lasted six innings, still above the league average — and settled into the happy medium that has housed the long careers of many productive major league players. In all, over his final 14 starts of the 1996 season, Wakefield went 8–4 with a 3.83 ERA during a time when the Red Sox were similarly making a wildly improbable turnaround.

The 1996 Red Sox made a memorable stretch run before ultimately succumbing, finishing with an 85–77 record that left them a mere three games behind the Baltimore Orioles for the final playoff spot in the American League. During the second half of the season, the Red Sox had posted a 49–28 mark that was the best in baseball and had almost everyone in and around the Boston team, including Wakefield, wondering how different the season's outcome might have been had they played better in April. *If only we had gotten off to a better start.* And yet, for the Red Sox and Wakefield both, the second half of the 1996 season was a critical step in their development, a sign that they might be headed in the right direction.

But now, at a time when the Red Sox and Wakefield seemed destined to suffer identical fates, things had gone differently. Wakefield had *survived.* He and the Red Sox had fought back. For the first time in his career, Wakefield had made it through an entire major league season, from the very beginning to the very end, finishing with a 14–13 record and 5.14 ERA in 211⅓ innings pitched. He had been one of the anchors of the Boston pitching staff. Wakefield's performance gave him more than three full years of major league service spread out over parts of four seasons, qualifying him for salary arbitration for the first time in his career and putting him in position to earn the first multimillion-dollar salary of his career.

As surely as Wakefield had harnessed his knuckleball, he now had a firmer grasp on his career.

But then the winds changed again.

For all of the success the 1996 Red Sox enjoyed on the field at the end of the season, they were a team in transition and, consequently, inner turmoil. Clemens and Greenwell, longtime cornerstones of the team, were at the end of their contracts and eligible for free agency. The goal of general manager Dan Duquette was to overhaul the roster, not preserve it, and the Red Sox were headed for one of the more unsettling seasons in their recent history.

Tim Wakefield was unsure of how all the changes in Boston would affect him, but his experience in Pittsburgh had taught him that everyone would feel the impact. Between 1992 and 1993, the Pirates had cut ties with, among others, outfielder Barry Bonds and pitcher Doug Drabek, the linchpins to that team. For any club, superstars are usually the building blocks. Wakefield knew he was not a superstar, and he also knew that he would be among those who felt the greatest impact in the absence of a staff ace if Clemens and the Sox could not agree on terms.

The message behind the eventual ugly breakup between Clemens and the Red Sox reverberated with Wakefield as harshly as it did with everyone else who had ever played in the major leagues. *If Roger Clemens can leave the Red Sox, then no one is safe.* Red Sox greats like Williams, Yastrzemski, and Rice had played their entire careers in Boston, long known as a place that conferred undying loyalty on its star players. Williams got most everything he wanted. So, too, did Yastrzemski. But now Clemens was leaving an organization that no longer seemed to want him. His departure was the biggest and most ground-shaking change during an off-season in which the Red Sox also fired manager Kevin Kennedy and cut ties with Greenwell, among others, all as Duquette tried to transfuse the Red Sox organization with younger, more dynamic players who did not need or expect to be coddled.

In the mind of Dan Duquette, who operated as if he were the new sheriff in town, the Red Sox needed an overhaul.

It was time to restore order.

Wakefield was headed for a bump in pay as a result of arbitration, but he wondered if that, too, could work against him. *Do they really want to pay me? Will I make too much?* For all of the money that major league players made, the game was also a ruthless business. At manageable salaries, many players had great value. But once those salaries began to escalate, players could price themselves out of a job, depending on their level of talent and contribution. If a team could get 80 percent of a player's production at 20 percent of the cost, that trade almost certainly was worth making. As long as teams drafted and developed reasonably good talent, signing cheaper and younger labor was always an option.

During the winter, amid the dramatic changes that were taking place in the Boston organization, the Red Sox sent out a letter to their season-ticket holders, a sales pitch intended to convince an increasingly skeptical fan base that the Red Sox had, well, *hope*. Seventy-eight years had passed since the Red Sox last won a World Series. Now the Red Sox were parting ways with arguably the greatest pitcher that had ever worn the Boston uniform in Clemens, someone who changed the culture in Boston by proving that a pitcher could lead the team. (Left fielders Williams, Yastrzemski, and Rice had all been position players.) During Clemens's time in Boston, statistics bore out the fact that the Red Sox were a playoff contender when he pitched and an extremely mediocre team when he did not. His presence made all the difference in the world. And while Clemens had skidded some recently — after he left, Red Sox officials were quick to point out that he had been a mere 40–39 in his final four seasons — the club also knew that Clemens's departure left an enormous void at the front end of the Boston rotation and stripped the club of its identity.

In their letter to the fan base, the Red Sox urged fans to renew their tickets, attempted to convince them that the Sox would be fine over the long haul, and insisted that life would go on without Clemens and that the Red Sox still had many capable players in the organization. The idea was to convince fans that the Red Sox were rebuilding the franchise and that the construction had already begun. To this end, the letter highlighted some of Duquette's shrewder maneuvers and identified some of the key players whom the club expected to be central contributors in 1997 and beyond.

One of the first names mentioned was Tim Wakefield.

With his arbitration case against the Red Sox looming, one of Wakefield's agents, Dick Moss, had caught wind that the team was using Wakefield as a marketing tool with its season-ticket base. Moss regarded this as leverage to use against the club if and when negotiations reached an arbiter. Although most teams avoid arbitration hearings with eligible players by coming to terms beforehand — think of it as a pretrial settlement — there are always cases that go the distance. Duquette himself regarded the arbitration process as "distasteful," as he often put it, but he had to admit that there was sometimes no other way to settle a dispute. In the arbitration process, a player enters the hearing with a proposed salary (Wakefield wanted $2.5 million) while the team comes in at another (the Red Sox offered $1.55 million), and the arbiter is required to pick one or the other based on arguments made by each side. Unsurprisingly, most cases settle before the hearing at the midpoint between the two exchanged figures, but every once in a while one side or the other (or both) feels so strongly that a hearing is inevitable.

If it goes that far, team representatives make arguments *against* a player whom the club soon will be asking to perform for them, creating a rather uncomfortable dynamic. Arbitration is a performance review to the nth degree, with sometimes millions of dollars at stake. Teams risk a great deal by taking a player to arbitration because, in the event of a team victory, the club often ends up with an unhappy, disgruntled player who is not likely to be especially productive. A player victory certainly might affect the team's budget, but such amounts are small potatoes to organizations like the Red Sox, who are worth hundreds of millions of dollars.

To a player like Tim Wakefield, however, every dollar made all the difference in the world, particularly during a young career that had been marked by instability.

Moss, who represented Wakefield when the matter went to a hearing, was not the same man who had represented Wakefield in negotiations with the team after Wakefield was released by the Pirates during the spring of 1995. Summoned by Wakefield's primary representative, Bill Moore, Moss was a longtime player advocate and staunch supporter of the Major League Baseball Players Association, the union that represented all major league players. Moss was far more familiar than Wakefield's old agent, Bill Moore, with labor issues, arbitration, and conflicts between players and teams. Though near the end of his career as an agent, Moss was an old-school, hard-nosed, no-nonsense businessman. Believing that Wakefield had the stronger case, he refused to settle. Just before the start of spring training, Moss and team representatives squared off in a hearing, Moss presenting both

Wakefield's statistics in Boston and the letter to season-ticket holders as evidence that Wakefield had considerable value to the franchise.

On the one hand, they're using him as a marketing tool. On the other, they're trying to argue that he should not be paid.

Wakefield won the case.

Still, as he prepared to report to spring training for the start of the 1997 season, Wakefield had his fair share of concerns. He was relieved that the matter had been settled in his favor, but he was still operating on a year-to-year basis. Because free agency was another three years away, his chance for a long-term contract might also have to wait that long. Wakefield desperately wanted the security of a long-term contract — wouldn't any knuckleballer? — and the arbitration hearing had been one of the colder, harsher reality checks that baseball could offer. *Why do I have to keep proving myself?* He had done everything the club asked him to do to that point in his Red Sox career — and succeeded — and he had made statistical sacrifices to accommodate the team. And yet, when he thought the club would acknowledge those sacrifices at contract time, Wakefield instead had to take the Sox to arbitration and argue his case.

Nonetheless, as spring training neared, Wakefield was more secure than he had been at perhaps any other time in his professional baseball career. The Red Sox needed pitching. He had a $2.5 million salary. And though Wakefield had been reintroduced to the cutthroat business side of the game, an underlying message he received throughout the winter had been impossible to ignore.

If the team was being truthful in its off-season letter to season-ticket holders, the Red Sox regarded him as a very big part of their future.

And that made Tim Wakefield feel wanted.

YOUNG KNUCKLEBALLER: After being drafted as a power-hitting first baseman, a desperate Tim Wakefield made the conversion to a knuckleballer in 1989. By the time he reached the Triple-A Buffalo Bisons in 1991, the Pittsburgh Pirates were beginning to realize what they had stumbled upon.

Courtesy of the Buffalo Bisons

THE BIG LEAGUES BECKON: At Triple-A Buffalo in 1992, Wakefield went 10-3 with a 3.06 ERA in 20 starts, earning a promotion to the major leagues.

Courtesy of the Buffalo Bisons

ELVIS HAS ENTERED THE BUILDING: Wakefield's arrival in the majors was nothing short of a whirlwind, producing an 8-1 record and postseason heroics. Years later, Pirates manager Jim Leyland would describe Wakefield the rookie as "the Elvis Presley of the National League."

© Dave Arrigo / Pittsburgh Pirates

KNUCKLE SANDWICH: After being released by the Pirates in the spring of 1995, Wakefield was able to resurrect his career with the Red Sox, thanks to the advice and guidance of knuckleballing brothers Phil Niekro (left) and Joe Niekro (right).

Chuck Solomon / Sports Illustrated / Getty Images

GRIP, KICK . . . : During his time in Boston, Wakefield has served as starter, closer, middle reliever, and long reliever, validating Phil Niekro's assertion that knuckleballers are among the most versatile and, therefore, valuable commodities in baseball. *Courtesy of Gary D. Ambush Photography*

. . . AND THROW: In the end, Wakefield became the Red Sox all-time leader in innings pitched, meaning he has recorded more outs than anyone in the history of the franchise. He ranks in the top three on the club's all-time list for victories. *Courtesy of Gary D. Ambush Photography*

THE FAB FIVE: During their historic championship season of 2004, the Red Sox starting rotation consisted of (from left to right) Derek Lowe, Curt Schilling, Pedro Martinez, Bronson Arroyo, and Wakefield. *Julie Cordiero / Boston Red Sox*

THE BOONE OF HIS EXISTENCE:
For the second time in his career,
Wakefield was on the verge of being
named Most Valuable Player of a League
Championship Series when his fortunes
rapidly turned. Aaron Boone's home
run against Wakefield in extra innings
of Game 7 of the 2003 ALCS sent the
Yankees to the World Series and had
Wakefield fearing he would be remembered as the Bill Buckner of his time. That
distinction, of course, ultimately belonged to Red Sox manager Grady Little.

ABOVE: *Julie Cordiero / Boston Red Sox*
RIGHT: *© Matt Campbell / epa / Corbis*

THE KNUCKLER ALSO RISES: One year after allowing the homer to Boone, Wakefield helped the Red Sox complete the most stunning comeback in baseball history. After the Red Sox rallied from a 3-0 series deficit to defeat the Yankees in the ALCS, Wakefield this time celebrated in the visiting clubhouse at Yankee Stadium.

Julie Cordiero / Boston Red Sox

G'DAY MATE: Wakefield spent a significant chunk of his Red Sox career paired with batterymate Doug Mirabelli, who became his personal catcher. *Julie Cordiero / Boston Red Sox*

GAME 1 STARTER: Following the 2004 series win over the Yankees, Red Sox manager Terry Francona named Wakefield his starter for Game 1 of the World Series against the St. Louis Cardinals at Fenway Park. Wakefield recorded a no-decision in the outing, the first of four consecutive Red Sox wins in Boston's climactic World Series sweep. *Brita Meng Outzen / Boston Red Sox*

FAN FAVORITE: An injured Wakefield pulled himself from the playoff rotation in 2007, but his contributions were not forgotten.

Paul Keleher / Flickr Unreleased / Getty Images

FINALLY, AN ALL-STAR: Just before Wakefield's forty-third birthday in 2009, Tampa Bay Rays manager Joe Maddon selected Wakefield for his pitching staff to represent the American League in the 2009 All-Star Game. Wakefield joined (from left to right) closer Jonathan Papelbon, starter Josh Beckett, first baseman Kevin Youkilis, and left fielder Jason Bay at the game.

Michael Ivins / Boston Red Sox

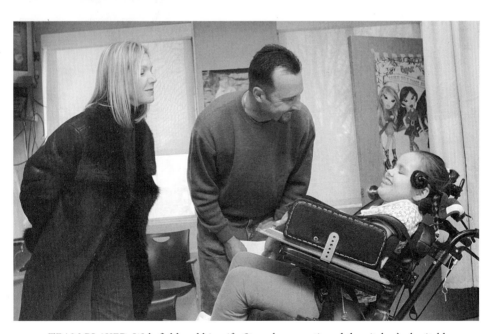

TEAM PLAYER: Wakefield and his wife, Stacy, have continued the pitcher's charitable endeavors throughout his time in Boston. In 2010, Wakefield was awarded the prestigious Roberto Clemente Award for his contributions to baseball on and off the field.

Julie Cordiero / Boston Red Sox

LOYAL TO THE END: At the conclusion of the 2010 season, Wakefield was among a most select group of active major league players to have spent fifteen or more seasons with one team. Entering 2011, he was a mere seven victories short of two hundred for his career.

Michael Ivins / Boston Red Sox

Seven

●

You live and die with it, and hopefully, you don't die too much.

—Knuckleballer Dennis Springer

AQUIRKY AND TRADITIONAL baseball fundamentalist who had a no-nonsense approach to most everything, Jimy Williams was the complete opposite of Kevin Kennedy, whose two-year stint in Boston had ended in ugly fashion. Tim Wakefield noticed the contrast immediately. While Kennedy had photos of movie stars in his office—Natalie Wood was a personal favorite for the California-based Kennedy, who was raised in the Los Angeles Dodgers organization—Wakefield saw Williams as the kind of manager who always seemed to be walking around with baseballs jammed into the rear pockets of his uniform pants, a fungo in his hands, the bill of his cap as flat as a serving tray. Williams looked like something drawn by an old newspaper cartoonist, and the new manager also possessed a wit that was, in a word, sharp.

On the field, too, Kennedy had catered to the superstars, while Williams embraced the role players, a priority that was made clear from the very first moment Williams addressed the Red Sox during spring training. He spoke of being *a team*. He stressed the value of all 25 men on the roster. Wakefield sensed that Jimy Williams took the job managing the Red Sox because he loved *baseball* and not necessarily the fame that came with being in the major leagues, an attitude that Wakefield found refreshing. To Tim Wakefield, Jimy Williams was *real.* And to someone like Jimy Williams, a hard-core baseball lifer who most recently had been the third-base coach of the wildly successful Atlanta Braves in the National League, Tim Wakefield was like every other player on his roster—someone who had value, no matter how specialized his skill or natural abilities.

Kennedy had treated Wakefield well during their two years together, but Kennedy's operating system also drew a clear line between the star players in the Red Sox clubhouse and those players who served more limited roles. Under the unconventional Jimy Williams, who frequently saw things that other baseball managers and coaches did not, Wakefield had no more or less value than anyone else, which was precisely the way Wakefield felt things should be.

"We're going to miss him dearly here," highly respected Braves general manager John Schuerholz said of Williams. "Jimy Williams was, to me, like a sidecar to [renowned Braves manager] Bobby Cox. That's how important he was to our team. Bobby relied on him immensely.... His strength is his absolute, top-to-bottom, in-depth knowledge of the game and a tenacity to succeed. He's a tough competitor. He has a real passion for baseball, and there isn't anyone that works harder than Jimy Williams. . . . Jimy is a guy who will leave no stone unturned to win."

Wakefield liked Williams almost immediately, largely because Williams not only treated all the players the same but was consistent in how he treated everyone in the organization, from the clubhouse attendants to the highest-paid players on the team. Every day, upon walking into the Red Sox clubhouse before the game, Williams would say hello to equipment manager Joe Cochran just as surely as he would say hello to someone like star first baseman Mo Vaughn, the power-hitting centerpiece of the team whom Williams would frequently call "Maurice." There were no theatrics, no melodrama, no hysterics. Every person deserved a hello. Williams's routine was almost always the same, win or lose, and it was very important to him to play the game properly. Once, Wakefield remembered, Williams apologized to the umpires for employing a positional player as a pitcher in a blowout loss, making it clear to the umps that he was trying to save arms, not make a mockery of the game. Williams avoided any self-promotion and said he was trying to *do* right, not *be* right, placing great emphasis on the values that any successful team had to possess and that Wakefield truly believed in.

This guy gets it.

On the field, Williams was a tremendous evaluator who knew almost instantly what types of contributions a player could make to the team. And he valued and gave considerable weight to every contribution, from the sacrifice bunt to the three-run home run, because he believed that such a perspective was necessary for both the success of his club and the health of his clubhouse. He had tremendous patience with young players and took the time to instruct them, work with them, and build their confidence. Williams understood the need for talent and appreciated those players who were truly gifted, but he had little use for the superstar *mentality*, which often gave managers headaches and could eat at the core of a team, the bonds of which he regarded as sacred.

For Wakefield, who never regarded himself as a superstar and never wanted to be one, the message was striking.

Jimy Williams has the same values I do.

The 1997 Red Sox were picked by few to be contenders for a playoff spot. The departure of Roger Clemens had left a gaping hole at the front end of the starting rotation, a group that now included, among others, left-hander Steve Avery, who had signed with the Red Sox as a free agent from the Braves. Wakefield and Avery had a great deal in common, both having been pitchers who burst onto the scene with National League playoff contenders. Their teams had faced one another in the 1992 National League Championship Series. In fact, a year earlier, Avery had been the phenom that Wakefield would become in 1992, posting an 18–8 record during the regular season and pitching absolutely brilliantly during the 1991 NLCS, when he won both of his starts (also against the Pirates) without allowing a run. Avery had seemed well on his way to a sensational career when suddenly he completely changed course: his combined 14–23 record over the 1995 and 1996 seasons ultimately inspired the Braves to cut bait and move on.

A tall, athletic left-hander whose fastball was clocked in the mid-90s at the peak of his career, Avery had all of the assets that traditional baseball evaluators want. He was big. He threw hard. He was even left-handed. And yet his career was fizzling rapidly, teaching a valuable lesson to anyone willing to notice.

That's just how the game works sometimes.

The knuckleball really has nothing to do with it.

It can happen with traditional pitchers, too.

Having had Avery in Atlanta, Williams lobbied for the Red Sox to sign the pitcher, and the move was precisely the kind that Duquette liked, too. Avery's stock was low. Like Wakefield in 1995, Avery was a good gamble, a low risk that could deliver potentially high rewards. He was an excellent competitor. He had played for a winning organization. The cost to the Red Sox was relatively minimal — $4.85 million for one year — and Duquette believed that, at worst, signing Avery could serve as a stopgap measure while the club tried to find a replacement for Clemens, who had anchored the staff since 1986. Further hedging his bets, Duquette also signed rehabilitating veteran right-hander Bret Saberhagen to an incentive-based contract that would pay huge dividends if the pitcher could regain form, though there was the question of when — or if — Saberhagen ever would return to full health.

Though Wakefield had no way of knowing it at the time, the arrival of Avery in particular would place Williams on firm ground in the Boston clubhouse. Unlike Kennedy, who could be volatile and often catered to star players, Williams was a hands-on manager who made almost every decision based on what was best for the team. In the season opener that year, against the Anaheim Angels, Williams had demonstrated the kind of instinct and perceptiveness that relatively few people in baseball possessed. The Red Sox were rallying in the ninth inning against Angels closer Troy Percival, an absurdly hard-throwing right-hander who had the potential for wildness. Percival was struggling with his control. Williams had opened that season with a platoon in right field — Troy O'Leary against right-handers, Rudy Pemberton against left-handers — and his initial plan was to have O'Leary pinch-hit for Pemberton against Percival in the ninth.

Once the manager saw Percival's wildness, he quickly changed course, pulling O'Leary back from the on-deck circle in favor of the right-handed-hitting Pemberton. The move seemed odd. While most major league managers would have embraced the opportunity to force their counterpart to make a move, leveraging someone like the typically dominating Percival *out* of a game, Williams did the opposite. He wanted to keep Percival *in*. A matchup of the left-handed-hitting O'Leary against the right-handed Percival might have inspired opposing manager Terry Collins to yank a struggling Percival from the game, and so Williams sent Pemberton up to bat instead.

Predictably, Collins stuck with Percival, who subsequently hit Pemberton with a pitch to force in a run and tie the game. His club now having blown a 5–2 lead, a frustrated Collins came out of the dugout and lifted Percival from the game. With right-handed-hitting catcher Bill Haselman due up, Collins called for right-handed pitcher Pep Harris. Williams then pulled back Haselman and sent up the left-handed-hitting O'Leary, who dribbled a ball up the third-base line that he beat out for a single to give the Red Sox a 6–5 edge.

After the Red Sox closed out the bottom of the ninth for a highly improbable 6–5 victory, Williams carefully explained himself, taking extra caution to make sure he did not belittle his counterpart, Collins. The game was humbling, Williams believed. Opponents were to be respected. And yet the simple truth was that Williams was two steps ahead of Collins throughout the ninth inning. He had managed the socks off the overmatched Angels skipper.

Wakefield took notice of Williams's strategy that night, recognizing the depth of the manager's knowledge, instinct, and evaluation skills. *He sees things that other people don't.* And while the 1997 Red Sox were a largely mediocre team that never threatened to make the playoffs—they went 78–84 en route to a fourth-place finish—there was reason for optimism. The Red Sox had a rookie shortstop, Nomar Garciaparra, who put together one of the great rookie seasons of all time. Wakefield marveled at his ability. And while Wakefield struggled through the early part of the season—difficulties that temporarily nudged him to the bullpen and required another (theretofore annual) visit from Phil Niekro, aka Dr. Knuckles—he finished 12–15 with a 4.25 ERA while leading the Red Sox with 201⅓ innings pitched. That last number brought Wakefield's three-year running total with the team to 608⅓ innings, a number that was easily tops on the club.

Along the way, Wakefield and others continued to feel the influence of their new manager, who proved to be as bold as he was unconventional. Late in the year, with the Red Sox fading from contention, Duquette ordered the demotion of Avery from the starting rotation to the bullpen, a move that had huge implications for the pitcher. When Avery had signed with the Red Sox, his contract included an option for the 1998 season at $3.9 million that would vest when the pitcher made his 18th start of the year. The provision had been designed to reward Avery, who had suffered some physical problems in Atlanta, if he remained healthy. With the Red Sox out of contention—and with Avery's performance having failed to meet expectations—Red Sox officials had instructed Williams to pull Avery from the rotation after his 17th start. This order became highly publicized (particularly in the absence of any meaningful games late in the year) and triggered a standoff between Williams and the man who had just hired him.

Like most every player in the Boston clubhouse, Wakefield took great interest in the Avery case, which was a classic struggle between an employee and his employer. Wakefield believed that Avery was in the right, and that Williams was caught in the middle. He believed that the Red Sox should allow Avery to pitch and honor the *spirit* of the agreement, which rewarded Avery if he stayed healthy. Avery had done everything the team asked to the best of his ability, and Wakefield already had experienced enough in his young career to feel that players in Avery's kind of situation deserved fair treatment.

Williams, for his part, stewed over the matter, and not solely because he had been a coach in Atlanta when Avery was there, nor because he had lobbied for the pitcher. Earlier in his career, as the manager of the Toronto Blue Jays, Williams had been involved in a similar incident involving pitcher Dennis Lamp, who had a similar incentive in his contract. Following the advice of Blue Jays upper management, Williams had refrained from using Lamp in games. The pitcher subsequently failed to qualify for bonuses that would have paid him hundreds of thousands of dollars, and he filed a grievance against the team through the Major League Baseball Players Association.

Lamp lost the grievance, but the matter never sat well with Williams, who felt that upper management was both telling him how to do his job *and* undermining his credibility with his players. The entire matter struck a very sensitive nerve with the manager and revealed a defiant streak that was both a strength and a weakness. As the manager of the club, Williams didn't like to be told what to do. If management hired him to run the team, management should let him do so. While every major league manager worked at the uncomfortable junction between players and upper management, Williams always regarded himself more as field personnel and less as an executive. Like his players, he wore a *uniform*. And in the case of Lamp, Williams knew that any future decisions he made would be looked upon with suspicion by the same players whom he would ask for sacrifices for the good of the *team*.

Years after the Lamp incident, Williams still regretted how he had handled the matter.

He believed that Dennis Lamp deserved to pitch.

And now he believed that Steve Avery did, too.

On September 25, 1997, with just four games remaining in a regular season during which the Red Sox had long since been eliminated from playoff contention, Jimy Williams named Steve Avery as his starting pitcher for a game at Detroit, all but spitting in the face of team management and stepping over a line drawn in the sand. Williams would stand side by side with his players. Wakefield was among the many Red Sox inspired by Williams's decision. One year after firing Kevin Kennedy, Duquette was in no position to fire another manager for insubordination, particularly after an off-season during which Clemens (who was en route to the Cy Young Award with the Toronto Blue Jays by that point) had left the club via free agency. Duquette had no leverage, and he knew it. Williams, by contrast, was trying to instill some trust in the Boston organization, which had been known throughout all of baseball as terribly dysfunctional. If the Red Sox ever were going to win, Williams reasoned, they needed to change the way they did things.

As it turned out, in his 18th start of the season — an outing that guaranteed his return to the Red Sox in 1998 at a salary of $3.9 million — Steve Avery shut out the Tigers for five innings of an eventual 3–1 Red Sox win. The game meant nothing in the standings, but it meant everything to a Red Sox clubhouse that was bonding with its new manager. And it meant everything to Wakefield, who had come to the conclusion that Jimy Williams was a man worth giving his best for, who respected his manager's knowledge and guts, who believed that Williams would help make him a better pitcher and player.

What Wakefield did not know at the time was that Jimy Williams would lead him to do things he had never envisioned and that no knuckleballer had been asked to do in decades.

Under the terms of the collective bargaining agreement between baseball players and owners, a player must qualify for salary arbitration for as many as three or four years before he can become a free agent. Tim Wakefield entered the off-season of 1997–98 eligible a second time for arbitration, which would allow him to continue increasing his salary as long as he pitched reasonably well.

But this time Wakefield never made it that far.

Facing the prospect of significant annual pay raises for a pitcher who was giving them an average of 200 innings per season — from 1995 to 1997, only 17 other pitchers in baseball won as many games as Wakefield (42) while pitching 600 or more innings — the Red Sox made the obvious and more prudent financial decision: they signed Wakefield to a long-term contract. Talks between the player and the club began on the final weekend of the regular season and concluded about a month later, the team getting a discounted rate for buying in bulk (three years) and Wakefield getting the kind of financial security (a guaranteed $12 million, an average of $4 million per season) that he never dreamed of while laboring for the Buffalo Bisons in Triple A during the summer of 1994.

Wakefield wasn't just a long shot anymore.

He was a bona fide success story.

On a broader scale, the timing of the deal was significant for other reasons. The winter of 1997–98 was expected to be a relatively volatile off-season, though nothing quite like the labor-dispute winter of 1994–95. Major League Baseball was inducting two new teams into the major leagues, the Arizona Diamondbacks and the Tampa Bay Devil Rays, which were set to begin play in 1998 after filling their rosters through the *expansion draft*. To prevent their core players from being available to either of the new teams, existing teams had to identify those players and, in some cases, secure them to contracts. The moment the Red Sox signed Wakefield, they effectively warded off any interested parties by identifying him as their sole property.

Keep off.

That winter, after a long, losing season, public confidence in the Red Sox was sorely lacking. As a result, Duquette was looking to reconstruct the franchise in history-making ways. In the days leading up to the expansion draft, Duquette put in place the pieces of a blockbuster deal that would bring pitcher Pedro Martinez to Boston. A 26-year-old Dominican right-hander who had been named that year's National League Cy Young Award winner, Martinez had just completed a season during which he went 17–8 with a microscopic 1.90 ERA and an eye-popping 305 strikeouts, numbers that bordered on the superhuman. Originally the property of the Los Angeles Dodgers, the 5-foot-11, 185-pound Martinez had been labeled early in his career by Dodgers ambassador Tommy Lasorda as someone who lacked the physical size to succeed in the major leagues as a starting pitcher; the Dodgers had promptly traded him to Montreal for a second baseman named Delino DeShields. At the time, Martinez was a young and especially raw talent whose natural ability piqued the interest of Montreal's general manager, then a young, budding executive who already had a knack for finding diamonds in the rough.

The executive's name?

Dan Duquette.

Now with the Red Sox, Duquette had the chance to acquire Martinez a *second* time, this time under far different circumstances. The Expos knew how good Martinez was, but the team could no longer afford him. Martinez was due for a considerable pay raise through arbitration and would be eligible for free agency following the 1998 season, so Montreal general manager Jim Beattie had little choice but to trade him. And because Duquette had drafted shrewdly through the first four years of his tenure as Red Sox GM, Boston was in a position to offer the Expos cheap, young pitching talent (right-handers Carl Pavano and Tony Armas Jr.) in exchange for Martinez, whom Duquette secured to a six-year, $75 million contract that included an option for a seventh season, bringing the value of the deal to $90 million over seven seasons.

For Wakefield, the impact of the Martinez deal was enormous — and he knew it. Martinez was a true ace among aces, someone whose ability would allow the other pitchers on the Boston staff to settle more comfortably into their roles. The idea of pitching on the same staff as people like Martinez and Saberhagen (who had two career Cy Young Awards to his credit) was beyond appealing. Suddenly, Wakefield found himself with a long-term contract to go along with ample help on the pitching staff and an offense built around affable slugger Mo Vaughn and dynamic young shortstop Garciaparra, all forming the nucleus of a team that could contend for a championship.

This is the best situation I've ever been in, Wakefield thought.

He was right.

And it showed.

"He's a lot more comfortable and a lot more relaxed," Red Sox pitching coach Joe Kerrigan noted of Wakefield at the start of spring training. "He's established himself now. He's a proven multi-game winner. He doesn't have too many ups and downs with the knuckleball anymore."

The 1998 Red Sox also enjoyed a relatively stable, solid ride, winning 17 of their first 23 games and rumbling to a 92–70 finish that earned them a return trip to the playoffs for the first time since 1995. Wakefield played an enormous role. Early in the season, he ripped off a stretch of eight consecutive starts during which he went 6–0 with a 3.20 ERA. Shortly thereafter, he went 4–1 with a 4.08 ERA over six consecutive outings. Suddenly, the good stretches were lasting longer and the bad outings were limited to isolated performances now and then, the kind of ebb and flow that was far more customary for reliable, traditional pitchers than it was for knuckleballers (at least in the eyes of the traditional baseball world). The Red Sox were rolling along, and Wakefield suddenly was blessed with the best of both worlds — the durability and resiliency of a knuckleballer and the consistency and reliability of a traditional starter — a blend that indisputably made him one of the very best pitchers in baseball on one of the best teams in baseball.

In fact, as Wakefield approached the end of the season, he had a chance at one of pitching's truly timeless accomplishments: a 20-win season. Superstitious as ever — and unforgettably battle-scarred — Wakefield dismissed that kind of talk out of hand, saying that such an achievement would be "nice," but that he was "not really thinking about that." Of course, the number was a clear and obvious goal. The tandem of Martinez and Wakefield in particular created quite the contrast: each was within range of 20 victories, the knuckleballer baffling hitters while the fireballing right-hander simply blew them away.

Two completely different pitching strategies, but with remarkably similar results.

Said Williams of his tandem, which was more like a trio when Saberhagen was thrown into the mix: "It's like, one day, you're on one of those really fast trains and you go where you're going. The next day, you go back to where you started and get on a stagecoach."

Whatever the analogy, the Red Sox were enjoying the ride.

Wakefield finished with a 17–8 record, a 4.58 ERA — the league average was 4.66 — and precisely 216 innings pitched, the last statistic ranking second only to Martinez, who faded down the stretch and finished with 19 wins. (No one attributed Martinez's slump to the unpredictable nature of the knuckleball.) The Red Sox faced the Cleveland Indians in the first round of the playoffs and were ousted in four games in the best-of-five affair — Wakefield pitched poorly — but there was nonetheless a feeling in Boston that the Red Sox were building again, primarily on a foundation that included Martinez, Garciaparra, Wakefield, and Tom Gordon, who turned in a spectacular season after being converted into a reliever.

In any given game, the Red Sox were good at the beginning, good in the middle, and good at the end.

For Wakefield, the 17 victories established a career best and gave him 59 wins in 824⅓ innings during his Red Sox career, numbers that translated into 15 victories and 206 innings per season. While those totals underscored Wakefield's value to the club, they also made him one of the best bargains in baseball. Martinez, for instance, had signed a six-year, $75 million contract that guaranteed him $12.5 million a year during the life of the deal, more than three times the average annual value of what the Red Sox were paying Wakefield in his three-year, $12 million deal. And while Martinez was a better pitcher, his bottom-line contributions (63 wins, 886⅓ innings) were not three times as great as those of Wakefield, offering even more evidence that baseball people were willing to spend for fastballs, but the knuckler still made them nervous.

And then there was this: while someone like Martinez had pitched exclusively as a starter during the span—all of his 127 outings were starts—Wakefield had also pitched out of the bullpen, filling gaps when the Red Sox needed him to. His individual statistics suffered as a result, and as he would be reminded throughout his career, his versatility and sacrifices earned him relatively little when it came time to sit down at the negotiating table.

Still, if they asked, he delivered.

To Tim Wakefield, the rise of Tom Gordon was, at the very least, instructive.

Though the Red Sox had signed Tom Gordon as a starter prior to the 1997 season, Gordon had spent his career shuttling to and from the bullpen, a pattern that continued during the 1997 season, his first in Boston. Out of the bullpen, Gordon had been used as a long reliever: he would pitch for two to three innings per appearance, but his outings were limited to roughly two a week. In 1998, in the kind of radical move that Jimy Williams was most unafraid to try, the Red Sox made

Gordon their closer, pitching him for one or two innings at a time at the end of games but increasing the frequency of his appearances to three or four a week. The change produced stunning results: Gordon secured a Red Sox record 46 saves in 46 opportunities during a total of 73 appearances, the highest total of his career.

But in 1999 the predictable happened.

Gordon injured his weary right throwing arm, suffering ligament damage that all but ended his season.

While Gordon's injury was unfortunate — most pitchers need the stability of a routine — it also further highlighted the value of someone like Wakefield, whose arm was not just effective but also resilient. Prior to 1998, Gordon had never pitched in more than 49 games in any of his 10 seasons. In 1998 he pitched in 73. And while Gordon's innings total in 1998 was limited to just 79⅓ — he had pitched in as many as 215⅔ innings in prior seasons — the change in routine was too much for his arm to endure over an extended period of time, leading to a physical breakdown. The bottom line was that Gordon's arm and pitching style were better suited for slightly longer stints, not shorter ones, though teams were far more interested in him as a short reliever (where he could be dominating) instead of as a starter (where he was generally mediocre).

With Gordon sidelined, Williams had one logical option at his disposal, young right-hander Derek Lowe. Acquired from the Seattle Mariners in 1997 as a starter, Lowe had been transitioned to the bullpen during the 1998 season, and the results were similarly striking. In 53 appearances out of the bullpen in 1998, Lowe went 3–2 with a sterling 2.88 ERA, becoming one of the more effective setup men in baseball. Lowe's arm had proven quite resilient during the span, and his skill set at that point in his career also was more suited for the bullpen. Baseball evaluators usually reason that a starting pitcher needs at least three effective pitches to succeed in the major leagues — a fastball, curveball, and changeup, for example — because the longer stints require starters to face the same hitter as many as three, four, or five times in a game. In each at-bat, a pitcher needs to be able to offer something different enough to keep the hitter off balance.

Derek Lowe had a truly dominating sinker that could handcuff even the most skilled right-handed batter, and so the Red Sox began using him in late-inning situations, particularly when a string of right-handed batters was due up.

The problem was that Lowe was still developing and still quite temperamental, which made him ill suited for the final inning of a game, when the competition intensified and the outcome was often on the line. He just wasn't ready for the stress of closing yet. Williams tried Lowe in the closer's role for a time, with varying degrees of success. The young pitcher had a hard time getting over his failures, suffering the kind of *hangover* that a manager could not afford in a game that provides precious few breaks along the way. In baseball, as the colorful Martinez liked to point out, there is no crying. There is another game to be played. Mental toughness is a prerequisite.

And so, with the Red Sox in the midst of a crisis — where were they going to find a closer? — Jimy Williams did something that led many people to wonder whether he was downright cuckoo.

He turned the responsibility of closing over to his knuckleballer.

"When [Gordon] got hurt, we put Lowe in that situation," Williams recalled. "To be very honest, he struggled at the outset. The one thing about Wake is that he would always take the ball. He would relieve in between starts — he didn't care. He just wanted the ball, and he was so strong mentally that I believed he could handle it."

On May 6, 1999, in a game the Red Sox led 3–1 in the ninth inning, Tim Wakefield was among a group of unsuspecting relievers when manager Jimy Williams lifted the receiver from the dugout phone and delivered a message to his relief corps: get Wakefield up. Wakefield glanced at the other relievers in the Boston bullpen, all of them wearing the same surprised facial expression as if it were part of the Boston uniform. *Is he serious?* The knuckleballer, as always, had made himself available for relief duty between starts, but the Red Sox were in a save situation. In this game, his time had come and gone. No one expected him to *close.* Wakefield hurriedly began his warm-up routine, his heart "racing a thousand miles an hour" — and his mind hurrying along at roughly the same speed — as left-hander Rheal Cormier began the ninth by retiring Rafael Palmeiro on a lineout. *Jimy must be joking.*

Texas catcher Ivan Rodriguez then singled before Todd Zeile doubled him home. The Red Sox now led by the slimmest of margins, 3–2, with one out and the tying run on second base.

Williams came out of the dugout and walked to the mound, raising his arm and signaling Wakefield into the game.

Here we go.

Now approaching his 33rd birthday, Wakefield had already pitched in an array of pressure situations during his career. He had shone in the 1992 National League Championship Series. On more than one occasion, he had felt as if he was pitching to save his career. And yet, no event during Wakefield's career had made him more nervous than his first closing opportunity, an occasion on which he "specifically felt like my heart was going to beat out of my jersey." Looking tight and restricted in his delivery, Wakefield threw ball one to the left-handed-hitting Lee Stevens. Then he threw ball two. And then, as Wakefield settled into the stretch position to throw his third pitch, a fan sprinted onto the field at Fenway Park, causing a temporary stop in play as security pursued and secured the trespasser. This interruption gave Wakefield a moment to step back off the mound and take a long, deep breath.

Whew.

"It was enough to calm me down," he said.

The third pitch to Lee Stevens was a strike. So was the fourth. The fifth produced a groundout to the left side for the second out, Zeile remaining at second base. Wakefield threw just two more pitches on the day, the last resulting in Luis Alicea's harmless fly ball to right field that landed in the glove of Red Sox outfielder Trot Nixon for the final out in a 3–2 Boston victory that successfully challenged conventional wisdom and earned Wakefield his first career save.

Wakefield made two more scoreless relief appearances — one in a save situation — before Williams returned him to the starting rotation on May 11. About a month later, when the Red Sox again had a need in their bullpen, Williams made a more significant, longer-term switch.

"I thought, *Wakefield can do this*," said the manager. "I went and talked to him, and he was all for it."

Or so he told his manager.

Willing as ever to fill a team need, Wakefield had his doubts about closing. He regarded himself as a starter and wasn't sure he was suited for the closer's role, which had an entirely different routine. And yet, as uncomfortable as he was with the switch, Wakefield took a great deal of pride in the fact that Williams had come to *him* to handle a part of the game that was an enormous *responsibility*. He felt the obligation to try. Closers are entrusted with leads, and it is their job to transform those advantages into wins. The job is completely different from the job of a starter, who must keep the team close and often has to let other factors determine the outcome.

For as much second-guessing as Williams endured for his strategy, his decision may not have been as unusual as many had deemed it. Knuckleballers had closed games before, after all, the great Hoyt Wilhelm chief among those who had done it effectively. Wilbur Wood had closed, too. But somewhere during the 20 years that separated the end of Wood's career from the heart of Wakefield's, the transformation in baseball had made some beliefs — for lack of a better word — outdated. As the salaries of all players rapidly escalated in the wake of free agency, starters were treated with great care, their outings shortened in hopes of preventing injury. Relievers were used and cast aside like disposable razors, particularly those who pitched in the middle of the game. And the relievers used at the end of a game were almost always intimidating, hard-throwing bullies expected to prevent contact and blow opponents away.

During that 20-year period, the responsibility of pitching the ninth inning had taken on colossal proportions, and so managers took no chances. They wanted strikeouts. Any contact on the part of an opposing hitter could be costly. Even brilliant and widely respected men like Jim Leyland fretted at the prospect of a ground ball to shortstop in the ninth inning, let alone a passed ball or stolen base, and so the idea of closing with anyone but a fireballer was deemed illogical.

A knuckleballer?

That was, in a word, crazy.

Maybe even stupid.

Nonetheless, between June 13 and August 17, 1999, Jimy Williams summoned Tim Wakefield out of the bullpen 25 times, 15 of those appearances coming in save situations. Wakefield successfully converted 12 and blew three. Though he remained skeptical about himself in the closer role, he got used to it. He adapted. During that stretch, the Red Sox went 17–8 in Wakefield's 25 appearances and remained in the thick of playoff contention. Once again, the knuckleballer provided great stability in an area where the Red Sox desperately needed it. During one game in Kansas City, Wakefield's knuckleball was moving so unpredictably that young catcher Jason Varitek simply could not handle it, the pitch producing the kind of results that led Williams's critics and other skeptics to offer a predictable *I told you so.*

Handed a 5–3 lead over the Royals, Wakefield began the ninth inning by striking out Chad Kreuter and Scott Pose. He then struck out Johnny Damon, too, but when the third strike eluded Varitek, Damon safely scampered to first base. Carlos Febles then belted a game-tying, two-run homer before Wakefield struck out a *fourth* batter in the inning, Carlos Beltran, in a succession of events that delivered all of the knuckleball's traits in one highly concentrated package: strikeouts, passed balls, and home runs. The Red Sox then rallied for four runs to take a 9–5 lead that ultimately would grant the Red Sox (and Wakefield) a win, but Williams was forced to pull Wakefield for right-hander Rich Garces with two outs in the bottom of the 10th inning after Wakefield had struck out two more *and* been charged with another passed ball.

"His knuckleball was so good that 'Tek couldn't catch it," Williams chuckled. "I had to take him out and bring in Garces to get the last out."

Of course, while a traditional closer might not have matched Wakefield's outing in terms of peculiarity, the reality is that a hard thrower might just as easily have blown the game in as frustrating a manner as Wakefield had. Two years earlier, after all, fireballing Anaheim closer Troy Percival had blown a game in such fashion against the Red Sox in the contest that marked Williams's managerial debut, and at the time Percival was regarded as one of the best in the business. And yet, while most baseball observers were willing to chalk up Percival's failure that night as a fluke, many of the same people looked at Wakefield's carnival ride in Kansas City as far more predictable, a just verdict for a manager who tempted the baseball fates.

The reality, of course, was that Wakefield was as good as most anybody else at closing games during the 1999 season, if not better. That season, of the 38 major league pitchers who finished with at least 10 saves — the Red Sox had three of them — Wakefield finished a respectable 16th in save percentage, the statistic that measured his efficiency in his new role. He successfully converted 15 of 18 opportunities, a conversion rate of 83.3 percent that placed him ahead of, among others, Percival of the Angels (79.5 percent), Armando Benitez of the New York Mets (78.6 percent), teammate Lowe (75 percent), Mike Timlin of the Baltimore Orioles (75 percent), and Scott Williamson of the Cincinnati Reds (73.1 percent).

Wakefield understood all of that, naturally.

Jimy Williams clearly did, too.

But there were others in the Boston organization who understood neither Wakefield's value to the team nor the many uses of the knuckleball.

Eight

●

The knuckleball screws up the mind.

— *Former major league coach Tim Owens*

AT ONE OF the darker and more disappointing moments of his Red Sox career, Tim Wakefield was blindsided. The Red Sox had just survived the 1999 American League Division Series with an emotional and draining comeback against the Cleveland Indians. They were delighted, but that hard-fought series had the team scrambling. And now they had the Yankees to face. Wakefield slept some on the team's flight from Cleveland to New York, but he was also busy wondering about his role in the next round of the playoffs.

The next day, seated at his locker at Yankee Stadium, Wakefield folded up his favorite section of *USA Today,* crossed his legs, and began working on the crossword puzzle as the team prepared for an off-day workout in anticipation of the rapidly approaching American League Championship Series. Wakefield had pitched twice in relief during the Indians series, but the outings were short. He was rested. And because the Red Sox pitching staff had been depleted during the Cleveland series, Wakefield believed that he was in prime position to aid the cause.

I wonder if they'll ask me to start Game 1.

Of course, Wakefield wanted to start Game 1, felt he deserved it, believed he could help. The Red Sox felt otherwise. Wakefield was still seated at his locker when he noticed manager Jimy Williams nervously walk by, avoiding eye contact, with no apparent destination. *That's weird.* For several minutes, the manager kept walking back and forth in front of Wakefield's locker. Maybe his sometimes quirky manager, he thought, was merely burning off nervous energy following a series and trip that had left them all drained, exhausted, operating on fumes.

Then Williams finally stopped and abruptly invited Wakefield into the visiting manager's office at Yankee Stadium, where he asked Wakefield to sit as he shut the door.

At that instant, Williams also shut the door on Tim Wakefield's 1999 season.

Believing he was about to be named the Game 1 starter, Wakefield instead sat in disbelief as Williams informed him that he would be left off the active roster for the ALCS against New York. Wakefield was not merely bypassed for Game 1; he would not be pitching *at all.* He did not know what to say or do. He asked Williams for an explanation but never really got one, the manager instead mincing his words and talking in circles. Williams had arrived at the ballpark early that day, he told Wakefield, and had been in his office "stewing for two hours." Then he had walked into the clubhouse, repeatedly checking to see if Wakefield had arrived. After Wakefield showed up and settled into the chair in front of his locker, Williams found himself still unable to engage his pitcher.

The more Williams talked, the more Wakefield wondered, *Is Jimy really the one making this decision?* Two years earlier, Williams had stood his ground with regard to Steve Avery, but that was a different case. Williams had felt he was being told *how* to employ his pitcher, and *how* fell under the jurisdiction of the manager. For someone like Williams, in any organization, roles were clear. The general manager got the players. The manager implemented them. Problems arose when boundaries were not respected. But if Wakefield was being left off the playoff roster, that decision had to be coming from higher up. There had to be other factors influencing the outcome of an organizational discussion on the matter.

To Wakefield, his manager seemed unusually evasive. Williams danced around questions about the decision-making process and his role in them, all of which led Wakefield to believe that pitching coach

Joe Kerrigan was the one who had argued against his presence on the roster. An ally of general manager Dan Duquette, Kerrigan had that kind of power when it came to the pitching staff. It was entirely possible that in the organizational decision-making about the playoff roster, Williams was outnumbered and thus overruled. And so a frustrated, angry, and dejected Tim Wakefield got up from his seat and walked out of the manager's office, feeling as if Jimy Williams had delivered a message that he himself did not believe in.

This is unbelievable.

I can't believe this bullshit.

Indeed, to that point, there was no way Wakefield could have forecast such a demotion. The Red Sox were on a high in the wake of their victory over the Indians, a five-game affair in which the Red Sox had overcome a 2–0 series deficit and won the last three games, the final and decisive affair behind six brilliant relief innings from a wounded Martinez, who had strained his shoulder in Game 1. Wakefield had pitched twice in the series, including an effective outing in Game 2, and a second, less effective performance had been fraught with confusion. In the fifth inning of Game 4, after Rich Garces walked lead-off man Roberto Alomar in a game the Red Sox were leading 15–2, Wakefield had been ordered to start warming up. He had not had sufficient warm-up time when he was summoned into the game, but he said nothing. Wakefield then issued a pair of walks and two singles to the four batters he faced, trimming the Red Sox lead to 15–4 and prompting his removal from the game.

As it turned out, that outing had hurt Wakefield, at least in the eyes of Kerrigan. And so, after a season in which he did everything the Red Sox asked him to, Wakefield was undone by four batters in a lopsided affair during which he felt rushed into the game.

They put more weight on four batters I faced in a 15–2 game than they did on what I gave them during the regular season.

Even Williams clearly and obviously sensed the unfairness of it all. Wakefield finished the regular season with individual totals that hardly illustrated his contributions to the team—a 6–11 record, a 5.08 ERA, and 15 saves in 140 innings pitched—but that was a trade that Williams and others were willing to make because of the emphasis placed on the ninth inning. Late in the year, Williams had made it a point to highlight Wakefield's contributions and had focused far more on the group results than the individual ones because those were what mattered.

"I don't think there's been a pitcher in this era who has done the things Wakefield has done," said the knowledgeable manager.

And yet, now Wakefield was *out.*

It made no sense to him.

Outraged, Wakefield returned to his locker at Yankee Stadium and later vanished into the more private areas of the visiting clubhouse, hoping to avoid reporters who undoubtedly would ask him about being slighted after the season of sacrifices he had just produced. When the media finally corralled him, Wakefield tersely declined comment. On the inside, he was angry and hurt, feeling that the team had deprived him of something he had dutifully earned. He wanted to go home and leave the team altogether, but teammates Mark Portugal and Rod Beck, both veteran pitchers, persuaded him to stay. *You're not the kind of guy who leaves. That's not who you are.* Wakefield watched the postseason from the dugout and the clubhouse, often wishing he were somewhere else throughout the balance of the postseason, a five-game series during which the Yankees rolled to a 4–1 series victory over Boston — and eventually a third World Series title in four years.

While Boston's problems in the series were primarily on offense — the Red Sox scored a mere eight runs in the four losses and truly dominated only in Game 3, a 13–1 victory behind the otherworldly Martinez — Wakefield believed that he could have helped. Still, that belief was causing only a fraction of his angst. Wakefield believed that the Red Sox owed him something, too, and he eventually became more convinced than ever that it was pitching coach Kerrigan who had undermined him. Following the '99 season, in a phone conversation with Wakefield, Williams suggested that the pitcher blame his manager for the slight at playoff time, but it was entirely within Williams's character to fall on his sword for the good of the team, just as the skipper had done in the manager's office at Yankee Stadium.

The more Wakefield thought about it, the more the pieces fit together. Wakefield's status as a knuckleballer frequently left Kerrigan helpless, just as Niekro had predicted. *Managers and pitching coaches, they can't help you much with the knuckleball.* And when push came to shove, when it came time to give Wakefield the smallest measure of thanks for a season filled with sacrifice, the Red Sox replaced him on the playoff roster.

Wakefield had never once thought that the sacrifices he made during the regular season would hurt him with regard to his place on the playoff roster.

As it turned out, the entire series of events left a mark on his soul that extended well beyond October 1999.

By most accounts, Joe Kerrigan was a fairly judicious pitching coach and a student of the game, but one who lacked the people skills that might have made him more popular and possibly more effective. In the major leagues, pitching coaches are often psychologists. Most of the pitchers have indisputable ability. The coach's job is to tailor his methods to the specific needs of each player, to enhance strengths and cover weaknesses.

Kerrigan's level of tinkering often went too far, as happened with a young Japanese right-hander named Tomo Ohka, who had gone a combined 15–0 with a 2.31 ERA in the minor leagues during the 1999 season before being summoned to the major leagues. When the young pitcher's results did not similarly transfer immediately, Kerrigan began overhauling his mechanics, changing the way he did things. Veteran Sox players took note and shook their heads. Ohka finished 1–2 with a 6.23 ERA that season and ultimately fizzled out in Boston before winning 10 or more games in three separate seasons with other teams. While Ohka hardly became a superstar, there was a sentiment in the Boston organization at the time that Kerrigan had hurt Ohka more than he had helped him, largely because Kerrigan wanted Ohka to do things *his* way rather than utilize the talents and style that had helped him in the minor leagues.

And then there was this statistic: during the 1997 season, the year before Martinez arrived in Boston, the Red Sox had ranked 12th in the

American League in team ERA with Kerrigan as their pitching coach. In the two years after Martinez joined the staff, Boston had ranked second in 1998 and first in 1999. The obvious conclusion was that the pitchers made a great deal more difference than the pitching coach, a fact that made Kerrigan's résumé look a good deal more like Ringo Starr's than John Lennon's or Paul McCartney's.

For Wakefield, Kerrigan was a positively terrible match, a pitching coach who had little use or desire to understand the true value of the knuckleball. What people like Duquette and Williams saw in the knuckler, Kerrigan did not. To him, it was as unreliable as a trick chair, likely to produce a fall or collapse for the next sap foolish enough to ride it. With conventional pitchers, Kerrigan often applied an analytical approach based on data accumulated over large chunks of time, numbers that inevitably revealed patterns and tendencies. If statistics showed that right-handed pitchers could neutralize someone like Cleveland Indians slugger Manny Ramirez with curveballs and sliders to the outside of the plate, then the Red Sox were likely to employ precisely that strategy, no matter who was on the mound. The evidence was what mattered. Kerrigan often molded the pitchers to the strategy instead of the other way around, discounting the specific skill sets of the pitchers on the Boston staff.

With Wakefield, of course, such an approach was futile because he almost always threw one pitch, the knuckleball, regardless of who was hitting, or where, or when. Wakefield believed, as Niekro had taught him, that the knuckleball was *the only pitch in baseball where, every time you throw it, it can be an out pitch.* Kerrigan, by contrast, saw the knuckler as something to which no hard data could be applied, the squarest of square pegs, a pitch that minimized his value as a pitching coach and rendered him virtually useless anytime Wakefield pitched.

In that way, Joe Kerrigan seemed to put his values before the contributions from his pitchers, a colossal error in judgment that greatly minimized Wakefield's contributions during a span of seasons in which the Red Sox, coincidentally or not, never reached their true potential as a team.

Wakefield did not have a terrible year in 2000 so much as he had a terribly unfulfilling one. At 33 years old, entering what should have been the prime of his career as a knuckleballer, Wakefield pitched in 51 games and made just 17 starts. He finished 13 games and did not record a save, which is to say that the Red Sox used him largely in mop-up situations in which the knuckleball's irregularities could not hurt them (or help them, for that matter). For Wakefield, the frustration boiled over in the middle of the season when he was summoned into a 15–1 game against the New York Yankees and asked to record the final four outs of a historic 22–1 defeat. In the span of a year, Wakefield had gone from bullpen savior to punching bag—at least in his mind—and he was at such a loss to explain his fall from grace that he did something very rare for him—he erupted.

"What do you want to know, that I was publicly embarrassed?" said an angry Wakefield. "I'm sick and tired of it. I feel like I'm being punished or penalized for being a team player. It's hard to swallow how I go from being a number-two or number-three starter, winning 13 games and pitching 200 innings a year, to being a fill-in guy, a mop-up. What they did to me was wrong, and you can ask any guy in here and they'd agree with you.

"People might think I'm crying, and I know I'm getting paid, but money is not the issue," he continued. "It's about respect. It's about loyalty. . . . There's nothing they can tell me that will make me feel better."

Indeed, while it was highly unusual for Wakefield to speak out, the pitcher had a point. Had he been ineffective as a closer a year earlier, the Red Sox might have left him in the rotation, and he just might have won his 14 or 15 games and pitched 200 innings. Instead, in helping the team, his individual performance as a starter suffered. The club moved him to the bullpen just before the beginning of the regular season, a decision that had Wakefield, if only for a brief time, wondering whether he should ask for a trade. The team's replacements for Wakefield in the starting rotation were grossly insufficient, and yet the Red Sox continued to use Wakefield out of the bullpen, in inconsequential situations, depriving both him and the team of valuable outs that might have helped them win more games.

In Wakefield's mind, none of it made any sense.

These guys don't know what they're doing.

Indeed, had it not been for Martinez, the Boston staff might have crumbled altogether. While Duquette had attempted to fortify the Boston offense by acquiring mercurial center fielder Carl Everett from the Houston Astros over the winter, a disproportionate number of innings in the starting rotation were falling on Martinez, who was performing at a level that would make him perhaps the single greatest player of his generation.

Like most everyone in Boston during those years, Wakefield found Martinez to be thoroughly entertaining and colorful, on the mound and off. Martinez had an infectious personality that permeated the Boston clubhouse, especially on the four days he did not pitch. He had the social impact of a class clown who was both loved by his mates and occasionally got on their nerves. Martinez's smarts, wit, and personality bridged the cultural gaps on the roster and endeared him to most everyone — he often referred to Wakefield as "Wakey" — and Wakefield felt that Martinez brought a blast of fresh air into a Boston market that sometimes needed to remember that baseball was a *game*. Martinez was *fun*. He was engaging. He said hello to anyone and everyone in and around Fenway Park, and Wakefield developed enormous respect for the way Martinez approached the game.

Off the field and on road trips, Martinez often kept to himself, but on the field he was the consummate teammate. Aside from possessing the desire to win, Martinez routinely retaliated for transgressions against Red Sox hitters, sometimes to a fault. In fact, his aggressiveness earned him, in some circles, a reputation as a head-hunter.

"Intense," Wakefield said of Martinez. "One of the best competitors I've ever seen."

In 1999 and 2000, too, Martinez put together arguably the two greatest back-to-back seasons of all time, winning consecutive American League Cy Young Awards (giving him three for his career) and performing at a level that was drawing comparisons to Sandy Koufax, among others. In those two seasons, Martinez went a combined 41–10 with a 1.90 ERA, a performance that only grew in magnitude when it was revealed that baseball was in the midst of an offensive era tainted by rampant steroid use. During the 1999 and 2000 seasons, when the overall ERA in the American League was 4.88, Martinez's total was almost *three full runs per game* better than the league average; as a result, the average outcome of a game he pitched was something in the neighborhood of 5–2, which qualified as one-sided. Beyond that, during the same two-year span, the next-best pitcher behind Martinez in terms of ERA was Baltimore Orioles right-hander Mike Mussina, whose aggregate ERA was 3.65. In other words, Martinez was roughly *twice* as good as the next-best starter in the AL. The gap between Martinez and everyone else, in a manner of speaking, was about as big as the gap between Wakefield and Kerrigan.

Wakefield, like most everyone else, relished opportunities to watch Martinez pitch, and he appreciated Martinez's presence on the Boston staff as much as anyone else. Wakefield knew what an ace like Martinez meant to both him and the team. In Pittsburgh, the demands on Wakefield had grown unrealistic following the departure of Doug Drabek. The departure of Clemens had created a similar dynamic in Boston. As much as the arrival of a pitcher like Martinez gave Boston an ace who could beat any team at any time, it also established a clear hierarchy on the Boston staff that slotted pitchers according to their abilities and ensured that each pitcher only needed to do *his* job.

If his impact on the team meant that Martinez was pampered some during his time in Boston — and he was — Wakefield could accept that as a necessary side effect. He liked Pedro, though he did not particularly care for how some Sox personnel, particularly Kerrigan, catered to him. But Wakefield would have been more than willing to live with some spoiling of the ace pitcher had the Red Sox simply allowed him to do what he did best — pile up innings. The disconnect there between him and Kerrigan was causing him great frustration.

For whatever reason, or for many, the 2000 Sox never really melded. They missed the playoffs and finished with an 85–77 record despite the efforts of their inimitable ace. Everett's troubled soul surfaced by year's end, explaining why such a talented outfielder had been available by trade in the first place. An outspoken, volatile, and sometimes frightening man who could also be charming, Everett had a chip on his shoulder the size of Fenway Park's famed left-field wall. Sometimes he would angrily rant and rave in the clubhouse, and at one point during the season he head-butted umpire Ron Kulpa. Everett made his teammates uneasy, and the tension he created ate at the fabric of the team, making it more difficult for players to succeed in a market where it was already nearly impossible.

Following the season, having reached the end of his three-year, $12 million contract with the team, Wakefield waited to hear whether the Sox would exercise their $5 million option for the 2001 season. When the team declined, he became a free agent for the first time in his career. He wondered whether Kerrigan was arguing against him again, just as the pitching coach had done during the 1999 playoffs. To that point, Wakefield had still resisted buying a home in the Boston area and putting down roots because he remained unsure about where his career and, more specifically, the knuckleball would take him. Despite all that had happened in Boston over the last two seasons, Wakefield told his agents that he still wanted to remain with the Red Sox. The Baltimore Orioles and Minnesota Twins had expressed some interest in signing him, but the pitcher instructed his agents to inform both teams that Boston was his priority. The Red Sox had given Wakefield a chance when few other teams did, united him with Niekro, rewarded him with contracts. His frustration over the last season or two did not change the fact that his time in Boston generally had been a good experience. He recognized what was important to him, and he had little desire to make decisions out of spite.

I can't preach about loyalty without showing it.

In December 2000, with Wakefield and the Red Sox facing a deadline, Wakefield agreed to a new two-year contract with the team for a guaranteed $6.5 million that included an option for the 2003 season. He was the property of the Red Sox again. In the rotation or out of the bullpen, he was going to pitch for Boston. Wakefield resented the way he was sometimes used—at one point he suggested that the Red Sox were "abusing" his versatility—but he also recognized that part of his value as a pitcher was that the team could ask him to do things that other pitchers could not. Again, Niekro's words guided him.

Knuckleball pitchers can start for you, they can be long men or middle men, and they can close. Wakefield had done all of those things during his six seasons in Boston, and there was no other pitcher in the Boston organization — or for that matter, anywhere else — who could claim to have helped his team in as many ways.

That is something to be proud of.

For the Red Sox, the 2001 season would prove to be a relative disaster, though it could have been far worse had it not been for the efforts and versatility of their familiar knuckleballer and the addition of players like slugger Manny Ramirez, whom Duquette had signed to a club record eight-year, $160 million contract during the off-season. The Ramirez signing came after the Sox had lost out on their pursuit of pitcher Mussina, but it nonetheless qualified as the biggest free-agent acquisition in Red Sox history. Many assumed that the Red Sox were increasing their payroll to keep up with the Yankees — New York won the 2000 World Series, its third straight title and fourth in five years — but the Red Sox had other motivations, too. For one, unbeknownst to most, the club would soon be up for sale, and a player like Ramirez would dramatically increase the value of the franchise. For another, the Red Sox had an 80 percent ownership stake in the New England Sports Network (NESN), which broadcast their games, and NESN was about to become part of the basic package on cable outlets throughout New England. Adding Ramirez at that point in time would increase television ratings, which would increase ad revenues, which would increase profits.

For the first time in club history, the Red Sox payroll eclipsed $100 million, coming in during the summer of 2001 at $110 million, $30 million more than the Sox had spent a year earlier.

Duquette and owner John Harrington were now chiefly focused on the sale of the club, but unfortunate events on the field undermined part of their plan. Early in spring training, wonder-boy shortstop Garciaparra had recurring symptoms from a wrist injury he had suffered earlier in his career, an issue that ultimately required surgery and effectively wiped out his entire season. (He played in just 21 games.) Stalwart catcher Varitek broke his elbow while making a diving catch during a game the Red Sox were winning easily in June, a mishap that ended the catcher's season as well. And on top of it all, the Sox effectively lost incomparable ace Martinez to a season-ending shoulder injury halfway through the season, the weight of the Boston staff having finally piled up on the team ace the way some had feared it would in the wake of two seasons during which the Red Sox got decidedly little from any other starter. Martinez's injury begged some questions:

Could Wakefield have made a difference?

Might he have helped preserve Pedro?

Along the way, Wakefield had merely continued to do his part, oscillating between the bullpen and the rotation with great efficiency. At midseason, he ranked among the American League leaders in ERA and had settled back into the rotation. And yet, with Martinez approaching a return from the disabled list in August, Wakefield learned he would be bounced from the rotation yet again, this time to accommodate Pedro. The move made no sense to him. He had pitched well all year. And so when Kerrigan informed him of the decision during a meeting in the players' lounge of the visiting clubhouse at Camden Yards in Baltimore, Wakefield uncharacteristically snapped, years of frustration pouring out in one damaging burst.

You don't get it. You don't know half as much as you think you do. You don't like me, and you never have. You know nothing about the knuckleball, and you don't want to because you want to take credit for everything.

The aftershocks, too, were damaging.

Three days after the win over the Orioles, Duquette fired Jimy Williams, with whom he had been feuding over, among other things, the renegade behavior of Carl Everett. The clubhouse was in turmoil. Veteran players were griping about inconsistent playing time. The Red Sox lacked chemistry and leadership during an injury-filled season in which frustrations had long since begun to mount. Wakefield was quite disillusioned to see a scapegoat made of Williams, whom he liked a lot and for whom he had a great deal of respect, despite some of the personal frustrations he had felt over the past two seasons. While some Sox players seemed relieved that Williams was gone, Wakefield almost always regarded managerial changes as a bad thing, an indication, above all else, that a team was failing. *It means we haven't been doing our jobs.* And yet, he also knew that teams were known to go on winning streaks in the wake of a managerial change, playing as if liberated from oppression or simply the monotony of a routine that had long since gone stale.

In the case of the 2001 Red Sox, there was no real such benefit, mostly because Williams's replacement was a man for whom Red Sox players had an even higher level of distrust: pitching coach Joe Kerrigan, with whom Wakefield had just had a very emotional falling-out.

You've got to be kidding me.

Oh, shit.

From the very start, like most everyone who had recently spent any time around the Red Sox, Wakefield knew that Kerrigan would be a disaster as a manager. Kerrigan had few, if any, allies in the clubhouse, and he was regarded strictly as a pitching specialist, a skill set that did not bode well for his performance managing the club.

Historically in baseball, for whatever reason, pitching coaches have generally made poor managers, though there have been some exceptions. Kerrigan would not be one of them. At team meetings during the early part of his tenure, the positional players on the Boston roster all but rolled their eyes whenever Kerrigan broached the subject of their offensive approach. Kerrigan knew how to pitch to hitters — pitching, by definition, is *proactive* — but the concept of a reactionary approach was lost on him. His offensive theories were strictly theoretical and based on no real experience. According to some Sox players at the time, Kerrigan would note that a player had good statistics in certain situations: he was batting .377 when the count was 2–2, for instance. Kerrigan would then encourage the player to swing every time the count was 2–2. Such an assessment was obviously simplistic and naive, overlooking the identity of the pitcher, the nature of the pitch, and the situation in the game.

If the 2–2 pitch was over the player's head, should he swing?

In the minds of some Sox players, they believed that Kerrigan would have answered *yes*.

Over the final six weeks of the season, pitching exclusively as a reliever, Wakefield went 1–3 with a 6.00 ERA. Had his performance been the only one that suffered, Wakefield might have spent the time soul-searching. As it was, the rebellion spread throughout the rest of the Red Sox clubhouse, and the team self-destructed in a collapse that proved an indictment of the managerial career and capabilities of Joe Kerrigan.

After treading water for the first week of Kerrigan's tenure, the Red Sox lost nine in a row, then 13 of 14, the nine straight making Kerrigan only the third Red Sox manager in nearly 40 years to suffer such a skid. Then, during a period that already qualified as one of the uglier stretches in Red Sox history, the world was shaken to its core by the terrorist attacks of September 11, a tragedy that only briefly awoke the Red Sox from their self-absorbed struggles. Before, around, and after September 11, Ramirez openly challenged Kerrigan on a team bus, Everett was suspended, and a rehabilitating Martinez threw off his jersey and walked out on Kerrigan in the middle of a team workout. The manager had completely lost control of the team, and the Red Sox were a laughingstock.

For perhaps the only time in his career, Wakefield was not proud to wear the uniform as the Red Sox concluded the season in inglorious fashion, each member of the team hurrying out of Boston for the off-season.

"It was embarrassing," Wakefield said.

I'm fine.
They're the ones bouncing all over the place.
From his home in Melbourne that winter, Wakefield watched with great interest as the Red Sox underwent massive changes at their very core. Christmas was fast approaching as the Red Sox convened for a morning press conference at Fenway Park on December 20, when the new ownership group headed by John Henry, Tom Werner, and Larry Lucchino was introduced to the media. Though that group would not officially take over operation of the team until the sale was finalized the following spring, the Sox continued to do business, announcing

the signing of outfielder Johnny Damon to a four-year contract later that same day, in the same room, to virtually the same cast of reporters. With the exception of the Damon acquisition, most of the Red Sox maneuvers had involved departures more than arrivals.

In fact, on some levels, Wakefield thought the entire winter felt like a cleansing. Carl Everett, for one, was traded to the Texas Rangers, and disgruntled veterans like Dante Bichette and Mike Lansing, who had been unhappy with their roles in Boston, left the club via free agency. Wakefield had healthy relationships with all of those players — as he did with most everyone — but he also felt that the Sox lacked chemistry and cohesion in 2001, and he knew the clubhouse needed changes. He wondered about the effect of his blowup with Kerrigan, with whom he had not reconciled, but he tried to prepare for the coming season as he had always done. He ran and got his legs in shape. He strengthened his upper body and core. He began throwing before camp and got his arm in shape. Baseball was his *job,* no matter who was in charge, and Wakefield believed that it was his responsibility to show up ready to contribute.

As it turned out, the changes in the Boston organization were broader and deeper than even Wakefield expected, and they shook the Red Sox at the highest levels.

When Wakefield arrived for spring training, the feeling was unlike any other spring during his time in Boston. More changes were coming, and everybody knew it. The uncertainty was palpable. Over the winter the Red Sox had installed former Sox catcher Mike Stanley as Kerrigan's bench coach, a move that Wakefield welcomed and thought was a good one. As a player, Stanley had been an enormously popular player in the clubhouse and someone to whom everyone went for advice, from superstars like Martinez to clubhouse attendant Joe Cochran. Wakefield and Stanley were friends and fellow Florida natives. As teammates, they had spent time fishing together during the off-season. Wakefield confided in Stanley throughout that winter, relying on the new bench coach as a conduit to his manager.

What's my role going to be, Mike? Just let me know how Joe wants to use me.

Mike Stanley never really had to answer Wakefield's questions.

Though the new owners of the Red Sox were not formally installed until early March, heads almost instantly began to roll. Duquette was fired and replaced by assistant general manager Mike Port, who was named Duquette's successor on an interim basis. Wakefield breathed a sigh of relief when the new administration similarly wasted little time in disposing of Kerrigan. A search for a new manager began immediately. Wakefield hoped that the changes would result in his return to the starting rotation, but there was no way of knowing that until the Red Sox hired a new manager. Boston's search was believed to include Grady Little, who had been a bench coach during the early years of Jimy Williams's tenure. Wakefield beamed at the prospect of playing for Little, particularly following the departure of Kerrigan, because Little was someone he liked and a baseball man who understood him.

The state of flux during this challenging time for the Red Sox was a feeling Wakefield knew all too well.

In some ways, I feel used to this.

My whole career has been a state of flux.

Midway through March, with opening day rapidly approaching, Wakefield showed up at the team's spring stadium, as he did every morning, and parked his car in the gated lot behind City of Palms Park. He walked through the back entrance, said hello to security personnel, and strolled to his locker at the far left corner of a rectangular Red Sox clubhouse. Wakefield changed into his uniform and spent much of the morning sitting in the chair in front of his locker, which was stationed next to a set of stairs that descended down to the runway, which led to the Red Sox dugout at their spring home. Beyond the stairs was a hallway that housed a bat rack and led to the team offices, a corridor that essentially connected the uniformed members of the Red Sox to management.

Later that morning, as Wakefield sat at his locker, a succession of Sox officials came through that corridor. Lucchino, Werner, and Henry all entered the room, and all three men were present as team president Lucchino addressed the team. The room was otherwise silent. Lucchino told the players that the Red Sox were going through a transitional time, that the changes could be hard on all of them, but that things were steadily beginning to settle. The new owners were committed to winning. And then Lucchino introduced the man who would be the next manager of the Red Sox. Grady Little strolled into the room from the corridor to Tim Wakefield's immediate left as Wakefield and his Red Sox teammates exploded into thunderous applause.

The worst is behind us.

We're starting over.

Though Little was unfamiliar to some of the new members of the Red Sox, many of the existing Sox knew him and adored him from his previous tenure as a bench coach with the club. Little spoke in a slow, southern drawl and never seemed to overreact to *anything,* and he had a clever wit to go along with his easygoing nature. He made others laugh and kept them loose, and he had enjoyed Williams's complete confidence as bench coach because both had most recently come from the Atlanta Braves organization, where Little had been an accomplished minor league manager. Little knew how to speak with players, and he knew how to treat them. Those skills made him a most refreshing and welcome change given the shortcomings of Kerrigan.

The moment Little appeared in the clubhouse, Wakefield felt an enormous sense of relief. *This guy knows me and knows what I can do.* Because the Red Sox were so late into camp, and because roster decisions had been made, Little informed Wakefield that he would remain in the bullpen to start the year. The simplest truth was that it was far too late to make changes. Wakefield still wanted to start, to be sure, but as he lamented his plight in the past to Little, he felt like he could communicate openly with his new manager. His specific role didn't seem to matter as much anymore. As bench coach of the Red Sox, Grady Little had heard out Wakefield on more than one occasion, and he had assured Wakefield that his contributions were valuable.

"I just felt like he appreciated me," Wakefield said.

And in the end, that was really all Tim Wakefield wanted.

In the first month of the 2002 season, thanks to unforeseen injuries and issues, Wakefield made two starts and three relief appearances, recording a win and a save while posting a 3.10 ERA. Over the next three months, he pitched almost exclusively out of the bullpen. On the morning of July 31, Wakefield was 4–3 with a 3.50 ERA and three saves, again having filled any and all gaps the Red Sox had asked him to fill. He was having another good year. The Red Sox had gotten off to a blazing start under Little before playing the final months of the season on a rather uninspiring plateau. They began the season 40–17 and finished it 53–52 — for a total of 93–69 — and ended up missing the playoffs by six games. Their spot in the standings was partly the result of a bullpen that undermined their efforts, but also partly the effect of an unusual season in which the fourth and final American League playoff spot, the wild-card entry, went to an Anaheim Angels team that had won 99 games.

Beginning on July 31, because of injuries, Little had permanently moved Wakefield into the starting rotation, a decision that paid enormous dividends for the team as well as the player. Over the final two months, Wakefield went 7–2 with a 2.01 ERA while the Red Sox went 8–3 in his 11 starts. He was positively brilliant. Opponents batted a paltry .193 against him, and he walked just 20 batters in 76 innings, a rate of 2.4 walks per nine innings that would have been commendable for a *traditional* pitcher. Wakefield finished the year with an 11–5 record, a 2.81 ERA, and three saves to go along with the lowest ERA of his Red Sox career, all as he approached an off-season during which the Red Sox again held an option on his contract.

Suddenly, all of the pieces for Wakefield seemed to be back in place. He had a manager who understood and appreciated him. He had acquired the wisdom and experience of a veteran knuckleballer. And he had reason to believe that the best years of his career were still in front of him and that the worst was indeed behind him.

Still, for Tim Wakefield, the damage done to his career during the Kerrigan years remained impossible to overlook.

During the four-year period from 1999 to 2002 — what should have been the heart and peak of his career — Wakefield pitched in 190 games and made only 66 starts, his versatility hurting him as much as it helped him. Given what Wakefield had contributed to the Red Sox prior to that span—and what he would contribute after—it is clear that the Red Sox badly misused him. From 1995 to 1998, a four-year period during which Wakefield was used as a starter (with relief outings when necessary), he had averaged 15 wins and 206 innings per season; during the period 2003 to 2005, the three years after his turbulent four-year stretch, Wakefield would similarly average 13 victories and 205 innings. The four-year period from 1999 to 2002 thus stands out as a time when the Red Sox failed to get maximum use out of their knuckleballer, depriving him of the victories that by 2010 would already have made him the winningest pitcher in Red Sox history.

Let's look at the numbers: Wakefield's contributions during those seasons was an 8–10 record and a 4.28 ERA over a yearly average of 157⅔ innings pitched. Wakefield did record 21 saves during that span, but the Red Sox cost themselves roughly 50 fewer innings (or 150 outs) per year while stripping Wakefield of a potential 20 to 28 wins—the figure that would have delivered him to the highest total in club history.

"There aren't a lot of people who understand the value of a knuckleballer on your staff," Duquette admitted. "There were people on Tim's [coaching] staff, in our clubhouse [from 1999 to 2002], who didn't understand Tim's value to the team. Those were misconceptions.

"Did Joe Kerrigan fail to understand Tim? Absolutely," Duquette continued. "That's part of the story. It boggles my mind as to why there aren't more knuckleball pitchers in major league baseball. It's a hard pitch to master, but you have more time to master it. Look at the amount of money that major league teams spend on pitching, and look at the amount of money that teams spend on pitchers who are on the disabled list."

Indeed, throughout the 1990s and 2000s, baseball was littered with so many bad pitching contracts that teams became increasingly wary of signing veteran, free-agent pitchers. The Yankees, for example, signed right-hander Carl Pavano (the same man whom the Red Sox traded for Martinez in late 1997) to a guaranteed contract worth $40 million over the 2005–08 seasons. When Pavano made just 26 starts and pitched only 145⅔ innings during that four-year period, New York ended up paying him slightly more than $91,743 *per out.* The Dodgers signed veteran right-hander Jason Schmidt to a three-year contract worth a guaranteed $47 million from 2007 to 2009, a period during which Schmidt made a mere 10 starts and pitched just 43⅓ innings, numbers that translate into a shade more than $361,538 *per out.* After experiences like these, teams came to the conclusion that they could pay younger, healthier pitchers far less and get far more, a realization that could dramatically shorten the prime earning years of an established major league pitcher.

And yet, during a period in which the Red Sox had one of the game's most efficient and cost-effective weapons in Wakefield, the team used him improperly. From 1999 to 2002, when used largely as a reliever, Wakefield cost the Red Sox a little more than $7,761 per out, a figure that *still* made him a valuable commodity. But in those seasons between 1995 and 2005 when Wakefield was used as a starter, the Sox got a *better* pitcher for even *less*—approximately $4,546 per out—while teams like the Yankees and Dodgers were spending tens (or hundreds) of thousands per out on damaged, inferior goods.

During that time, Joe Kerrigan did not merely cost Tim Wakefield wins.

He hurt the Red Sox, too.

Fortunately for the knuckleballing Wakefield, the new owners and operators of the Red Sox were not about to make the same mistake.

Nine

•

It's like snowflakes — no two are ever alike.

— *Red Sox catcher Jason Varitek describing
Tim Wakefield's knuckleball*

THE RED SOX had far more pressing questions than their veteran knuckleballer entering the 2003 season. Theo Epstein, the team's new and progressive young general manager, was planting the seeds of dramatic change.

Tim Wakefield, for once, was a constant far more than a variable, the Red Sox having signed him to a new three-year contract for slightly more than $13 million almost immediately after the season. During the winter, on numerous occasions, Epstein and Little had made it quite clear that Wakefield would be a starter. The knuckleballer's personal life similarly tumbled into place over the winter when he married his girlfriend, Stacy Stover, a Boston-area native to whom he had been introduced by a friend at a kickoff party for a charity golf tournament.

Finally, I feel like I can stop worrying so much.

Indeed, almost everyone around the Red Sox was focused on other things. Much of the skepticism surrounding the Red Sox concerned the absence of a true closer, a deficit that raised eyebrows around baseball given that an effective closer was now thought to be a fundamental ingredient of any winning team. That was only one of the long-held beliefs that Epstein was willing to challenge. The new general manager had signed a handful of relievers during the off-season — right-handers Mike Timlin, Chad Fox, and Ramiro Mendoza chief among them—and his idea, shared by manager Little, was to employ them in situations that best suited their specific skill sets. With left-hander Alan Embree and right-hander Bobby Howry in the mix, too, the idea was to give Little as many options as possible on any given night to effectively play a game of musical chairs with both his bullpen and opposing lineups.

Some nights, Mendoza might close. The responsibility might belong to Fox in the next game. Timlin and Howry both had some closing experience to their credit, as did Embree, though none of them had excelled in the role. Regardless, Epstein and Little theorized that, since sometimes the most important outs of a game are recorded not in the ninth inning but in the seventh or eighth, it made little sense to have a closer and to earmark him exclusively for the ninth. They believed that their *closer-by-committee* system, as it came to be called, could work.

Of course, the experiment failed miserably. With no clear responsibilities on a nightly basis, Red Sox relievers struggled mightily. For as much as their theory made perfect sense—it had been promoted by longtime statistical analyst Bill James, whom the Red Sox had hired—it completely disregarded the human element. Relievers, like most baseball players, are accustomed to specific job descriptions and responsibilities. Some pitch in the seventh, some pitch in the eighth, some pitch in the sixth. Some face only left-handers, and others face largely right-handers. The uncertainty that came with the closer-by-committee approach required the Red Sox pitchers to be ready at all times. They were left unsettled, uncertain of when or how they would be used on any given night.

Performing under those kinds of conditions was extremely difficult.

And given his experience as a starter or reliever at a moment's notice, Tim Wakefield could have told them that.

Fittingly, the Sox blew the season opener in the ninth inning of a game at Tampa Bay (then a vastly inferior team) when Fox surrendered a three-run home run to Carl Crawford on the final pitch of the game. For Epstein and Little, the game was their worst nightmare come true. The Red Sox had held a 4–1 lead entering the ninth thanks to the typical brilliance of Martinez, but both Embree and Fox melted in the heat of a closing situation. Culminating with Crawford's homer, the pair of relievers allowed five runs and dealt the Sox a 6–4 defeat. The bullpen problems continued for much of the first two months of the season, ultimately forcing Epstein to make a trade for a closer. At the end of May, he acquired enigmatic Korean right-hander Byung-Hyun Kim, who also came with question marks. Most recently, he had been starting for the Diamondbacks after a tumultuous experience trying to close for Arizona against the Yankees in the 2001 World Series. He was just 24 years old, however, and possessed dynamic talent, a combination that appealed to someone like Epstein.

"It hasn't been good enough. We've got to be better," Little said of his team's pitching woes. "I don't think very many times in our careers can we look at the stat sheet and see a team ranked in pitching where we are and be in the standings where we are. That speaks a lot for our offense."

While Epstein refused to entirely give up on the closer-by-committee approach, leaving the door open for another attempt sometime during his baseball career — "I still believe it can work," he said — the 2003 Red Sox had too much at stake for the experiment to continue any longer. Wakefield had suspected that the Sox might come to that realization. During his time with the Red Sox, Wakefield had effectively shuttled between the starting rotation and the bullpen, which was difficult enough to manage. But at least on many of those occasions Wakefield had known what his role would be and could mentally prepare himself for it. On the one most obvious occasion when he was caught by surprise — the first time Williams brought him into a game to close in 1999 — Wakefield had nearly been overcome with anxiety and was able to calm himself only through the serendipity of a spectator running onto the field and stopping the game. Wakefield did not know Mike Timlin, Alan Embree, and the other new relievers especially well at that point, but he knew that if all players, like most anyone, need time to *prepare,* that was especially true for relievers, who are usually thrust into games under already difficult circumstances.

Adding an additional level of uncertainty to the reliever's role would turn the final innings of a game into a fire drill.

Still, on the more positive side, the events of the first two months had made two other things quite clear. First, Little was right about the prolific Red Sox offense: Boston had an extremely potent lineup that could overcome deficiencies in the pitching staff. Second, the early-season developments proved that Theo Epstein was fearless when it came to challenging the establishment and that the young general manager was, in many ways, a revolutionary thinker open to all kinds of ideas and suggestions. At just 29 years old, Epstein was willing to try things that others were not. A lifetime spent in the game had not tainted him. Epstein believed in performance, for sure, but he also had a more modern, analytical approach to baseball that allowed him to measure things that others could not or would not.

For Wakefield in particular, this was an important development. Epstein might have looked like a prep school student, but he was smart enough to know the value of a knuckleballer who was being used properly.

While the Red Sox continued to pound away at opponents — over the winter Epstein had reinforced the lineup, too, with the acquisitions of Todd Walker, Kevin Millar, Bill Mueller, and David Ortiz — Wakefield took his turn every five days and gave the Red Sox exactly what he was supposed to: innings. For his fourth consecutive season as a Red Sox starter — omitting the bullpen years from 1999 to 2002 — Wakefield recorded at least 600 outs. Only Lowe (203⅓ innings) had pitched more than Wakefield (202⅓). On August 3, with a victory at Baltimore, Wakefield became just the ninth pitcher in Red Sox history to win at least 100 games for the franchise. A month later, Wakefield reached a milestone that meant as much to him at the time as any other; he had accrued a full 10 seasons of major league service time, no small feat for a man who had been tossed to the scrap heap by the Pittsburgh Pirates during the spring of 1995.

His 10 years of service afforded Wakefield certain privileges, the most significant of which was spelled out in the terms of the collective bargaining agreement between owners and players. Because he now had 10 years of service in the major leagues, and because at least the last five were with the same team (the Red Sox), Wakefield not only qualified for a full pension from the Major League Baseball Players Association but was also a *10-5 player,* which gave him one enormous power: the right to veto any trade. The Red Sox could not ship Wakefield elsewhere unless he agreed to the deal. He alone got to choose where he would play. And so, when the clock struck midnight on September 11, 2003, Tim Wakefield knew from that moment that, so long as he had a contract, the Red Sox could not part ways with him without his consent — another bargaining chip that brought him great comfort.

They can't get rid of me now even if they want to.

Nonetheless, by the time the regular season ended, Wakefield and the Red Sox had other things on their minds. Despite the acquisition of Kim and Epstein's continued efforts, the bullpen problems persisted. Epstein acquired another potential closer, Scott Williamson, via trade on July 30, and the results of that deal, too, were mixed. No matter which pitcher Grady Little tried in the ninth inning, the Red Sox seemed to remain vulnerable late in the game, and the entire bullpen situation grew more unstable. In Williamson and Kim, Little had inconsistent pitchers who alternated between dominance and vulnerability. Their performance was impossible to predict. Since the start of the season, the Red Sox had gone from no closers to *two,* further complicating what had been a muddled situation to begin with.

Grady Little had become the managerial equivalent of a knuckleballer — unsure of how his offerings would turn out no matter how consistent he tried to be.

Tim Wakefield understood that feeling.

Welcome to my world.

And yet the Sox still won, thanks largely to the strength of their starting rotation and an offense that set a major league record for slugging percentage while leading all of baseball in runs scored, securing Boston a place in the postseason for the fourth time during Wakefield's nine years with the team.

At this stage of his career, Wakefield knew what the opportunity for a championship meant, especially in Boston. During the season, he had celebrated his 37th birthday. Eleven years had passed since he broke in with the Pirates in 1992. Boston had made three trips to the playoffs during his time with the team, but never advanced past Game 5 of the American League Championship Series. Wakefield had never played in a World Series game, not with Pittsburgh and not with Boston. The new owners of the Red Sox had put a great deal of emphasis on character and on chemistry, and there was now a sense of camaraderie not only in the Red Sox clubhouse but in the entire Boston organization. For the first time in a long time, particularly in contrast to the 2001 Red Sox team that represented the end of the previous ownership, Wakefield felt that Red Sox players and executives were in it *together,* that the lines of communication were more open than they ever had been before, that any tension or friction between the clubhouse and front office was gone. There was an inarguable sense of harmony. Everyone was focused on the same thing.

For Wakefield especially, all of these developments were reassuring and signaled that the Red Sox finally had figured out the secret to winning a championship, something they had not done as an organization since 1918. He had prided himself on his team play since arriving in the major leagues, but he had especially demonstrated a selflessness and willingness to sacrifice for the greater good since arriving in Boston. *Even though I wanted to start, I did my job as a reliever.* He now felt that the entire Boston organization was operating with a togetherness that had been absent from teams like the 2001 Sox, who grumbled about roles and playing time during a year that resulted in the firing of manager Williams. The 2003 club had little or none of that attitude. *Winning* was the objective. If that meant that some people got more playing time and others got less, so be it. Selfish wants and needs could only hurt the cause.

As a result, Tim Wakefield *believed* these Red Sox could win.

The idea of another outcome did not even cross his mind.

At least not yet.

Along with the Red Sox, the Oakland A's, New York Yankees, and Minnesota Twins qualified for the postseason in 2003, the Red Sox as the American League wild-card entry given their second-place finish to the Yankees in the East Division. The Red Sox had won more games (95) than the Twins (90), and just one fewer than the A's (96). Since Major League Baseball prohibited teams in the same division from facing one another in the first round of the playoffs, Boston drew Oakland, which made for a fascinating matchup.

During the regular season, while the Sox had scored more runs than any major league team and set a major league record for slugging percentage, the A's had allowed the second-fewest runs in the American League and finished the year ranked first in pitching. The battle of Boston's bats against Oakland's arms was seen as baseball's version of the irresistible force and the immovable object.

"I think everyone knows what kind of offense we have," said Red Sox manager Grady Little. "A lot of times you'll have a well-pitched game going against the best offense I've ever been around and do a number on them. But it hasn't happened very often this year. We know what our offense is capable of doing, we know what that pitching staff over across the way is capable of doing. It should be a good series."

Of course, for all of the attention paid to the matchup between Red Sox batters and Oakland pitchers, the opposite matchup was equally vital: Red Sox pitchers versus Oakland batters. During the regular season, Oakland's lineup had been extremely mediocre, finishing ninth in the AL with 768 runs scored. The Red Sox, by contrast, had scored 961. Boston's starting pitchers, meanwhile, had finished fifth in the league in ERA thanks to the performance of people like Martinez, Wakefield, and Lowe, whom Little had scheduled, in that order, to pitch Games 1, 2, and 3 of the series. Because the first round of the American League Division Series was a best-of-five affair, neither Little nor Oakland manager Ken Macha scheduled his rotation beyond Game 3.

If the A's had any noticeable advantages in the series, two were obvious. First, because Oakland won the AL West while the Red Sox finished second in the East, Oakland was afforded home-field advantage: Games 1, 2, and 5 would be played at the Network Associates Coliseum in the Bay Area. Second, the A's had an effective bullpen, anchored by closer Keith Foulke, that had finished third in the American League in ERA; by contrast, Red Sox relievers finished 12th. The prevailing theory was that Oakland would have the edge in games that were close entering the late innings — a likely scenario in any postseason game.

Sure enough, the bullpens decided Game 1.

With Boston starter Martinez and Oakland ace Tim Hudson effectively neutralizing one another, the Red Sox took a 4–3 lead in the seventh inning on a two-run home run by second baseman Walker, his second homer of the game. The score remained that way until the ninth, when Little summoned Kim, whose three most recent career postseason appearances in the National League (all with Arizona) had produced disastrous results. On this occasion, Kim fared no better. He walked one batter and hit another, prompting Little to call upon left-hander Alan Embree with two on and two outs in the bottom of the ninth. Embree promptly allowed a single to the left-handed-hitting Erubiel Durazo, tying the game at 4–4 and sending the affair into extra innings.

In the bottom of the 12th, with the bases loaded, Oakland won the game on an improbable two-out bunt single by catcher Ramon Hernandez that scored third baseman Eric Chavez. With the rest of his teammates, Wakefield looked on in disbelief. *You've got to be kidding me.* No member of the Sox was more stunned than Lowe, the scheduled Game 3 starter who had been summoned to pitch the final 1⅔ innings of Game 1 after Little had run through the only trusted members of his relief corps — Timlin, Kim, Embree, and Williamson.

And thanks to the Game 1 performance of Kim in particular, Little's circle of relievers he trusted was getting even smaller.

By then, Wakefield had already addressed the media with regard to his upcoming start in Game 2. As was customary in baseball, the Game 2 starters had taken questions from reporters in formal press conferences held before Game 1 was even played, a schedule designed to accommodate newspaper reporters working on deadline. Game 1 of the series was played on a Wednesday, and Game 2 was scheduled for a Thursday. Back in Boston, by dawn on Thursday, fans could pick up the morning paper and read about Game 1 while seeing what Wakefield had to say about the now all-important Game 2.

This is the beauty of baseball: win or lose, there is little use in dwelling too much on what happened because another game is fast approaching and demanding focus and attention.

"I really feel this team, there is something special about it," Wakefield said when asked to compare the 2003 Sox to other playoff teams on which he had played. "I don't know if it's chemistry or offense, but one thing the organization did great this winter was get a bunch of ballplayers, a bunch of gamers. The chemistry we have among each other can't be bought. You can't go out and buy that. You have to tip your hat to the organization with Theo and Grady and the acquisitions that they made in the off-season to put together such a great team."

Still, Wakefield suddenly had a great deal on his mind, none of which had to do with the A's. Shortly after the Red Sox had arrived in Oakland, Wakefield received a call from his wife, Stacy, who was six weeks pregnant with the couple's first child. Stacy Wakefield had just come home from her first ultrasound exam, where doctors had been unable to locate the baby's heartbeat. They immediately scheduled another ultrasound in hopes of better assessing the status of the pregnancy, but Wakefield could discern from the tone in his wife's voice that she was scared.

I'm afraid, too.

I wish I were there with you.

Wakefield shared the news with very few people outside of Red Sox clubhouse attendant and equipment manager Joe Cochran, who had become a close friend. He was thus preoccupied when he took the mound for Game 2, which proved to be an effective distraction in the sense that it required Wakefield's concentration and focus, but it also proved frustrating. Paired against a near-perfect Barry Zito, Wakefield pitched a scoreless first inning before his control and defense briefly escaped him in the second inning, when the A's erupted for five runs, the final two of them unearned as the result of an error by second baseman Todd Walker.

Wakefield found the inning maddening. He had good stuff and he knew it, and yet the knuckleball—as it was wont to do—ran wild for a short burst of time, causing enough damage to put the outcome in great jeopardy. Wakefield reclaimed control of the pitch in the third and allowed just one hit while racking up five strikeouts over the next four innings, but the early mistakes were too much for the Red Sox to overcome against Zito, who was brilliant. In seven innings, Zito allowed just one run while striking out nine, pitching Oakland to a 5–1 victory in a mere 2 hours, 37 minutes. The A's now had a 2–0 series lead.

Just 24 hours into the playoffs, the Red Sox had already lost twice and were one defeat away from elimination in the best-of-five series. Wakefield was reminded that the postseason, unlike the regular season, allows almost no margin for error. During the press conference with reporters after the game, he said nothing about his wife's visit to the doctor, preferring to keep the matter private and unwilling to make an excuse for his performance.

I just didn't get it done.

Still, as the Red Sox returned home and the series shifted to Fenway Park for Games 3 and 4, Wakefield believed that there was reason for optimism — for his family and the Red Sox both. After all, the 2003 Red Sox had frequently done their best work at the 11th hour, demonstrating a mental toughness that had made them almost impossible for opponents to knock out. Meanwhile, doctors had stressed to Stacy Wakefield that the absence of a heartbeat was not cause for alarm and that the next visit might very well alleviate the couple's concerns.

In either case, Tim Wakefield was happy to be home, where the 2003 Red Sox had been nearly unbeatable and his wife now needed him. As a team, for the season, the Sox had batted .316 at home and averaged an insane 6.6 runs per game. Almost nobody had been able to shut them down. During one game in June against the Florida Marlins, the Red Sox scored 10 runs in the first inning before an out was recorded and scored 14 runs in the first inning overall. When the first 11 Boston batters of the game reached base — 10 on hits that included five singles, three doubles, a triple, and a home run — the baseball world was summarily warned of Boston's potency when all cylinders were firing properly.

Despite his Game 1 relief appearance, Lowe started Game 3 and performed brilliantly, effectively matching Oakland starter Ted Lilly

throughout the first seven innings. Just the same, the game was tied at
1–1 entering the eighth. Wakefield found these kinds of games intoxi-
cating. When he had been asked to work as a reliever between starts,
he had learned the routine in the bullpen during the game, how the
tension built in the middle and late innings. *Time to get ready for work.*
Some relievers, knowing they would not pitch before the late innings,
did not even make the trip out to the bullpen until the third or fourth
inning. Depending on the specific role each pitcher filled, the preparation was different. But in this game—an *elimination game*—late-
inning relievers like Timlin, Williamson, and others were on high
alert from the middle innings on. Any joking and banter had faded
and finally stopped as the game progressed. They did exercises to get
their bodies loose. When the call came from the dugout, they began
to warm up until they were, as the relievers like to say, *hot,* which was
an indication they were ready to enter the game. Then they had to stay
hot by throwing at their own pace, one eye on their warm-up routine,
one eye on the game.

Because he had started Game 2, Wakefield was among those pitchers not likely to be used in Game 3. But he knew that he would be on
call for Games 4 and 5 if needed, especially because Game 2 projected
to be his only start of the series. The Red Sox had planned to use four
starters in the first round, with only Martinez scheduled to go twice,
and Wakefield understood as well as anyone what that meant for the
bullpen.

I know what those guys are going through out there.

Just before Game 3, Wakefield joined his wife for a follow-up ultrasound exam, which produced the sound they longed to hear: a heartbeat. The baby was fine. Doctors quickly determined that they had
merely miscalculated the child's due date, news that the Wakefields
accepted with both tears and an enormous sigh of relief. Tim could
now turn his attention back to the task at hand.

Baseball.

This time, in Game 3, the A's relievers were the ones who cracked.
After Timlin and Williamson combined for four scoreless innings, Sox
outfielder Trot Nixon, a gritty fan favorite, belted a game-ending, two-

run homer to center field against A's wonder boy Rich Harden that gave the Sox a 3–1 victory and extended the series to a fourth game. The Red Sox, demonstrating to Wakefield and everyone else a familiar toughness and resiliency, particularly at Fenway Park, suddenly had a jolt of momentum. The A's, like many other teams, had been unable to put the Sox away.

We're not dead yet.

With Game 4 set to be played the next day, Sunday, October 5, Wakefield was among those pitchers again being placed on call. Just as Lowe had pitched in relief during Game 1, Wakefield knew a similar responsibility might be thrust upon him in Game 4 or Game 5 — or both. While Red Sox fans clamored for Little to bypass John Burkett and start Martinez on short rest in Game 4, Little resisted the idea because he knew the limitations of his ace. Unlike Lowe and Wakefield, Martinez's history of shoulder problems made him unavailable between starts. He could not pitch effectively on short rest. The Red Sox had never asked Martinez to pitch with fewer than four days between starts, and they weren't about to start now, on the brink of elimination.

The A's, by contrast, turned back to Hudson, who took the mound on three days of rest and left the game after one inning with an injury to his oblique muscle. Nothing could have better highlighted the value of resilient pitchers like Lowe and Wakefield, who could pitch frequently and on little or no rest. When other pitchers made such attempts, the quality of their pitches suffered. Or they got hurt. As Martinez watched from the dugout and Hudson left the mound early, Wakefield was in the bullpen, ready to go, sitting alongside Timlin, Williamson, and Embree. Theirs was a perspective that pitchers like Martinez and Hudson had never really been asked to learn.

Unlike the way Kerrigan used him, Wakefield knew that any role he filled out of the bullpen, whether in the regular season or the playoffs, could come at a critical time. Little trusted him. Wakefield enjoyed the camaraderie in the bullpen, a team within the team on which all the relievers seemed to pull for one another. Whether the call from the dugout resulted in work for Wakefield, Timlin, or Embree — or any combination of relievers — the response from the others was almost always the same. *Go get 'em.* The Red Sox bullpen came with its own support structure. There could be a closeness among relievers in a game, particularly during the postseason, that did not exist on other parts of the club. The relievers were like a relay team, one man handing the ball to the next, the entire group effectively running the anchor leg for the bigger group that was the entire 25-man roster.

Game 4 was tied entering the sixth inning, when the A's began to rally and Little called down to the bullpen. *Get Wake up.* As was the case when Jimy Williams had unexpectedly asked Wakefield to close for the first time, Wakefield's pace quickened. Again, it was time to go to work. When Burkett allowed a two-run homer to Jermaine Dye, Little yanked his starter and called upon his knuckleballer to do exactly what he had been unable to accomplish during his Game 2 start: stop the bleeding. Wakefield made a final warm-up toss and strolled toward the bullpen door—*Go get 'em, Wake*—then jogged in from right field to the Fenway Park mound, where Little placed the ball in his knuckleballer's glove.

No instructions were necessary.

The game is in my hands.

Making just his third relief appearance of the season, Wakefield coolly closed out the sixth before teammate Walker (him again) hit a solo homer in the bottom of the inning to make the score 4–3. *Now keep the score right there.* Taking the mound in the top of the seventh, Wakefield retained the command that had escaped him only in the second inning of Game 2, pitching a critical inning without allowing a run. His focus was sharp. The deeper the Red Sox went into that postseason, the better his command seemed to get. Wakefield walked off the mound with the Sox still facing a 4–3 deficit but still very much within striking distance given the strength of their offense and their knack for dramatic finishes.

Attaboy, Wake. We can still win this thing.

Answering the bell like Timlin (in Game 3) and Wakefield (in Game 4) before him, Williamson pitched a perfect eighth before Oakland manager Macha summoned his closer, Foulke, with hopes of closing out the series. The move backfired. With the A's still holding a 4–3 advantage, there were two on and two out when David Ortiz awoke from a postseason slumber and belted a two-run double to right field that gave the Sox a 5–4 advantage, a lead Williamson nailed down with a dominating, perfect ninth during which he recorded two strikeouts.

The Boston bullpen was scrambling, to be sure, but the Red Sox were finding ways to win. With the series now tied at two games each, the teams packed their belongings in anticipation of cross-country flights and Game 5, scheduled for the next day.

"They deserve everything they get," Little said of his players. "This ball club, the fans of Boston, they just keep grinding all the way to the last out. And we've had some players come through for us this year, day after day, and they continue to do that. And we feel we have a chance. As long as we have a uniform on and they have a schedule for us telling us there is another game, we feel like we have a chance."

In line with the rest of the series, Game 5 was a classic, further defined by the invaluable versatility of pitchers like Wakefield and, again, Lowe. Pitching on three days of rest, like Hudson, left-hander Zito outdueled Martinez for the first five innings and took a 1–0 advantage into the sixth. With Zito tiring, the Sox erupted for four runs, the last three coming on a home run by cleanup hitter Manny Ramirez. Oakland scored once against Martinez in the sixth to make it 4–2, but the Sox ace made it through the seventh without incident before Little, still shaken by the season-long performance of his bullpen, sent Martinez back out for the eighth. The move proved, yet again, how little trust the Red Sox manager had in virtually anyone specifically assigned to his bullpen, a distrust that had been highlighted by his reliance on starters like Wakefield and Lowe to pitch in relief between scheduled starts.

As a pitcher, Wakefield knew what a manager's distrust could feel like, particularly after having experienced it under Kerrigan. Players almost never look at it the same way a manager does. Wakefield could always believe another pitcher explaining what went wrong in a game for him, if for no other reason than the fact that Wakefield had been in a similar place. Like hitters, pitchers have slumps. The only way they can endure slumps is to continue pitching. If a manager starts changing things, the result can be a chicken-and-egg routine that frustrates players to no end.

How can you expect to have confidence in me if you won't pitch me when it matters?

You're giving up on me.

Wasting no time against Martinez, the A's opened the eighth with a double by Chris Singleton and a run-scoring single by pinch-hitter Billy McMillon, trimming the score to 4–3 and putting the tying run at first base with nobody out. Little then quickly turned to left-hander Embree, who retired the next two batters — lefties Erubiel Durazo and Eric Chavez — before surging right-hander Timlin entered to retire shortstop Miguel Tejada on an inning-ending groundout. The Red Sox had escaped a tie by the skin of their teeth, but with one inning to play, they were operating with no margin for error. The stage was set for the rebuilt but nonetheless rickety Boston bullpen to be tested to the fullest.

Much to the dismay of Red Sox fans watching back in Boston in the late hours — the game had started at 5:18 PM Pacific Standard Time, so it was now approaching midnight on the East Coast — Williamson followed his sterling Game 4 performance by walking the first two batters of the inning, Scott Hatteberg and José Guillén. The Red Sox and their fans started to fret. By that point, Little had completely eliminated the self-doubting Kim as an option, and Embree and Timlin already had pitched. His options were limited. Once again, the manager's only option was a starter, Lowe, who entered the game with nobody out and runners at both first base and second — the potential tying and winning runs.

Wakefield took particular note of all of this, recognizing that Lowe was being asked to do precisely what he himself had done the day before, to bounce between the starting rotation and bullpen at a time when the Red Sox could not afford even a hiccup.

C'mon, D-Lowe. You can do this.

After catcher Ramon Hernandez sacrifice-bunted the runners to second and third — in Game 1, remember, it was Hernandez who bunted for a hit against Lowe to win the game in extra innings — Lowe faced three consecutive left-handed batters: pinch hitter Adam Melhuse, outfielder Singleton, and pinch hitter Terrence Long. Lowe struck out Melhuse, walked Singleton to load the bases, and then whiffed Long on a banana-bending two-seam fastball (or sinker) that started at Long's right hip and darted over the inside corner. Long froze, the bat remaining on his shoulder. Lowe squared his hips and thrust his fist downward — over his right hip and between his legs — touching off a Red Sox celebration that ended the game, 4–3, and the series, 3–2, and sending Boston back to the American League Championship Series for the second time in five seasons.

In the series, Lowe threw the final pitches of Games 1 and 5 and the first pitch of Game 3. Wakefield had started Game 2 and relieved in Game 4. The two most versatile members of the Boston staff accounted for 52 of the 146 outs recorded by Red Sox pitchers during the series, including at least one out in every game.

Boston's two most valuable performers in the series were easily its most pliable pitchers.

"If you had any doubts about his heart, there are absolutely no doubts now," Epstein said of Lowe after Game 5. "That was as clutch as you can possibly be. I don't know how many pitchers in the game have the guts to make those pitches."

Given the results of Game 5, the Red Sox were not about to change their strategy entering Game 1 of the ALCS, where they would face their longtime rivals, the New York Yankees, in a series that was expected to be downright apocalyptic. If relievers like Williamson and Timlin showed the first signs of cracking, Little was likely to call starters like Wakefield and Lowe out of the bullpen between starts. The Red Sox couldn't sacrifice games during the playoffs the way they could during the regular season, when every team managed for the long haul. The playoffs were a sprint, and every loss moved a team one step closer to winter.

Even though the Yankees finished 2003 with the best record in baseball, even the most level-headed baseball observers acknowledged that the Red Sox had a certain spunk that was impossible to ignore. For all of the pain the Yankees had inflicted on the Red Sox over the course of their history, there was a sentiment throughout New England that these Red Sox were different, that Boston now had a team capable of rising to any challenge, which spoke to the competitiveness and professionalism of the Boston roster.

From Wakefield and Lowe and on through the roster, the Red Sox had a team of players willing and able to do whatever was *necessary*.

To that end, Little named Wakefield his starter for Game 1, calling for the knuckleballer to appear a third time in seven days since the start of the postseason. While Little's decision again highlighted his dependence on Wakefield and Lowe — slated to start Games 1 and 5, Wakefield could pitch out of the bullpen in between — it also had great meaning to the knuckleballer, for obvious reasons. The last time the Red Sox faced the Yankees in the postseason, during the 1999 American League Championship Series, Wakefield had been unceremoniously left off the roster. That decision as much as any other made by any manager, coach, or executive during Wakefield's career had stung him deeply and reflected how uneasily traditional baseball observers regarded the knuckleball when the stakes were high and the pressure intense.

We just can't trust that thing.

Now here was Wakefield, four years later, assigned the responsibility of leading the Red Sox into Yankee Stadium to face an awesome Yankees team, with a trip to the World Series at stake. This time, while someone else had to suffer the indignity of being omitted from the active roster at the most critical time of year — the psychologically brittle Kim — the Red Sox were confidently standing behind Wakefield. His days as a full-time reliever were but a distant memory, and his philosophical differences with pitching coach Joe Kerrigan were long gone. Finally, he had bosses and teammates who regarded him as an invaluable multipurpose tool, an asset. By contrast, Kim had proven incapable of handling the pressure and constant shuttling from the starting rotation to the bullpen. That instability had left his career in a state of upheaval from which he would never really recover.

To almost anyone who had followed Wakefield's career, in fact, it was clear that the knuckleballer had become *stronger* as a result of his travails. He spoke openly and unemotionally about the past and embraced his versatility as a strength. In the days before Game 1, he spoke of his versatility as "a weapon," noting that he and Lowe "just did whatever we had to do to try to win games." Four years after being snubbed, Wakefield saw the 2003 ALCS as "a totally different story." He spoke of the chemistry the Red Sox possessed as a team, using words like *fun* and *exciting*. Wakefield's manner suggested a supreme confidence in his organization and his teammates, and his unspoken message was equally as apparent.

I'm confident in myself, too. I'm as ready as I have ever been for this.

Maybe it was no surprise, then, that he made the most of the opportunity.

In the bullpen before Game 1, Wakefield's pregame routine was systematic and precise, his mind free of any of the clutter that had weighed him down in previous years. *Grip, kick, throw.* Throwing knuckleballs for strikes had rarely seemed so simple. Yankee Stadium fans were renowned for razzing opposing pitchers before, during, and after their warm-up sessions, but Wakefield heard relatively little of the taunting. When he did hear it, he just chuckled to himself at the creativity of New York hecklers. He could not be derailed. During any warm-up session — or for that matter, during games — Wakefield's target behind home plate was the mask and chest protector worn by his catcher (in this case Doug Mirabelli), with the idea that the ball would dip just before reaching the hitter, the pitch all but landing in the catcher's lap. *Plop.* When Wakefield found his rhythm, as he had done in all but the second inning of Game 2 of the series against Oakland, he could effortlessly drop knuckleballs in Mirabelli's lap as if he were Michael Jordan shooting free throws.

Dribble, *swish,* dribble, *swish,* dribble, *swish.*

Matched against the crafty and talented Mike Mussina — a traditional pitcher in the truest sense of the word, Mussina could throw hard and change speeds effortlessly — Wakefield took his brilliance from the bullpen and transferred it to the mound. While Red Sox batters stung Mussina for three homers — a two-run drive by the awakening Ramirez and solo shots by the sizzling Walker and Ortiz — Wakefield shut out the Yankees for the first six innings. He allowed just two singles and did not walk a batter. The Red Sox held a 5-0 edge when Wakefield opened the seventh by walking both Jason Giambi and Bernie Williams, at which point Little wisely decided that he had asked enough of his knuckleballer, who had thrown 91 pitches in the game, 220 during the first week of the playoffs. Yankees catcher Jorge Posada promptly greeted Embree with a double that made the score 4–1, but Embree retired the next three batters — one on a sacrifice fly — to allow the Red Sox a 5–2 advantage entering the eighth. Timlin and Williamson each followed Embree with 1-2-3 innings, closing out a 5–2 Red Sox victory in which unpredictable Sox relievers retired the final nine Yankees of the game. Adding in Wakefield's mastery, Red Sox pitchers retired 27 of New York's 32 batters on the night, allowing New York just three hits in 29 official at-bats.

The Red Sox concluded the victory 48 hours after the win over the A's, a period of time during which the Sox made a cross-country flight and endured a light off-day workout, leaving little time for rest.

Said a matter-of-fact Little when asked about Wakefield's performance: "We saw the same thing with Tim tonight that we've seen most of the season."

As it turned out, Wakefield's performance only grew in magnitude over the coming days. Asked to start Game 2 and make his fourth appearance of the postseason in eight days, Lowe struggled, allowing seven hits, six runs, and a pair of walks in a game the Red Sox led only briefly, 1–0. The workload seemed to be catching up with him. The series subsequently shifted to Boston for a highly billed matchup featuring Martinez and Roger Clemens, the erstwhile Sox ace whom the Sox had ravaged in Game 3 of an identical matchup during the 1999 American League Championship Series. This time, however, Martinez was the one who had nothing on his pitches from the very start. Staked to a 2–0 lead in the first inning, Martinez allowed one run in the second, another in the third, and two more in the fourth. Before that inning was over, however, with his pitch count escalating, Martinez's patience wore thin: he cracked and buzzed Yankees outfielder Karim Garcia with a pitch, igniting the ever-present tensions between the teams. Two innings later, Sox slugger Ramirez overreacted when the intimidating Clemens fired a fastball up and in, triggering a bench-clearing scrum during which 72-year-old Yankees bench coach Don Zimmer charged at Martinez, who, while defending himself, pushed Zimmer to the ground. The enraged Yankees held on to a 4–3 victory that left the Red Sox to deal with both a 2–1 series deficit and the shameful behavior of their ace.

"I know there's no question in my mind that Pedro hit him on purpose," Yankees manager Joe Torre said when asked about the pitch that whizzed by Garcia. "He was probably frustrated with the fact that we hit some balls hard. You know the kind of respect I have for Pedro's ability to pitch, but, you know, I didn't care for that. After that, Roger threw one high to Ramirez. It wasn't even over his head — it was over the plate. It was just high. And Manny — I think everybody's nerves were a little frazzled by that time — and he overreacted. Again, I can understand the overreaction because of the tensions and everything. Aside from that, that's all I know."

Wakefield, too, felt that Martinez had allowed his competitiveness to get the better of him, a reaction that was not entirely unusual for any player in a tight game, particularly the Red Sox ace. Martinez could be temperamental, but that came with the package. Most pitchers are at their best when operating with an *edge;* Wakefield himself had had that air about him in Game 1. Martinez had lacked it in Game 3. In the mind of Wakefield and many others, that made Martinez's actions not so much excusable as *understandable.* Wakefield had experienced his own times on the mound when he felt like whipping a ball at a batter's knees, only to think better of it.

Of course, there was also the question of whether his knuckleball or fastball could have the same effect.

With the battle lines between the Red Sox and Yankees now clearly drawn, the teams were offered a much-needed reprieve from Game 4 when nature intervened. While reporters followed up the Game 3 brouhaha in the hours prior to Game 4 — a crying Zimmer apologized in a press conference — rain dampened Fenway Park and forced a postponement of the game until the next day. For the Red Sox, the change in schedule was a welcome respite given the taxing nature of the Oakland series, from which the Red Sox were still puffing when Wakefield took the mound for Game 1. Now they could use the unscheduled day off to recover from an emotional drama of a different kind. Beyond that, the extra day of rain allowed both clubs to reshuffle their pitching rotations — Little could bypass the soft-throwing John Burkett in favor of Wakefield, who was throwing the ball as well as any pitcher on either team.

Torre responded by also going back to his Game 1 starter, Mussina, but the results proved no different. Wakefield again dominated. The bullpen routine before this game had gone precisely like the bullpen routine before Game 1 — albeit in Boston this time — and Mirabelli had concluded the session with precisely the same words he had uttered in New York. *You're pretty locked in right now.* Wakefield's answer also had been the same. *I know I am.* Wakefield then took the mound and pitched seven assembly-line innings, thwarting the Yankees with an array of knucklers that safely darted and danced their way into Mirabelli's lap. When the Sox scored a run on pinch hitter Jason Varitek's groundout in the bottom of the seventh, they gained a 3–1 advantage and needed just six outs for a victory that would even the series at two games apiece.

Though his bullpen was now pitching extremely well — Boston relievers had pitched 6⅓ scoreless innings to that point in the series — Little nonetheless sent Wakefield out to the mound for the eighth, albeit on a very short leash. When Wakefield opened the inning by walking Giambi on his 100th pitch of the game, Little hooked his knuckleballer and turned the game over to Timlin, who retired the next three batters. Williamson followed and surrendered Boston's first bullpen run of the series on a solo home run by Ruben Sierra, but the reliever responded by striking out both David Dellucci and Alfonso Soriano to preserve a 3–2 Red Sox victory that stabilized the series in every way imaginable.

Two days after questioning the methods of the Red Sox starter, Torre found himself now praising a Boston pitcher.

"He was terrific. . . . I have a great deal of respect for him," said the esteemed Yankees skipper. "He's probably great for a manager because you can start him, you can relieve him, he's pretty durable, and he's a class act."

Said Little: "He has come through very big for us in the two games he's started here in this series. It couldn't happen to a better fella. This guy has pitched well for us, and he's been very consistent throughout the season. We're just glad he's on our side right now."

Indeed, there was no telling where the Red Sox would have been without Wakefield at that point. In his last three appearances — Game 4 of the Oakland series and Games 1 and 4 of the Yankees series — the Red Sox were 3-0. In the ALCS, now tied 2-2, Wakefield had both Boston victories. Wakefield had pitched in four postseason games overall and posted a 2.61 ERA, evoking memories of his performance for the Pittsburgh Pirates as a 26-year-old unknown in 1992.

For the Red Sox, however, Game 4 had come at a price. Because of the rainout, Boston and New York lost an off-day that had been scheduled between Games 4 and 5. Beginning with Game 4, and barring additional weather issues, the clubs would be required to play the final four games of the series in four days. That schedule would make it harder for Little to make the best use of Wakefield's versatility — and Lowe's as well — at least until the series reached a seventh game.

Fearful of matching Burkett against the Yankees, Little went to Lowe for Game 5. Torre, by contrast, opted for the more rested David Wells, who had yet to pitch in the series. (By doing this, Torre lined up Andy Pettitte, who had defeated Lowe in Game 2, to pitch Game 6.) The Yankees scored three times in the second inning to take early command of Game 5 and stake Wells to a 3-1 lead through seven innings. Once more, Little sent his starter back out for the eighth inning, a decision that again backfired when Lowe walked the leadoff man. Little left Lowe in the game for two more at-bats. The second was Jorge Posada, who stroked a one-out single that placed runners at first and third base — the key blow during an inning in which the Yankees would extend their lead to 4-1.

Though Embree was on the mound when the Yankees extended their lead that inning, the run was officially charged to Lowe, who left the runner in scoring position when he departed the game amid more questions about Little's unwillingness to trust his bullpen. Lowe finished the game with 119 pitches, a total surpassed only by Martinez in any postseason game played by the Red Sox after 1990 (the point in time when teams became increasingly cautious about overburdening their starters). Martinez, for his part, had thrown more than 119 pitches on only two occasions during his Red Sox career, but one of them was Game 1 of the Oakland series, when Little had allowed his ace to throw a preposterous 130 pitches.

Torre, by contrast, yanked Wells after the seventh and turned the game over to rested and trusted closer Mariano Rivera, who closed out a 4–2 Yankees win and sent the series back to New York with the Yankees holding a 3–2 series edge.

Once again, the Red Sox were on the brink.

And yet, as the team traveled to New York, Wakefield felt exactly as he had all year long — that the Red Sox were far from dead.

This is when we do our best work.

Now faced with almost no choice but to start Burkett in Game 6, the Red Sox came out and made an early dent in Pettitte, erasing an early 1–0 deficit with four runs in the third inning. After the Yankees responded with an outburst of their own and took a 6–4 lead into the seventh — Burkett was long gone by then — the Sox scored three times in the seventh against reliever Jose Contreras and twice more in the ninth on a towering home run by Trot Nixon, cruising to a 9–6 victory that evened the series at 3–3 and forced a decisive Game 7. Despite Burkett's difficulties, the Red Sox had shut down the Yankees over the final 5⅓ innings thanks to the continued and entirely unexpected brilliance of the Boston bullpen, which was redeeming itself tenfold.

As usual, Game 7 left no uncertainties. In a rematch of the emotional Game 3, Martinez and Clemens were the scheduled starters. Both managers were expected to exhaust all options on their pitching staffs. The Red Sox quickly came out and hammered Clemens for three runs in the second inning — two on a homer by Nixon — then extended the lead to 4–0 in the top of the fourth. Boston seemed poised to break open the game when a desperate Torre summoned *his* starter in Games 1 and 4 — the surgical Mussina — in hopes of preserving any chance at a Yankees win. And just as Lowe and Wakefield had done for Little and the Red Sox at earlier points during the postseason, Mussina stabilized what was a very shaky situation for the Yankees, preventing major damage and keeping New York within striking distance.

Martinez, meanwhile, shut the Yankees out for the first four innings before allowing solo home runs to Giambi in the fifth and seventh. On the latter occasion, the Yankees followed with consecutive, two-out singles by pinch hitter Sierra and outfielder Garcia before Martinez struck out Alfonso Soriano, leaving the Red Sox with a 4–2 lead entering the eighth inning and leaving Little in an eerily familiar situation that had presented itself over and over again throughout the playoffs.

His starter or his relievers?

Which way should he go?

Seated in the Red Sox bullpen by that point — it was Game 7, after all — Wakefield similarly wondered which option his manager would choose. It was one of the major disadvantages of being a reliever. In any baseball game, the dugout served as master control, that place where things were discussed and decisions made. Out in the bullpen, particularly during intense postseason play, relievers could feel lost and detached. *Okay, what are we going to do here?* Little could call down to the bullpen and ask relievers to begin warming, as he did in Game 7, but nobody in the bullpen was privy to the discussions taking place in the dugout on a pitch-by-pitch basis. It was not as if Little could keep them on speakerphone. Relievers could do nothing but watch through the tensest moments, like spectators, until a call came or a decision was made. *Okay, now go!* The situation was unsettling for the relievers, who could get just as anxious as any nervous fan glued to the television set.

After the Sox extended the lead to 5–2 in the top of the eighth on a home run by Ortiz, Little sent Martinez back out for the eighth despite the availability of a bullpen that had pitched brilliantly throughout the series. Wakefield did not wonder so much about whether that was the right decision as he did about when relievers might be thrust into duty. Timlin and Embree had warmed and were *hot,* fully prepared to enter the game, as Martinez allowed one hit, then another, then another. The Yankees strung together four hits in all, the last a two-run hit by the switch-hitting Posada that locked the game at 5–5. Like the rest of the Red Sox relievers, Wakefield only watched. As much of New England groaned in horror and disbelief, Embree and Timlin finally were summoned and worked out of the inning, but the damage had been done. The game was now tied, and New York had the momentum. Martinez had thrown 123 pitches — the second-highest total by a Sox pitcher since 1990 in the team's postseason history — and there was the indisputable feeling that the Sox had just blown their chance.

Red Sox fans had seen this kind of thing far too many times, after all, to think that things would end well.

With each manager now operating as if the next run would determine the outcome of his team's season — *next run wins* — Torre turned the game over to his closer, the incomparable Rivera, already by then regarded as one of the great postseason performers of all time. Because the game was in New York, that option was also a luxury afforded Torre that Little did not possess: even if the Red Sox went ahead, Little still needed someone to get the last three outs. Torre, by contrast, needed to shut down the Red Sox first and score later, a fact that inspired him to use Rivera for three full innings, the second-longest postseason relief appearance of the pitcher's career. Little countered by using Timlin for 1⅓ innings, then did what he had done throughout the playoffs.

He turned to one of his starters.

And given the early developments of the series with the Yankees, he called upon Tim Wakefield over Derek Lowe.

Taking the ball with only two days of rest after his Game 4 performance — Wakefield, in fact, had speculated that he might be able to pitch as soon as Game 5 if needed — the knuckleballer jogged to the mound for the 10th inning with the same confidence he had possessed throughout the series. *I still feel locked in.* He set the Yankees down in order in the bottom of the 10th. Wakefield then returned to the mound for the bottom of the 11th and took his customary warm-up pitches before Mirabelli fired the ball down to second base — Mirabelli, unsurprisingly, had entered the game precisely when Wakefield did — before Wakefield stepped onto the mound for one of the most devastating and unforeseen moments in his career.

As he had done so many times, Wakefield planted his fingernails into the cover of the baseball and spun on his right heel, kicking his left leg into the air as he cocked his arm. *Grip, kick, throw.* He lofted a knuckleball that harmlessly floated to home plate, targeted for the lap of his catcher, but Yankees third baseman Aaron Boone swung and connected squarely, lofting a parabolic blow that headed like a final cannonball into the left-field seats at a delirious Yankee Stadium.

Before the ball had even landed, a knowing Wakefield slumped off the mound as Boone raised his arm triumphantly and jogged to first base, declaring a 6–5 Yankees win that delivered New York to the World Series. The knuckleballer lowered his head and dropped his shoulders, disappearing down the runway steps and into the Boston clubhouse, where he broke down and confessed his greatest fear to his close friend and confidant Joe Cochran, a New England native and longtime Red Sox employee.

"I just became Bill Buckner," he wept.

In a somber Boston clubhouse after the defeat, as some Red Sox players refused to concede that the Yankees were a better team, Wakefield stood before his locker and wondered how one of the best years of his career could have ended so badly. He never saw the end coming. Just a few innings earlier, with Boston holding a 5–2 lead, he had stood to be the Most Valuable Player of the American League Championship Series. Now he had trouble seeing himself as anything other than Buckner. Prior to Boone's homer, the Red Sox and Yankees had played 64 innings in the ALCS and scored precisely 29 runs each, a testament to just how evenly matched the teams were. Red Sox players repeated over and over again that Wakefield was not to be blamed for the loss, that he was to be praised for the manner in which he performed, that he was to be lauded for the grace he demonstrated to the bitter end.

Wakefield felt inconsolable. *I let us down.* He had spent an entire career priding himself on being a team player, on doing whatever was necessary for his team to win, on doing the grunt work. He did that for his teammates, for *them,* more than he did it for anyone else. Now he felt as if he had failed them. Now he felt like a bad teammate. Almost to a man, the Sox players took turns attempting to console him — Timlin, Mirabelli, all of them — and yet Wakefield simply could not shake the feeling that he had ruined things for them, that he would be regarded as an eternal failure by Red Sox fans, that he forever owed an apology to anyone who had invested in the 2003 Red Sox as he had.

I'm so sorry.

Of course, Wakefield had nothing to be sorry for.

The end of Game 7 in 2003 proved to be nothing more than a beginning.

And Tim Wakefield soon would learn that the curse of being the next Bill Buckner would descend on someone else, and that the life of a knuckleballer could rise again as acutely as it dipped.

Ten

●

You don't catch a knuckleball, you defend against it.

— *Longtime catcher and manager Joe Torre*

ROUGHLY THREE MONTHS after Aaron Boone ended Boston's 85th consecutive season without a World Series championship, Tim Wakefield fidgeted at the base of a small staircase, waiting for his introduction to a dinner crowd of about 1,000. As always, the knuckleballer tried to get a handle. Wakefield had become a regular attendee and crowd favorite at the annual Boston Baseball Writers dinner, but this year he simply did not know what to expect.

While dinners like this one had died off in most every other major baseball market in America, the annual event in Boston was still thriving, further evidence of the passion the city held for the Red Sox.

The dinner represented Wakefield's first opportunity to assess public sentiment in the wake of the Boone homer, which had caused him great anxiety over the winter. He was still worried about his legacy. He still wondered whether fans would forgive him. At the dinner, Wakefield mingled with his teammates, members of the media, and Sox officials beforehand, his typically pleasant manner disguising his concerns as he approached the dais to address the crowd. *What if I get booed? What if they won't take me back?* Thoughts like these weighed on him. Wakefield had spent nine full seasons with the Red Sox, and he had found a home in Boston. He knew, however, that Red Sox history was littered with tragic figures, from Johnny Pesky (who allegedly held the ball as Enos Slaughter scored the winning run in the 1946 World Series) to manager Joe McCarthy (who bypassed young lefty Mel Parnell in favor of veteran righty Denny Galehouse in a one-game playoff in 1948) to Buckner himself. In a place like Boston, there was no outrunning your past.

What if they don't forgive me?

Later, as Boston baseball writers and various baseball players, coaches, and executives lined up to be introduced to the crowd, Wakefield's pulse quickened. His mind raced, too. Had things turned out differently, he might have won a World Series by now, maybe been the Most Valuable Player of *two* League Championship Series. Instead, he was left to wonder whether a single, floating knuckler could undo the work of a career during which he had thrown thousands upon thousands of pitches.

His name was finally announced to the crowd, and as Wakefield stepped up the small staircase onto the dais the room erupted with applause. Fans stood and clapped wildly. Not a single person dissented. Wakefield's body and mind eased all at once, relief and emotion washing through him. Red Sox fans seemed to embrace him the way a father would a dejected Little Leaguer.

It's not your fault. You did your best. We're proud of you.

"I had tears in my eyes," Wakefield said.

Indeed, for all of the criticisms Red Sox fans had absorbed over the years, they could prove to be an extremely compassionate lot. Had Wakefield thoroughly reviewed the tale of Buckner, for instance, he would have discovered the ending to be far happier than most realized. Released by the Red Sox during the 1987 season nine months after his historic blunder against the New York Mets in the 1986 World Series, Buckner returned three years later during spring training of 1990. Then an aged, broken-down veteran, he was a long shot to make the team. Buckner nevertheless had a productive spring and played his way onto the team's opening day roster, and he hobbled onto the field from the top step of the dugout when he was customarily introduced, along with the rest of the Red Sox, to the opening day crowd at Fenway Park.

To the surprise of no one that day, Bill Buckner was cheered wildly, a sellout crowd at Fenway Park standing throughout the ovation.

Bill Buckner, like Tim Wakefield in January 2004, felt like a hero.

During the 88 days between Boone's homer and Wakefield's first public appearance in Boston, the Red Sox had undergone dramatic changes and another scapegoat had been identified. Shortly after the Game 7 loss to the Yankees, amid escalating public outcry about the manner in which Grady Little had handled his pitching staff throughout the postseason and, more specifically, in Game 7 of the Yankees series, the Red Sox fired their manager. Grady Little, as it turned out, was the one who would be labeled the scapegoat for their failure in the ALCS and lumped with Bill Buckner. From owners John Henry and Tom Werner down to team president Larry Lucchino and Epstein, the Red Sox seemed more determined than ever to improve a team that possessed a champion's heart and drive — if not the pitching staff. Even though the Red Sox front office felt that Little had become an obstruction during the playoffs, they also acknowledged that the manager frequently was forced to play musical chairs with a pitching staff that was a little short on both ends. Several changes were in order.

First, following Little's firing, the Sox hired the more cerebral Terry Francona as manager, hoping for a leader who could both handle modern players and effectively manage the game. Second, Epstein orchestrated a blockbuster trade with the Arizona Diamondbacks that brought ace and certified big-game starter Curt Schilling to Boston for a package of prospects. Third, the Sox signed A's closer Keith Foulke as a free agent to bring order to a bullpen that had lacked a reliable anchor until the final days of Boston's postseason.

The message was clear.

The Red Sox weren't fooling around.

Watching and listening with great interest from his home in Melbourne, Wakefield was surprised and saddened at the dismissal of Little, who had been a key element in returning the knuckleballer to his rightful place in the starting rotation. He liked Grady. He believed in Grady. He felt that teams won and lost together, and the reality of the game sometimes frustrated him. Little might have summoned Embree and Timlin in place of Martinez in Game 7, and the Red Sox still might have lost. Had Martinez been more effective, the Red Sox might have won. There had been countless points in that game, as in every other, where events could have turned, both teams missing opportunities along the way that might have changed the outcome.

Sure enough, even had the Sox beaten the Yankees, there was no guarantee Boston would have won the World Series. When the Yankees themselves lost the championship to the Florida Marlins in six games, many theorized that the Yankees were physically and emotionally drained after their seven-game epic with the Red Sox.

In the eyes of Tim Wakefield and many others, Grady Little was indeed made a scapegoat.

It could just as easily have been me.

Beyond the changes they made, the Red Sox explored countless others that would have shaken the team to the core. Every time word leaked that the Sox were even *considering* these major changes, the news had the same effect. Frustrated with both the contract and attitude of Manny Ramirez, who was just three years into a whopping eight-year, $160 million contract, the Red Sox placed the slugger on waivers with the small hope that another team might claim him and assume the financial obligation of his remaining contract. Naturally, there were no takers. Still, news of the club's dissatisfaction with Ramirez sparked some trade discussion with other teams, most notably the Texas Rangers, who similarly had a disgruntled superstar in shortstop Alex Rodriguez. The deal made great sense for both teams but came with a very large string attached — the fate of Red Sox shortstop and face-of-the-franchise Nomar Garciaparra.

By that point, the new Sox officials had also grown frustrated with Garciaparra, who had flatly rejected the team's latest attempt at a contract extension and was entering the final year of his deal. Because the new officials had no real ties to Garciaparra — he had been drafted and developed under former general manager Dan Duquette — they had no reservations about trading him. During Major League Baseball's annual winter meetings in December, Epstein agreed to the framework of a deal that would send Garciaparra to the Chicago White Sox for talented outfielder Magglio Ordonez, but the proposed trade came with the condition that the Red Sox first complete a deal with the Rangers that would swap Ramirez for Rodriguez.

The idea was simple: trade an outfielder for a shortstop, then trade your shortstop for an outfielder.

While Garciaparra publicly bristled at the idea that the club would trade him — he called both a Boston-area newspaper and an all-sports radio station from his honeymoon in Hawaii with soccer star Mia Hamm to express his shock — the deal between the Red Sox and the Rangers crumbled. Seeking the help of the Major League Baseball Players Association to restructure Rodriguez's deal (10 years, $252 million) and make the contract more feasible, the Red Sox failed miserably. In a very public affair, the players' union shot down Boston's proposed reconstruction of Rodriguez's contract, igniting a spat between Lucchino, agent Scott Boras (who represented Rodriguez), the MLBPA, the Rangers, and the Red Sox.

Nonetheless, there was no disputing that the Red Sox had made major upgrades to a team that came within five outs of going to the World Series — and that Boston was very much a threat to unseat the Yankees in 2004.

Following all of that winter activity, Wakefield had lots of questions about its impact, especially about the effect of newcomers Schilling and Foulke on a team bond that was as strong as Wakefield had ever experienced during his career. He was not alone. Prior to the Boston Baseball Writers dinner in January, Wakefield and first baseman Kevin Millar privately took their questions about the two pitchers to Francona, who had shared a clubhouse with both Schilling and Foulke at various points during his career as a manager and coach. Francona had most recently served as the bench coach in Oakland — he was in the opposing dugout when the Red Sox came back to defeat Foulke and the A's in the 2003 American League Division Series — and he also had dealt with Schilling during a four-year stint as manager of the Philadelphia Phillies from 1997 to 2000.

Schilling, in particular, with his reputation as a strong and opinionated personality who could grate on teammates, concerned the Red Sox players, who worried about the clubhouse dynamic.

"You're going to want to tell him to shut up every once in a while," Francona told Wakefield and Millar as Sox representatives, dressed in tuxedos, waited in line to be introduced to fans at the dinner. "But he's a good guy."

Satisfied by his new manager's assessment, Wakefield nodded at the time, though his mind was obviously elsewhere.

In failing to make the deal for Alex Rodriguez, the Red Sox never imagined that they had opened the door for their rival New York Yankees to close the deal. Just before the start of spring training, in a stunning development, the Yankees announced that they had acquired the great A-Rod, pulling off the blockbuster deal the Red Sox had been unable to execute. Almost nobody saw it coming. The Yankees already had a Hall of Fame–caliber shortstop in Derek Jeter, so nobody regarded New York as a potential destination for Rodriguez. In fact, the Yankees had an unexpected vacancy at third base because Aaron Boone, of all people, had suffered a major knee injury while playing basketball during the off-season. No one imagined A-Rod at third. But there he was, and the 2004 season had already elevated to an arms race before the pitchers even reported to camp.

Among Red Sox fans, the response was predictable. *Woe is us.* The Yankees had just replaced the hero of the 2003 ALCS with the best player in baseball, even if the Yankees were required to sacrifice talented second baseman Alfonso Soriano in the process. Some Red Sox fans who had gone generations without celebrating a world title feared that history was merely repeating itself, that Rodriguez ending up in New York was akin to Boston's decision to sell Babe Ruth to the Yankees in 1920, a decision that forever altered the histories of the two franchises and spawned *the Curse of the Bambino.*

But inside the walls of a Red Sox clubhouse fortified with off-season acquisitions and now stuffed with both talent and moxie, Rodriguez's arrival in New York was seen as something altogether different.

"Nobody said it would be easy, and George [Steinbrenner, the

Yankees' owner] is going to do whatever it takes to stop us," said Embree shortly after arriving at camp in Fort Myers, Florida. "I think it's kind of exciting . . . [because] they're worried about us. They know we have a very good ball club."

Said backup catcher Mirabelli: "I think there's definitely respect for the Red Sox there, but I don't know if they'd admit that. They know they've got a fight on their hands every time they play us, regardless of who they've got on their team. . . . Look, A-Rod would help any team, but still, on paper, the Red Sox are right where they need to be."

Tim Wakefield felt this as strongly as anyone.

While first-year manager Francona had some egos to mas-sage—Garciaparra in particular was still vexed by the Red Sox pursuit of Rodriguez in the first place—there was no disputing the talent on the Boston roster. The Red Sox were stacked. They had some major contract issues: Garciaparra and catcher Jason Varitek as well as start-ing pitchers Lowe and Martinez would all be eligible for free agency at the end of the year. But there was a potential benefit in that—the Red Sox were likely to get the best possible performance from these players in their final contract years. There was a great deal at stake, and Red Sox officials were wise enough to recognize that the players' concern about protecting their own individual futures as well as their collective legacy could provide key motivation.

For many of the Red Sox who preceded the new owners and team administrators, the 2004 season had the feeling of the last roundup.

"They've made it pretty apparent this is probably the last time the four of us [Varitek, Lowe, Martinez, and Garciaparra] will be together," the typically soft-spoken Varitek said late in spring training. "We've got to hold on to that and win."

Amid all of that, Tim Wakefield found himself in a most unusual place.

For one of the first times in his Red Sox career, during a potentially unsettling time, he had stability that others did not.

The Red Sox burst from the starting gate with a vengeance. The team won 15 of its first 21 games, making it clear from the outset that they were a team on a mission. During the first three weeks of the season, the Red Sox played seven games against the Yankees—four in Boston, three in New York—and won six of them. The first meetings came on April 16–19 at Fenway Park, where the revamped, reinforced teams played for the first meaningful time since Boone's homer the previous October.

As fate would have it, Wakefield pitched the first game, which doubled as his first start of the season. He went seven sterling innings and backboned a resounding 6–2 Boston win. For the knuckleballer, the game brought full closure to his 2003 season and, like the writers' dinner, was impossible to forget. Wakefield was cheered as he walked from the dugout to the bullpen for his warm-up tosses, cheered when he was announced to the home crowd, and cheered when he walked off the mound at the end of the seventh. He felt as if the crowd was speaking directly to him at times, celebrating his career and contributions to the team and vowing to do exactly what Red Sox fans had learned to do each spring.

Let's give it another try together, Tim.

For that matter, Wakefield had long since learned the same lesson.

"To me, I could see it in his face—there was a relief. I think he was waiting for this outing for some time," Mirabelli said of Wakefield. "We were all in shock [last year]. . . . The season was over, and we felt like we had a lot of game left in us. He was the MVP in that series. There was no doubt in my mind about that, and for it to turn that quickly on him . . . it was a shame it ended like that. But without him, we wouldn't have been in that situation."

With the page now officially turned on 2003—for the Red Sox and Wakefield both—the team settled into the rhythm of the regular season at a relatively uninspiring pace. After starting the season 15–6, the Red Sox went a positively mediocre 41–39 over the next 80 games, a chunk of the schedule that constituted almost exactly half the season and brought Boston to the brink of the annual July 31 trading deadline. During that stretch, some of the team's internal issues began to eat away at it from the inside. Garciaparra remained unhappy and was playing poor defense in the wake of a heel injury he had suffered during spring training. Matters came to a head during a 5–4 loss to New York in 13 innings on July 1 at Yankee Stadium. Even though Garciaparra did not play in that game because he had been scheduled to have the day off as part of his rehabilitation from the injury, his teammates seemed irked that he did not fight his way into the lineup. The defeat concluded a three-game series sweep by the Yankees that increased New York's lead in the division from 5½ games to a whopping 8½, and many believed that Garciaparra had abandoned his teammates, acting selfishly in the midst of his ongoing issues with club management.

Whatever the case, Epstein had had enough, and by the time July 31 rolled around, he pulled the trigger on a blockbuster deal that sent Garciaparra to the Chicago Cubs in a three-team trade that landed shortstop Orlando Cabrera and first baseman Doug Mientkiewicz in Boston. In a separate deal, the Sox acquired speedy outfielder Dave Roberts from the Los Angeles Dodgers. All of Epstein's moves were designed to improve Boston's defense and athleticism — Cabrera and Mientkiewicz were excellent defense players — while simultaneously ridding the club of a holdover from the previous regime who seemed to be growing increasingly disgruntled.

"I like the club as is. The safe thing to do would have been to play it out. The safe thing to do would have been not to touch it," Epstein said. "But in my mind, we were not going to win the World Series as is."

Wakefield, for his part, had seen this sort of thing before, albeit under different circumstances, with different people. Roger Clemens had departed via free agency after the 1996 season. Mo Vaughn did the same late in 1998. The Red Sox had undergone considerable turnover during Wakefield's time in Boston — players, managers, general managers, owners — and his experience in Pittsburgh had long since hardened him to the realities of the game. People came and people went, and there really wasn't a damned thing that anyone could ever do about it.

Wakefield, in fact, had learned of the Garciaparra deal in unusual fashion. Despite trade rumors that involved the Red Sox shortstop, Wakefield never believed that Garciaparra would be traded, right up until the moments before the annual trading deadline. Garciaparra simply had meant too much to the franchise.

That day, Wakefield had left the team hotel in downtown Minneapolis and taken a taxi to the Metrodome, where he was dropped off in the rear of the building, as usual. He entered the stadium near the loading dock, where he greeted and walked past building security, then walked through the cavernous main hallway that circled the Metrodome and served as the central access point to all the locker rooms in the building — college and pro football, baseball. Finally, he arrived at the door that led to the visitors' clubhouse.

Just as Wakefield was headed in, Garciaparra was headed out.

Where are you going, Nomar?

The answer: *To Chicago.*

Indeed, Garciaparra was headed to the Cubs. Wakefield had no idea what to say to his teammate. *Are you kidding? What happened?* The news caught him completely off guard. Garciaparra did not know who the Red Sox were receiving in return. He just knew he was out. Wakefield wished Garciaparra luck and told his former teammate he had enjoyed playing with him. Garciaparra did the same. Then the two shared a quick embrace before Wakefield walked into the Red Sox clubhouse and Garciaparra began the long walk out.

Once in the Boston clubhouse, Wakefield learned that the Red Sox had acquired Cabrera from the Montreal Expos and Mientkiewicz from the Twins, and that Mientkiewicz had been put in a most amusing position. A night earlier, Mientkiewicz had worn the uniform of the Twins and sat in the dugout opposite the Red Sox. Now that the deal had been made, all he had to do was change locker rooms. Mientkiewicz woke up in the same city and went to the same ballpark on consecutive days, but he played for different teams.

The visiting clubhouse at the Metrodome felt like a bus station. Wakefield told reporters that he was "sad" to see Garciaparra leave, but that he also recognized "the business side of this sport." He was still processing the moves himself. The Red Sox had a great deal invested in the 2004 season, and now they were changing course, again.

I wonder how this is going to play out.

More dips and turns.

For all the large-scale changes going on, their starting rotation had remained remarkably intact, and the Red Sox would play the entire year without a starting pitcher missing so much as one turn on the mound. They treaded water for the next two weeks. When the Sox suffered a 5–4 loss to the Chicago White Sox on Sunday, August 15, they were a season-high 10½ games behind the first-place Yankees with a mere 46 games to play. They had gone a mediocre 8–7 since the changes that cast off Garciaparra and brought Cabrera, Mientkiewicz, and Roberts to Boston. Time was dwindling, and the Red Sox needed to get their act together quickly. While Epstein had expected an acclimation period after the changes, the Red Sox soon might risk missing the playoffs entirely.

If that happened, Wakefield knew that Boston's failure in the 2003 American League Championship Series would take on even greater significance and that the team could face even more dramatic changes.

As if flipping a switch, the Red Sox then morphed into their season-opening form, ripping off a succession of victories that seemed downright effortless. From August 16 through September 8, the Red Sox won six straight, lost one, won 10 straight, lost one, won four straight. Wakefield could not remember a time when the Red Sox ever played better as a team. When the surge was complete, Boston had gone 20–2 over a scintillating 20-game stretch that had brought the club within 2½ games of the first-place Yankees and all but secured a playoff berth as the American League wild-card entry.

During the streak, almost every Boston player contributed in some way, shape, or form—and most of them were playing at a very high level. In his final three starts of August, Wakefield went 3–0 with a 2.57 ERA and limited opponents to a .231 batting average. To that point, the season had been far more of a struggle for him than 2003—Wakefield would finish the 2004 regular season at 12–10 with a 4.87 ERA and pitch 188½ innings in 32 outings (30 starts)—but he made his usual contributions and sacrifices during a campaign in which the Red Sox finished 98–64, posting their highest win total since 1978 and finishing with the third-best record in baseball.

Though the Red Sox failed to catch the Yankees for the division title, that was a failure of relatively little consequence. Boston and New York were both going back to the playoffs, and the teams seemed to be on a collision course given all the events of the previous 12 months.

Said a succinct Francona, capturing the essence of the moment: "This is the beginning."

Or more appropriately, another *new* beginning.

As had happened with great regularity over a two-year span, the Red Sox once again found themselves starting anew. They had changed owners. They had changed general managers. They had changed managers. They had made the playoffs and lost to the Yankees, revamped their roster, and started anew. They had traded Garciaparra and started over yet again. Then they had made the playoffs and recalibrated once more.

Quite accustomed to new beginnings, Wakefield was earmarked to start Game 4 of the playoffs. The addition of Schilling had reordered the starting rotation, with Martinez slipping into an uncharacteristic number-two spot. The stringy Bronson Arroyo was third. Squeezed out of the rotation, for a handful of reasons, was Lowe. First, because the postseason typically included an abundance of travel days on which no games would be played, teams generally operated with a maximum of four starters, not five. And second, among a deep group that included Schilling, Martinez, Arroyo, and Wakefield, Lowe had been the least effective down the stretch, and that performance had now left him on the outside looking in.

And then there was this: because Wakefield threw the knuckleball, he was almost always paired with catcher Doug Mirabelli, who was more adept at handling the knuckler than the customary starting catcher, Jason Varitek. Pitching Wakefield in relief during the postseason might require two substitutions in the middle of the game — the pitcher *and* the catcher — and the Red Sox believed they were better off using the knuckler early in the game as a result.

In that way, the knuckler was now working *for* Wakefield, not against him.

As it turned out, Wakefield never pitched in the best-of-five, first-round series against the Anaheim Angels. The Red Sox didn't need him to. Behind Schilling, Martinez, and Arroyo, the Red Sox wiped out the Angels in three straight games, winning by scores of 9–3, 8–3, and 8–6. The Angels simply had no answers. Boston batted a whopping .302 as a team and dominated the series on both sides, save for a hiccup in Game 3 when reliever Timlin allowed a game-tying grand slam to outfielder Vladimir Guerrero. The Red Sox closed out the series when they won in the 10th inning on a two-run homer by Ortiz, a decisive blow that made a winner of Lowe, who had emerged from the bullpen to pitch the final inning.

While the Red Sox celebrated in typical rowdy fashion, the focus immediately shifted to the upcoming American League Championship Series, where the Red Sox would face either the Yankees or the Minnesota Twins. At that moment, New York led the series by a 2–1 count. To a man, Red Sox players said all the right things and insisted that they had no preference with regard to their next opponent, but the sentiment in the clubhouse was unanimous. Boston wanted to face the Yankees again, and no member of the Red Sox wanted another crack at New York more than Wakefield, who had been on the verge of being named the ALCS Most Valuable Player in 2003 when it all went *poof.*

One night later, Wakefield and the Red Sox got their wish when the Yankees defeated the Twins in Game 4 for a 3–1 series win. Just like that, Boston and New York were slated to meet in a rematch that had all the makings of a *Rocky* sequel, but with one significant distinction.

The second version would prove even more riveting than the original.

We're going to get another crack at these guys, and nobody wants that more than me.

Because things went so swimmingly against the Angels, Francona had the luxury of lining up his pitching precisely as he wanted it again, which meant a Game 4 start for Wakefield. The knuckleballer was fine with that. As badly as Wakefield wanted another chance at the Yankees, he also knew that the Red Sox rotation was set in a way that would give him the best position to succeed. *I'll get my chance.* For as much as Curt Schilling helped the Red Sox during the regular season—he finished 21–6 and would finish second in the American League Cy Young Award balloting—the Red Sox had acquired Schilling for October, for moments like this. Wakefield knew that and welcomed it. *The more good pitchers we have, the better we all can be.* In 2001, as a member of the Arizona Diamondbacks, Schilling had started three games against the Yankees, the last two on three days of rest, posting a 1.69 ERA. He was the starting pitcher when the Diamondbacks toppled the Yankees and Mariano Rivera in a decisive Game 7. For all of the criticism Schilling historically had taken for being outspoken and opinionated, he was a winner and a fierce competitor. Wakefield had come to respect Schilling greatly during his first season with the Sox.

The Yankees, too, knew of Schilling's importance, his arrival in Boston having elicited a response from the most respected Yankees that revealed more than a hint of concern.

"They've made some good additions," Yankees shortstop Derek Jeter had said during spring training. "They've added some quality guys, and the big one is Schilling. Obviously, you win with pitching and defense, and they've added a quality guy."

With all the hype that had accompanied meetings between the Red Sox and Yankees for several months, Game 1 of the American League Championship Series took on enormous proportions, particularly for New York. Despite being the defending American League champions and the reigning AL East Division champion in possession of home-field advantage, the Yankees entered the series as improbable underdogs. Incredibly, the Las Vegas oddsmakers had installed the Red Sox as favorites. Wakefield and his mates shrugged this off as nothing more than media hype and said all the right things publicly, but privately they couldn't help but see it as further evidence of their inevitable success. *Everyone else knows what we know. We're the better team. Now we just have to go and prove it.* Confidence in the Red Sox had never been higher, in and out of the Boston clubhouse.

And then, with little warning, the Red Sox found themselves reeling.

From the start, Wakefield was among those who could see that Schilling was laboring. *He doesn't look right.* Pitching on an ankle that he had recently tweaked — or so everyone thought — Schilling was battered in Game 1, allowing two runs in the first inning and four more in the third. He never came out of the dugout to pitch the fourth.

Boston's series game plan was immediately thrown into a state of chaos as Francona found himself forced to use six relievers, including Wakefield, for no more than an inning each. Yankees starter Mike Mussina — an unsung hero of Game 7 in 2003 — flirted with a perfect game as the Yankees built an 8–0 lead through six innings, at which point the Red Sox began a near-historic comeback that whittled the score to 8–7. The Yankees ultimately won, 10–7, but the nature of the game made a handful of things clear from the outset.

Whenever the Red Sox and Yankees were involved, there was no way of predicting anything.

Favorites or no favorites, all bets were off.

With or without Schilling, Wakefield felt that the Red Sox still had the pitching to defeat the Yankees. Depending on the severity of his injury, Schilling's absence would certainly be costly, but the Red Sox still had great depth. Not many teams had someone like Martinez lined up to pitch Game 1, let alone Game 2. Fewer teams still had someone like Lowe, who had been a postseason hero only a year earlier, in the bullpen. The 2004 Red Sox were a carefree lot — loud and entertaining — but they were also confident more than they were cocky. There was an unspoken trust between them. Wakefield did not have to say anything to Martinez following Game 1 — or vice versa — because everyone *knew* the reality. In a pitching rotation, as in the bullpen in some respects, the baton passed from one man to the next, albeit from game to game. There was a certain camaraderie among starters, who were another team within the team intent on helping one another. If one failed, the next one covered for him, and so on. Pedro Martinez had been around long enough to understand what he needed to do.

But once again, the Red Sox failed to hit until it was too late. While Martinez pitched quite well, Jon Lieber was brilliant, and the Boston lineup was shut down by a Yankees starter for a second consecutive night. New York built a 2–0 series lead as the ALCS shifted back to Boston, and the Red Sox suddenly found themselves in what seemed to be a virtual must-win situation. Francona entrusted Game 3 to slinky right-hander Bronson Arroyo, but he, like Schilling, was treated like a punching bag by the Yankee batters. Though the Red Sox offense had awakened to force a 6–6 tie entering the fourth inning, the Red Sox simply had no answers for the New York lineup. Francona desperately tried to clean up the developing mess by going through relievers as if they were paper towels, but the game was rapidly getting out of control and threatening to destroy Boston's season.

Because rain had postponed Game 3 by a day, the clubs lost a scheduled travel day between Games 5 and 6 of the series, a loss that was now affecting the Red Sox far more than the Yankees. If the Red Sox were to win the series — somehow, some way — they would have to play the final five games without a day off, putting even more strain on a bullpen that had endured a season's worth of wear and tear. Consequently, Francona found himself in the unenviable position of both losing Game 3 *and* burning his bullpen for the balance of the series, however long that would be, a combination that would have left Boston with even less of a chance to win a best-of-seven set in which they were already being thoroughly embarrassed.

Like Martinez entering Game 2, Wakefield assessed the situation without any prodding. *We're getting killed. And if we're going to have a chance from here on out, we have to save the bullpen.* The knuckleballer got up from his seat in the dugout and walked over to his manager, asking the obvious question. *Do you need my arm tonight?* Francona needed the innings, to be sure, but he also needed a starter for Game 4. If Lowe was prepared to start the following night, the manager said, Wakefield would be used. Wakefield turned, walked over to Lowe, and asked the demoted starter whether he could start the next game, and Lowe nodded yes. Wakefield grabbed his glove and ran down to the bullpen between innings to warm up, all with the idea of preserving the late-inning relievers for a future game the Red Sox might actually be able to win.

To that extent, without question, Wakefield's outing proved an enormous success. Though Embree appeared in the game in the eighth inning — by which point the Yankees had built a 17–8 lead — he threw just 14 pitches. Timlin and Foulke did not appear in the game at all. With the exception of Wakefield, who pitched 3⅓ innings (10 outs) and threw 64 pitches in *relief,* no Sox reliever to that point had been exposed to the carnage for more than an inning or 20 pitches, a method Francona had similarly employed in Game 1. By distributing the workload and asking every full-time reliever to do *a little,* Francona had avoided overburdening any of them, ensuring that he would have as many weapons as possible at his disposal for subsequent games.

And yet, for that same plan to work in a Game 3 loss that produced a humiliating, lopsided score of 19–8 and all but knocked the Red Sox out cold, the manager needed his knuckleballer to take a bullet and sacrifice his Game 4 start in service to a long-term approach that Wakefield had long since learned from Jim Leyland and Kevin Kennedy and Jimy Williams and Grady Little.

Taking a loss today might help produce wins during the rest of the week.

Of course, the Red Sox were focused on taking one step at a time, something they hoped to begin doing in Game 4. They had no more margin for error. They trailed in the series 3–0. One more loss would end their season. Making his first start since the regular season, Lowe effectively neutralized a cresting Yankees offense that had battered both Schilling in Game 1 and Arroyo in Game 3, giving the Red Sox, for just the second time in the series, a *chance* at victory entering the late innings. Wakefield saw this as a good sign. *Derek did his part.* Though facing a 4–3 deficit against the inimitable Rivera entering the ninth inning, the Red Sox rallied to tie the game on a walk by Kevin Millar, a stolen base by pinch runner Dave Roberts, and a game-tying single by Bill Mueller. Just like that, the Red Sox came back to life.

Wakefield, for one, saw it fitting that the rally began with Millar, whose arrival in Boston had dramatically transformed the makeup of the Boston clubhouse. Millar had defied all the odds to build a successful major league career after being discovered in the low-budget independent leagues, and he had what Wakefield playfully described as a "strong personality." Millar was loud and defiant, and he brought a mentality to Boston that had been sorely lacking at Fenway Park for decades. Every day Millar would walk around the Red Sox clubhouse and needle someone like Manny Ramirez or David Ortiz as easily as he would Wakefield or Bill Mueller, bridging the sort of cultural and communication gaps that were common in many clubhouses throughout baseball.

He's our glue.

With Red Sox relievers pitching a sterling 6⅔ innings during which they allowed just one run in relief of Lowe, Boston won Game 4 in dramatic fashion, the outcome decided on a two-run, game-winning home run by David Ortiz that produced a 6–4 victory in the bottom of the 12th inning. Just as Wakefield had done a year earlier in Game 7, Yankees reliever Paul Quantrill, a onetime member of the Red Sox, walked off the mound in dejected fashion as the home team celebrated. The Red Sox repeated the scene the following night when Ortiz punched a game-winning single to center against right-hander Esteban Loaiza to give Boston a 5–4 win in 14 innings that whittled New York's series advantage to 3–2, and it was in that victory that Wakefield made his second and most significant contribution in what became an epic series.

Because Game 4 lasted 12 innings, despite Lowe's solid performance, Francona again had relied heavily on his bullpen. His relievers continued to carry an undue portion of the workload. Thanks to a radical procedure performed on Schilling's ankle by team medical staff, the Red Sox believed they could have Schilling back for Game 6 in New York, assuming the team could extend the series that far. To do so, Boston would need a strong performance in Game 5 from Martinez, who pitched his team into the seventh.

Much to the chagrin of his manager, Martinez's contribution of six innings would prove to be less than half the game.

Trailing 4–2 in the eighth, the Red Sox again rallied to even the score, the tying run scoring in eerily similar fashion to Game 4. After Ortiz opened the eighth with a homer against reliever Tom Gordon — another former member of the Red Sox — Millar again walked. Pinch runner Roberts advanced to third on a single by Nixon before scoring on a sacrifice fly by Jason Varitek, whom Rivera had been brought into the game to face. The Red Sox and Yankees then ventured into extra innings again, the drama building through an array of missed scoring opportunities in the ninth, 10th, and 11th innings.

Francona had already used Timlin, Embree, Foulke, Mike Myers, and Game 3 starter Arroyo, so once again he summoned Wakefield, his human spackling compound. *I need to fill the gaps again.* The image of Wakefield trotting onto the field in extra innings of an elimination game evoked immediate and obvious images of Game 7 in 2003, but Wakefield never allowed the thought of Aaron Boone to enter his mind. With a man in scoring position in the 12th, Wakefield retired both Jeter and Rodriguez on flyouts. The Red Sox failed to score in the bottom of the inning, setting the stage for a freakish 13th inning that served up evidence that the luck of the Red Sox and their loyal knuckleballer had changed for the better.

Paired with Varitek, who had not caught him all season, Wakefield began the inning by striking out Gary Sheffield. But Sheffield reached first base because Varitek couldn't hold on to the third strike. Yankees outfielder Hideki Matsui then forced Sheffield at second base for the first out of the inning, and Wakefield seemed on the verge of escaping without any damage when Bernie Williams was retired on a flyout to right field.

And then, as if trying to avoid capture, Wakefield's magic knuckler began darting about as if it were a schizophrenic butterfly.

With two outs and Matsui still at first, Wakefield threw a knuckler that averted Varitek's grasp and advanced Matsui to scoring position. *Another passed ball.* When Wakefield missed the strike zone with a subsequent pitch that moved the count further in favor of the batter, Jorge Posada, Francona ordered an intentional walk. *There were now runners at first and second.* The count on designated hitter Ruben Sierra was in Wakefield's favor, 1–2, when the knuckler escaped Varitek yet again, a third passed ball that advanced the runners to second and third bases and brought Fenway Park to a virtual state of panic. *Can Tek even catch this thing?* The count had run full, 3–2, and as Matsui aggressively crept in from third, Posada moved from second, and the home crowd held its breath, Wakefield rocked into his delivery.

The pitch, of course, was a knuckleball, possessing every bit as much movement as Wakefield's other pitches in the inning. Had Sierra been batting right-handed, as many switch-hitters opted to do against

Wakefield, the ball would have darted in and landed near his right foot. Sierra had chosen to bat from the left side, however, and so, when he began his swing, the pitch looked as big as a beach ball, but when he came around the ball had suddenly darted down and away from the man who might have sent the New York Yankees back to the World Series for a second consecutive season and the seventh time in nine years.

As Sierra swung and missed, Jason Varitek, like part of a tandem doing everything possible to win an egg toss, desperately and awkwardly sprawled to his knees and caught the knuckler, the ball disappearing into his glove for a safe, secure strike three.

Inning over.

Disaster avoided.

Comeback intact.

Whew.

An inning later, after Wakefield retired the Yankees in order in the top of the 14th, Ortiz delivered his second game-winning hit in as many nights. The Red Sox and Yankees packed their belongings and headed to New York for Game 6, Tim Wakefield having earned the honor as the winning pitcher in Game 5 after sparing Red Sox relievers in Game 3.

"Last year is last year," Wakefield succinctly told reporters after the game.

The message was obvious.

That's history.

Now we have to make some of our own.

In fact, even as Varitek was wearing out a path to and from the backstop, Wakefield never lost confidence in his new batterymate, their relationship having been forged through their years together in the Boston organization. Varitek, like Wakefield, had come to the Red Sox from elsewhere, acquired in a 1997 trade that brought him along with Derek Lowe to Boston from the Seattle Mariners. Wakefield had pitched to him extensively in the late 1990s. Wakefield, Lowe, and Varitek were now among a group of Red Sox personnel who had been in Boston longer than many other Sox employees, a list that included the owner, general manager, manager, and many teammates. Wakefield *trusted* Varitek. He believed in him. And even as Varitek struggled to harness Wakefield's knuckler at its dancing best, the two repeatedly made eye contact, mutually reassuring each other that they remained unshaken.

It's okay. We've been through worse. Let's just keep going.

The wind now firmly at their backs, the Red Sox went to New York and defeated the Yankees, behind a sewn-up Schilling, by a 4–2 score in Game 6. The Sox then took the field and routed the Yankees in Game 7 by a decisive 10–3 margin. Taking nothing for granted at Yankee Stadium, Francona employed Martinez out of the bullpen in the seventh game and had Wakefield, among others, ready to go again if necessary. As it turned out, Wakefield was not needed. Originally scheduled to start Game 4, Wakefield instead pitched out of the bull-pen in Games 3 and 5. He also was prepared to enter in relief in Games 4 and 7. For the seven-game set with New York, Red Sox relievers pitched nearly as many innings (33⅔) as Red Sox starters (35⅓), a ratio that almost certainly should have produced defeat. And yet, the Red Sox instead were celebrating on the Yankee Stadium lawn, an unrelenting team having completed an unthinkable comeback under unimaginable circumstances.

Dealt a crushing blow by the Yankees a year earlier, Tim Wakefield and the Red Sox climbed up off the mat and belted the Yankees with their own knuckle sandwich.

In the immediate aftermath of Game 7, the Red Sox clubhouse had the feel of Bourbon Street at the peak of Mardi Gras. The Red Sox still needed four more victories to record their first World Series championship since the days of World War I, but they had every reason to celebrate, to extend and cherish the moment. The Red Sox owners, executives, and players openly embraced one another and celebrated what was arguably the greatest victory in the history of the franchise, even though the Sox still had another series to play before reaching their ultimate destination.

Wakefield quietly stood off to the side of the visitors' clubhouse at Yankee Stadium, a room that had been draped, in customary baseball practice, in protective plastic sheets as the Red Sox were routing New York. It was team equipment manager Joe Cochran who oversaw the process during the game, anticipating a Red Sox celebration that would be like no other in the history of the franchise. In the visitors' clubhouse at the old Yankee Stadium, there were stalls with one shelf (on top), a bunk (at the bottom), a chair (which usually faced the stall), and two hooks (one on each post that framed the space). Everything was painted white. Visiting players would come in and sit on the chair or bunk before putting on their uniforms, draping their clothes on the hooks, and stashing any other belongings on the shelf above. Equipment was strewn about — gloves and cleats could be on the floor, on the bunk, or on the shelf, depending on the player's preference — and it was Cochran's responsibility to make sure that everything remained dry in the inevitable champagne celebration that would follow such a monumental victory.

Wakefield had elected to station himself in the general area of his locker, which had been in the same place for as long as he could remember. This, too, is quite customary in baseball. Every team has personnel who oversee both the home and visitors' clubhouses, and every team tries to make players as comfortable as possible. Baseball is, after all, a game of routines. A small plate just above the space was engraved with Wakefield's number 49, and his game jersey hung on one of the hooks, but the pitcher no longer had to look for either the plate or his jersey to find his space. The older a player got, the less the routine changed.

In the major leagues, long-standing membership, especially, had its privileges.

With friend and fellow veteran Mike Timlin stationed in the locker next to him — Timlin wore number 50 — a smiling Wakefield sipped from a can of beer while many of his rowdier teammates were spraying champagne wildly and pouring beer over one another's heads. Predictably, the area near Wakefield and Timlin was far more controlled. At that point in their careers, Wakefield and Timlin had a combined 27 years of major league experience — some good, some bad — and each man was quite content to leave the heavy-duty partying to the younger members of the team. Wakefield had not pitched in Game 7, but media members streamed toward his locker upon being allowed into the Boston clubhouse — some because Wakefield stood in one of the safer parts of the room, but most because they had all congregated in precisely the same place a year earlier, albeit under far, far different circumstances.

"This is as big as the World Series," said a beaming Wakefield. "To be down 3–0, losing Game 3 the way we lost it (in blowout fashion), with the way we won Game 4 and the way we won Game 5, then coming back and winning Game 6 and Game 7 here, it's tremendous, not only for this organization but for the city and the fans that stuck around through thick and thin for us."

Reserved as ever, Wakefield resisted talking too much about 2003, but the big, bright smile on his face spoke for him.

Redemption.

While reporters scribbled away on notepads and poked their microphones into the scrum to capture the knuckleballer's every word, the extension phone in the back of the Red Sox clubhouse began to ring, unbeknownst to Wakefield and the reporters surrounding him. Yankee Stadium was a workplace, after all, and there was an interoffice phone system that connected most every part of the ballpark. Anyone with a master phone list could pick up the phone and call just about anyone else, just as a hotel guest might call a friend staying in a nearby room.

As Wakefield continued to speak with reporters in front of his locker, one of the attendants in the visiting clubhouse at Yankee Stadium leaned in and delivered a message to the pitcher.

"Joe Torre's on the phone," he said. "He asked to speak with you."

Joe Torre, his clubhouse eerily quiet following what is still regarded as the greatest collapse in the postseason history of major league baseball, returned to the solitude of his office, sat behind his desk, and picked up his phone, dialing the numbers that connected him to the Red Sox clubhouse. Excusing himself from the group, Wakefield promptly departed and joined the attendant at the rear of the clubhouse, an area sectioned off from reporters and the merrymaking and typically reserved as what players referred to as their *lounge* before and after games. This room was off-limits to the media so that players could eat, read, and socialize without any interference. As new ball-parks were constructed, lounges would become rather sizable areas with large flat-screen televisions and card tables as well as sofas and chairs. At Yankee Stadium in 2004, however, the room was far more like a small kitchen, the proverbial heart of the home where, in this case, Wakefield picked up the receiver and accepted the well wishes of one of the most accomplished and respected managers in baseball.

Joe Torre had spent a lifetime in the game as a player, manager, and broadcaster. From failure to success, he had experienced everything the game could muster. It was Torre's impeccable people skills, com-bined with his comfortable, easygoing manner, that had allowed him to be a successful and longtime manager of a storied franchise like the Yankees, in a boiling media kettle like New York, for a megalomaniacal owner like George Steinbrenner. The 2004 ALCS Game 7 loss to the Red Sox was the indisputable nadir of Torre's tenure with the Yankees, but he nonetheless felt compelled to call Wakefield in the fallout of Game 7 and deliver the simplest message.

I'm happy for you. You deserve this. Good things happen to good people.

"First of all, I always admired the fact that he's taken the ball and gone to the post. He's never been an excuse-maker, and he's been a great competitor," Torre remembered. "The thing that obviously came to mind was when he walked off the field after giving up the home run to Boone in Game 7 in 2003. He had pitched really well in that series, and yet, I knew his year was going to be defined by that home run. I didn't think that was fair.

"Despite all that was going on with [the Yankees], that was all that came to mind for me. It was just like a flashback. It was a lasting image for me. We all say sometimes that life is unfair, and when I saw him walk off that field in 2003. . . . I don't know if this is the right word, but it was sort of a redemption."

Wakefield graciously accepted Torre's thanks and returned to the Red Sox clubhouse. The New York manager's call would forever re-main one of the highlights of his career.

The Red Sox and Yankees of 2003 and 2004 were bitter rivals and true peers — in the 52 times the teams played in two years, the Red Sox held a 27–25 edge and each team won a seven-game postseason series over the other — but Wakefield was the only member of the Boston organization who spoke with Torre on the clubhouse phone that night. The Yankees made an incredible 12 consecutive postseason appearances during Torre's 12 years with the team: four of them culminated in victories that delivered a world title to New York, and eight of them ended with disappointing Yankees defeats. The Game 7 loss to the Red Sox in 2004 was easily among the most disappointing of those losses, and yet Torre expressed his respect for an opposing player by calling immediately afterwards to convey his congratulations.

Wakefield knew that such a gesture was special and unusual, and so he made sure he took the time to reciprocate. Shortly after the baseball season ended, Wakefield wrote a personal note to Torre, thanking him for taking the time to call in the wake of Game 7. Torre, in turn, locked away that memory, forging a relationship that remains intact, the two men greeting one another with heartfelt appreciation whenever their paths cross.

"He has since written me notes," Torre said, "and the one he sent me after that year said something to the effect of, 'That call meant as much to me as winning the World Series.' I tucked that one away."

Added the longtime manager: "You know, as a person, when you express yourself to someone and they express the same thing back, that's a nice feeling. When he made the All-Star team for the first time [in 2009], I went over and congratulated him. I think he gets lost in the shuffle sometimes because nobody wants to take a knuckleballer on an All-Star team. I think you get afraid that you might have to put him in the game."

For Wakefield and the Red Sox, thankfully, Boston manager Terry Francona had shown no such trepidation during the playoffs, using Wakefield out of the bullpen in Games 1, 3, and 5 of the League Championship Series. In Game 5, the decision had paid off enormously. Francona, as any manager would do, had told all of his pitchers to be ready for duty in Game 7, a series-deciding game being the one scenario in which baseball managers universally manage for the short term and throw all caution to the wind. Just the same, Francona took the time to tell Wakefield before Game 7 that the knuckleballer would start Game 1 of the World Series against either the St. Louis Cardinals or the Houston Astros, so long as the Red Sox could beat the Yankees. Despite the exhilaration of their historic comeback against the Yankees, no one on the team had lost sight of the importance of that last game.

"There's more baseball to be played," Francona pronounced after the Game 7 win. "I hope [Red Sox fans] are dancing in the streets. This is why we play and why we show up."

But then, following a career marked by ups and downs, Tim Wakefield already knew that.

Between Game 5 in 1986 and Game 1 in 2004, 93 World Series games were played at various locations throughout North America. Many of them were played in New York. Some were played in traditional baseball cities like Cincinnati, Philadelphia, and Cleveland. Others were played in places like San Diego, Miami, and Phoenix, homes of baseball's trendy nouveau riche. There were even World Series games played in Canada.

During that span, not a single World Series game was played in New England.

That all changed on the night of Saturday, October 23, 2004, when the Red Sox played their first World Series home game in 18 years and manager Terry Francona identified Tim Wakefield as his starting pitcher. Wakefield had anticipated this moment for as long as he could remember — flashbulbs rippling throughout Fenway Park like strands of blinking Christmas lights — and the significance could not, would not, be lost on him. Had things gone differently in 2003 — if deposed manager Grady Little had yanked Pedro Martinez after the seventh inning and the Red Sox had closed out Game 7 against the Yankees, like they should have — Wakefield would have been in line to start Game 1 of the World Series. Instead, Boston's epic eighth-inning meltdown had taken that opportunity away from him. When Wakefield ended up making his next appearance as a reliever in Game 7 of the ALCS instead of as a starter in Game 1 of the World Series, the enormous repercussions of that change included the firing of Little and the acquisitions of key contributors Curt Schilling and Keith Foulke.

For Wakefield, the repercussions had rippled all the way into late October 2004.

After all of that . . . I get to throw the first pitch.

By then, almost everyone was aware of Torre's affection for Wakefield, even if the details of the Yankees manager's call to the Red Sox clubhouse were not known. Following any clinching game of any postseason baseball series, the first person escorted into the interview room is always the losing manager, a man roughly 10 minutes removed from one of the most heartbreaking defeats of his life. Torre handled the event with predictable dignity. Two days later, as the Yankees cleaned out their clubhouse and took time to reflect on the events of the historic series with the Red Sox, Torre told members of the New York press that the flipside of defeat came in the fact that "guys like Tim Wakefield get to go to the World Series," a comment that quickly traveled all the way up to Boston as the Red Sox and St. Louis Cardinals convened at Fenway Park to prepare for Game 1 of the 2004 World Series.

Sitting at a podium in an interview room jammed with reporters from all over the world, an elated Wakefield happily spoke about the responsibility of pitching Game 1, which was to take place the next night. This was his moment. This was the payback for being unceremoniously omitted from the Boston playoff roster in 1999 and for being jerked back and forth from the bullpen as if he were hooked to guide wire. This was the chance Wakefield had been waiting for since he first began throwing the knuckleball, the opportunity to lead his team into one of the biggest games of the season while being showered with praise by a rival manager, Torre, one of the most respected managers in history.

"It means a lot that Joe would actually mention my name in his interview when they were packing up going home," Wakefield said. "I have a lot of respect for that man. I've played against him for a long time and watched him win a lot of championships over there. And for him to say something that nice about me really shows how passionate he is for not only the game, but for other players on other teams.

"You know, I'm excited. This is the first time I've ever experienced a World Series, and it's the first time the city of Boston has experienced the World Series since '86. I think it's a real honor that I'm getting the nod for Game 1. It's kind of ironic that, you know, if Derek [Lowe] doesn't pitch as well as he does in Game 7, I don't get to start. So I have him to thank for that. He pitched his tail off in Game 7 to give us a chance to win, and it's really amazing what he accomplished."

Of course, Wakefield was right. As much as anyone, he understood the realities of being part of a team, and Wakefield also knew that Lowe's career had included a transition from starter to reliever and back with which he himself was quite familiar. Wakefield wanted to make that clear. In Lowe, he saw some of himself. Entering Game 7, Lowe was operating on a mere two days of rest. In a best-case scenario, the Red Sox hoped Lowe could give them five innings; in a worst-case scenario, Wakefield was one of their many options in the bullpen. As it turned out, Lowe gave the Red Sox six sterling innings during which he allowed just one hit, one run, and one walk while throwing a mere 69 pitches, all while the Red Sox built a bulging 8–1 lead.

Over the course of his Red Sox career, more often than not Wakefield had been the one making the same sacrifices that Derek Lowe also had made.

And everybody knew it.

"I think I spoke about it after Game 3 [of the ALCS, the 19–8 loss], the traumatic night here. We got kicked around a little bit," Francona said. "I know I told Wake after the game that as tough as that night was, I was so proud of him and what he did for us that it really helped get me through that night. . . . He saved a couple of our pitchers, and that actually helped us win [Game 4]. Dave [Wallace, the pitching coach] and I were in the dugout trying to figure out where we're going in [Game 3], and [Wakefield] was over my left shoulder with spikes on and his glove. It wasn't halfhearted — he was ready to go — and an inning later he was down in the bullpen throwing. That's the type of guy he is. Joe Torre commented on how happy he was for Wake to be in the

World Series. On the flipside of that, not only is he a very good guy, but he's a very good pitcher, and he's feeling very good about himself. There were some periods this year that were a little rough on him. He feels good about himself. His confidence is high."

Said Red Sox catcher Jason Varitek of Wakefield: "We asked a tremendous amount of him in the last series, and he threw a lot of pitches in different ways. Tim's been through the war quite a bit, and he's been through the war in this city for a long time, and I couldn't be happier for him."

By the time Game 1 finally started at precisely 8:09 PM, the New England weather, precisely as one would expect, was something of a factor. The game-time temperature was a crisp 49 degrees, but of far greater concern to Wakefield was the wind blowing in from the northeast. At Fenway Park, that meant Wakefield would take the mound with the wind at his back, which was always something of a concern for him. While conventional pitchers preferred to have the wind behind them — which made it far more difficult to hit home runs and allowed them to operate with a greater margin for error — Wakefield preferred a slight wind blowing *against* him. Though this increased the likelihood for home runs — particularly because knuckleballs produced more fly balls than ground balls — Wakefield found that wind resistance increased the movement on his pitches. Again, it was a matter of physics. A well-executed knuckler, thrown against the wind, resulted in more acute movement of the pitch. The ball might travel farther if it was hit into the air, but it was also much harder to hit squarely. Wakefield had long since discovered the benefit of this trade-off.

By contrast, when the wind was at his back, Wakefield had great difficulty controlling the pitch. The knuckleball frequently would sail when aided by any significant gust of wind, which worked against Wakefield on multiple levels. For one thing, wind made it even harder to throw strikes with a pitch that was extremely difficult to harness in the first place; for another, if the ball sailed, it was less likely to have the sharp, downward movement that Wakefield needed to get outs. Instead, his ball would remain elevated through the strike zone, and every hitter knew the mantra with regard to hitting the knuckler.

If it's high, let it fly. If it's low, let it go.

In the hours leading up to Game 1, Wakefield treated the outing as he would any other game, though his concerns centered on one highly unusual variable: the flashbulbs. Wakefield wasn't quite sure how he would deal with them. The first pitch of every World Series all but went off like a starter's pistol, no matter where the game was played, and flashbulbs inevitably flickered like fireflies the moment the ball left the pitcher's hand. Wakefield wondered if it would break his concentration. He wondered what would happen if leadoff man Edgar Renteria swung and made contact, whether he would be able to see the ball coming off the bat, whether the ball might just look like one of the many bursts of bright light at Fenway Park. That moment, Wakefield knew, was something he simply could not prepare for.

Beyond that, the knuckleballer had shown up at the ballpark, as always, and changed into his uniform before sitting at his locker and finding ways to pass the time. Because the media was prohibited from access to the team before postseason games, the clubhouse was more controlled, less chaotic. Only players, coaches, and team personnel milled about. Wakefield had seen many players develop superstitions over the course of their careers—Garciaparra had been one of the most obsessive—but he always resisted becoming a slave to them himself, joking with people that he found superstitions to be "bad luck." Baseball was baseball. As much as anyone else who played the game—or more so—a knuckleballer knew there was only so much he could control. And so Tim Wakefield focused on the things he could.

Wakefield had nerves, to be sure, but he wasn't *nervous,* per se, at least not about anything other than flashbulbs.

The first pitch, as it turned out, was far less worrisome than Wakefield expected: his knuckleball fluttered to home plate amid the succession of camera shutters that popped like corn kernels. Renteria did not swing. *Strike one.* Renteria swung at the second pitch and missed, took the third for a ball, then swung at and missed the fourth pitch, recording the first out of the 2004 World Series by strikeout in what would be a scoreless first for the St. Louis Cardinals.

By the time Wakefield took the mound for the second, the Sox had a 4–0 lead courtesy of yet another home run from David Ortiz and a run-scoring single by Bill Mueller. Over the next two and two-thirds innings, a span covering 15 batters, Wakefield allowed just two hits, but he also hit one batter and walked five others. The Red Sox were supporting him with tremendous offense — Boston scored three more times in the third and had a 7–2 advantage going into the fourth, Wakefield's final inning — but Wakefield simply could not harness the knuckler. When Wakefield issued his fifth and final walk — this one to Renteria with two outs in the fourth — Francona felt he simply could not wait any longer. The score was now 7–5, and even though Wakefield was at least partially victimized by an uncharacteristically poor defensive game — the Sox had committed four errors — the manager summoned right-hander Bronson Arroyo from the bullpen.

"You know, going into the game, we thought it had a chance to be tough because the wind was blowing straight in, which doesn't help his effectiveness," Francona said. "But he came out and threw the ball very well. And then the start of the [fourth] inning with the walks, I mean, when you score, the last thing you want to do is walk somebody, and you walk three. Once he did that, he started getting outs, but we started to throw the ball around and put ourselves in a tough spot. But, you know, when you have a four-run lead or five-run lead, it's hard to walk people and get away with it."

Still, the Red Sox ultimately did. Though the Cardinals tied the game twice — at 7–7 and 9–9 — both times the Red Sox immediately took back the lead. The second time came in the bottom of the eighth inning, when Boston second baseman Mark Bellhorn hooked a drive to right field that struck the foul pole for a two-run home run. The home run was the final blow in an eventual 11–9 Red Sox victory that extended the club's impressive postseason winning streak, leaving Wakefield with the only thing that really mattered whenever a pitcher took the mound: a win for his team.

As it turned out, Wakefield did not pitch again in the World Series because the Red Sox simply did not need him to.

With the wind now indisputably at their backs — the Game 1 victory was Boston's fifth straight after trailing the Yankees by a 3–0 series count in the ALCS — the Red Sox did not let up. Boston won the next three games of the World Series by scores of 6–2, 4–1, and 3–0, completely dominating a series in which they outscored St. Louis by a final count of 24–12. During the entire four-game set, the Red Sox never trailed. Even in Game 1, St. Louis was always chasing. Three outs from postseason elimination late in Game 4 of the ALCS, the Red Sox had improbably rallied for eight straight wins, outscoring the Yankees and Cardinals by a combined 38–15 over the final six games of the playoffs. Since Jason Varitek's game-tying sacrifice fly against Mariano Rivera in the eighth inning of ALCS Game 5, the Red Sox had been no worse than tied for their final 60 innings of the 2004 baseball season.

In the bowels of an aging Busch Stadium following the Red Sox victory behind Derek Lowe — yes, him again — in Game 4, reporters once again were lined up outside the visiting clubhouse, just as they had been in New York. The lockers were once again draped in plastic. Officials from Major League Baseball rushed commissioner Allan "Bud" Selig past reporters and into the room for the official presentation of the Commissioner's Trophy, a ceremony that took place every October in the clubhouse of the victorious team. Baseball lifer Selig understood the magnitude of what the Red Sox had accomplished in the context of baseball history, and he offered reporters a succinct assessment of the seeming chain reaction that had delivered Boston to the world title.

"Wow," Selig said without breaking stride.

Inside the walls of the Red Sox clubhouse, the scene was very much like the one that had taken place in New York, though Francona had no reason to remind anyone that there was still baseball to be played. Redemption for the Red Sox was now complete. The season was over. Boston effectively had run the table and finished the 2004 campaign by going a sensational 45–15 in its last 60 games, 46 during the regular season (during which the Red Sox went 34–12) and the final 14 in the playoffs (during which the Red Sox went 11–3). The most senior members of the Red Sox had an intimate understanding of what this outcome truly meant, their sentiments bouncing from one to another amid a clubhouse filled with otherwise deafening revelry.

"We're finally winners," said Lowe. "We're not the happy guys that came in second, the so-close-but-so-far kind of thing. There are so many people who deserve credit for this. I was happy to see Johnny Pesky here, and I saw a tear in his eye. I hope the Red Sox bring everybody back (from the past to celebrate). This isn't just the 2004 Red Sox. This is 86 years here."

Said Wakefield from the opposite side of the celebration: "We'll never hear the '1918' chants again. It's huge for the franchise. Ever since Mr. [John] Henry and Mr. [Tom] Werner and Larry [Lucchino] took over, they've pointed us in the right direction. People that have lived there longer than I have had too many sad days. Now they can rejoice in the city of Boston."

Tim Wakefield was all too happy to join them.

Eleven

•

There are two theories on hitting a knuckleball. Unfortunately,
neither of them works.

                 —*Renowned hitting coach Charlie Lau*

T HE CHAMPIONSHIP PARADE was everything Tim
Wakefield had imagined in every respect but one: it was too
darned short.
Projecting crowds of Red Sox fans in the hundreds of thousands,
Boston city officials responded to the team's first World Series win in
86 years by organizing a *rolling rally,* eschewing the standard celebration at City Hall Plaza for a road trip on *duck boats* through the city's
streets and neighborhoods, even venturing into the Charles River.
Despite cold temperatures and light, persistent drizzle, an estimated
1.6 million fans turned out. Wakefield rode on a float with fellow veteran starters Curt Schilling, Pedro Martinez, and Derek Lowe—one
of the teams within the team—and stood alongside his wife, Stacy,
while toting their six-month-old son, Trevor. Fans seeking autographs
tossed items into the boats with the hope that each would be signed
and tossed back, and three-fourths of the starting rotation found it
particularly amusing when one fan tossed a baseball that plunked an
unaware Pedro Martinez on the head, the oft-accused head-hunter
getting a playful dose of his own medicine.

Then it was all over, and the Red Sox quickly dispersed after an
event that Wakefield somehow had expected to endure.

Is this it?

Wakefield's ears were ringing, as if he had just left a rock concert, and reentry would require some time, for him and for all of the Red Sox. The subsequent days and weeks featured a succession of opportunities to sign memorabilia in one hotel conference room after the next, and Wakefield agreed to some, passed on others. Similar ripples of the championship extended into winter and beyond, and when the Red Sox finally arrived in Fort Myers, Florida, the following spring, in some ways it felt as though the 2004 season had not yet ended.

And yet, as Wakefield knew, the Red Sox had another season to play when February arrived far more rapidly than anyone had anticipated, a reminder that all good things, like bad things, come to an end. *We have to start playing again sometime.* While Red Sox manager Terry Francona knew that questions would abound throughout camp about the team's extraordinary comeback in the 2004 playoffs, he, too, knew that he and his team needed to prepare for another season.

For Wakefield, the winter had served as yet another reminder that baseball is a business. The Red Sox continued to make difficult personnel decisions over the winter; the front office allowed pitchers Martinez and Lowe to depart via free agency while re-signing catcher Varitek and formally entrusting him with the title and responsibilities of team captain. Wakefield, for his part, was entering the final year of a four-year, $13 million contract that would pay him slightly more than $4.6 million in 2005, but the events of the off-season only cemented the thoughts he'd had throughout his Red Sox career. *I want to finish my career here. I want to have what Varitek has. I want my career to be worth something more than just a pile of pay stubs.* Winning a World Series in Boston was the consummate achievement, Wakefield believed, and now he wanted to focus on solidifying his legacy as a Red Sox lifer during an age when the game had been defined by mercenaries who toted big contracts — and who were in pursuit of bigger ones.

The way I can be different is to be loyal, he thought.

The feeling was mutual.

For the Red Sox, the Fenway Park opener on Monday, April 11, would be a day unlike any other in the history of Fenway Park. With the Yankees again scheduled as the opponent, the Red Sox would raise their World Series championship banner and hand out their championship rings, a moment that the Red Sox and the entire New England region had been awaiting since the days of World War I.

The Red Sox, to their credit, planned the event perfectly, down to every last detail.

That day, Tim Wakefield would be their starting pitcher.

Wakefield learned of the team's intentions during spring training, and almost everyone involved with the club acknowledged that Wakefield was the obvious choice. *He's been here the longest. He's endured the most.* Wakefield regarded the assignment as an honor every bit as meaningful as pitching Game 1 of the World Series, and a fitting culmination to an off-season that had been an absolute blur.

Worn and weary from the events of the fall, winter, and spring, the Red Sox had generally sputtered to start the season, losing four times during their season-opening six-game road trip. Wakefield had backboned one of the two victories, dueling New York right-hander Mike Mussina for more than six innings in an eventual 7–3 Red Sox win in the second game of the season on April 6. Precisely five days later, on April 11, Mussina again was the pitcher Wakefield was paired against, though the start of the game almost seemed anticlimactic. Some of the players who had left the Red Sox over the winter, including Lowe, returned to Boston for the ring ceremony and created a minor stir with fans in their new markets by wearing their old Sox jerseys. (Lowe, for instance, took some criticism for adorning his old number 32 after having signed a four-year, $36 million deal with the Los Angeles Dodgers.) But to the Boston fans, it was as if the players had never left, each member of the Sox receiving a resounding ovation for his part in Boston's historic victory.

Wakefield, predictably, received one of the loudest ovations from the Fenway crowd.

We know you better than them. Thanks for sticking it out.

But then, Wakefield believed the cheers spoke to everyone in a different way.

"The fans are so knowledgeable about the game and so passionate about the team. You can hear that when all of our players are an-nounced for the starting lineup or even on opening day," Wakefield said. "Each player has a uniqueness to the fans. There's a special con-nection there. I know I feel that special connection every time I walk on the field to take the ball."

The game was anticlimactic, as it turned out, at least in the competi-tive sense. The Red Sox rolled. Wakefield threw 110 pitches in seven superb innings, allowing just five hits, two walks, and one unearned run as the Red Sox rumbled to leads of 4–0 and 7–1. The eventual 8–1 win gave the Red Sox their third victory in seven games—two of the victories coming in the only games started by Wakefield—and gave Sox players the grateful feeling that finally the party was over. They could move on with their lives and careers and turn once again to the business of trying to win another championship.

"As special as it was, I think we all felt like we could finally put that to bed," Wakefield said.

Wakefield also had other things on his mind, most notably a con-tract extension that would all but ensure his commitment to the Red Sox and their commitment to him. In discussions with agent Barry Meister, whom Wakefield had hired to handle his negotiations after the retirement of Dick Moss, Wakefield confided that remaining in Boston was his priority. He didn't want to go to free agency. He didn't want to play anywhere else. He had become as much a part of the com-munity in Boston as his wife, Stacy, who had grown up in the Boston area. Wakefield considered himself a Bostonian as much as he consid-ered himself a resident of Florida, and the idea of playing for another team did not appeal to him. When Meister reminded Wakefield that such an approach would hurt his leverage in negotiations—the agent was merely fulfilling his professional obligation—Wakefield expressed his complete understanding.

Then he told Meister to negotiate the deal anyway.

"I explained to him that the free-agent market is a strange and won-derful place," Meister said. "Tim kind of waved me off and said, 'This is not about the money.' He said, 'I prefer that we approach Boston now and that we make it clear I want to play with Boston for the rest of my career.'"

And so, slightly more than a week after the opening day victory against the Yankees, Wakefield and the Red Sox conducted a press conference at Fenway Park to announce one of the most unique and creative deals in baseball history, if not all of professional sports. With Wakefield headed to free agency, the Red Sox extended his contract by one year for a salary of $4 million, with an option for the 2007 season at $4 million. If and when the Red Sox exercised that option, another $4 million option would be generated. And then another. And then another. In fact, the option *regenerated* every time the Red Sox exercised it, making Wakefield's contract essentially an infinite loop. So long as he continued to pitch reasonably well, and so long as he wanted to continue pitching, the deal all but ensured that Wakefield would pitch for no other team than the Red Sox, that he would never go to free agency, and that if and when the time came that the Red Sox no longer deemed him a worthwhile $4 million investment, he would effectively call it a career.

Beyond the annual $4 million salary, Wakefield also could earn incentives based on health that could bump his earnings over $5 million annually, though those were just perks that would further reward him for a job well done.

Under normal circumstances, throughout the business world of baseball, a contract like Wakefield's might have been frowned upon, even scoffed at by super-agents like the renowned Scott Boras, who forever claimed to be representing the small man, the player, in the never-ending negotiations between "millionaires and billionaires." Such deals seemed to be far too team-friendly and failed to compensate the player adequately. But there was decidedly little objection to the contract that Wakefield signed with the Red Sox, and in fact his deal was heralded as groundbreaking—a creative device that allowed a team and a player to achieve a common goal together in unique circumstances.

So, almost exactly 10 years after he first pitched in a game for the Red Sox, in May 1995, Wakefield indeed had become a unique case. The man whose career had been on the scrap heap was now seen as the consummate loyalist, the company man whose gold watch had taken the form of a contract for his professional life. Tim Wakefield had become synonymous with the Red Sox franchise, with perseverance and hard work, with resiliency and selflessness. In committing to being a part of something much bigger than himself, he had become bigger than he could ever have imagined.

The man with perhaps the most unique pitch in baseball history now had a contract to match.

The beauty of experience, assuming one stays healthy, is that relatively little becomes unsettling. Most everything becomes a case of *been there, done that.* With the weight of 86 fruitless years having been lifted off the Boston organization, with a contract that would cover his professional life like an insurance policy, Tim Wakefield settled into some of the more comfortable years of his career. He entered the 2005 season with 114 career victories for Boston, needing just 10 more to surpass Bob Stanley (115), Pedro Martinez (117), Smoky Joe Wood (117), Luis Tiant (122), and Mel Parnell (123) and move into third place on the Red Sox all-time wins list.

At that point, only two men would sit ahead of him, tied at 192 wins for the most in the history of the Red Sox franchise: Cy Young, a man for whom baseball's top pitching achievement was named, and Roger Clemens, who had just won the award for a record seventh time.

Still four months shy of his 39th birthday, Wakefield started to see landmarks on the horizon that he had never imagined he would see.

I could actually catch them.

By then, there was relatively little that could fluster Wakefield, who had not mastered the knuckleball — who really does? — so much as he had harnessed it. Often, even the unforeseen could no longer derail him. For a knuckleballer, something as seemingly insignificant as a broken fingernail could become a relative crisis, but Wakefield had long since learned to manage the situation by treating his fingernails as his tools. He carried his suitcases and travel bags with his left hand so as to avoid breaking a nail on his right, and he always tried to snap together the metal buttons on the waistband of his uniform pants using his glove hand.

Wakefield typically used clippers to trim the nails of the thumb, ring finger, and pinky finger of his right (pitching) hand, but on his index and middle fingers, which he used to grip the baseball, he used a file with the precision of a sculptor. Wakefield had an array of methods for fixing broken nails, ranging from athletic tape to Q-tips or cotton swabs, all of which were made up of very fine fibers. Wakefield would sit in front of his locker or in the trainer's room, delicately plucking the individual fibers from a strand of tape or swab, and lay them across the broken area of his nail. Then he would apply small amounts of super glue that instantly bonded with the fibers and his skin, creating a hard, shell-like solid that allowed him to grip the baseball with familiar feel.

Voila.

Take that, Elizabeth Grady.

Phil Niekro had taken similar care of his nails, as he and Wakefield had discussed more than once. Niekro remembered taking the mound sometimes with fake, plastic fingernails marketed for women, and everyone knew the story of his brother, Joe, being ejected from a game for carrying an emery board in his back pocket. Accused of illegally scuffing up the baseball while on the mound, Niekro was ordered by umpires to empty out his pockets on the field, at which point he realized that he effectively was carrying a piece of sandpaper in his pocket, something that would not sit well with the umpires.

Recognizing that the emery board would all but cement his perceived guilt, Niekro unsuccessfully tried to cast it aside, away from the view of the umpires, only to get caught red-handed.

"I used to carry an emery board with me in my pocket all the time, too," cracked Phil Niekro, who defends his brother to this day. "Those two fingers are the most important part of my body. A lot of people talk about that game, about how he got suspended and thrown out of the game, but think about it: four umpires are out there on the field at all times. How are you going to get that thing out of your pocket and file down the ball without anybody seeing?"

Of course, Niekro was right.

The only place a pitcher might have been able to extract a file from his pocket was in the dugout, where he wouldn't have possession of the baseball being used in the game.

Wakefield often could be seen filing his nails at his locker before a game, when he was similarly seen doing crossword puzzles. Later in his career, these habits gave him the look of a man comfortably settled into the middle and later stages of his life — or in this case, his career. He looked to be in complete control now. Even something as free-spirited as the knuckleball could not rattle him. The 2005 Red Sox struggled with an assortment of issues — injuries, undying interest in the 2004 season, a positively wretched relief corps — but Wakefield seemed almost entirely unaffected. He had one of the best and most consistent seasons of his career, going 8–7 with a 4.05 ERA before the All-Star break, 8–5 with a 4.26 ERA after it. The Red Sox seemed to be running on fumes throughout 2005 — the 2004 season, after all, had come *after* the similarly grueling postseason of 2003 — and the season ended as it began, with Wakefield pitching the final home game, a 5–3 defeat that completed a three-game sweep by the White Sox in the first round of the playoffs and sent Chicago along on its own historic course.

The White Sox had not won the World Series since a 1919 season that produced the great *Black Sox scandal* in which Chicago players were paid to lose. In 2005, the White Sox finally won *their* first World Series title in exactly 86 years.

Though Wakefield was the losing pitcher in Game 3, the outcome hardly put a damper on an individual season during which he was, quite simply, the best Red Sox pitcher. Wakefield led the team in victories (16) and innings pitched (a career best 225⅓), and he blew past Stanley, Martinez, Wood, Tiant, and Parnell into sole possession of third place on the team's all-time list for victories. For an organization as old as the Red Sox, however pitching-deprived they might have been during some long stretches, Wakefield's accomplishment qualified as positively astounding.

"He's been doing this a long time," Red Sox manager Terry Francona said of Wakefield. "And I don't see him slowing down."

Indeed, in many ways, Tim Wakefield felt like he was just starting to hit his stride.

• • •

In the months immediately following the 2005 season, the Red Sox deteriorated into a state of civil war. Theo Epstein and team president Larry Lucchino, protégé and mentor, were locked in a bitter contract dispute for the young and already accomplished general manager. The matter turned public and rather ugly, at times feeling far more personal than businesslike, as if the younger man was trying to escape from the shadow of the older man who had schooled him.

Tim Wakefield watched from afar, staying careful not to choose sides and wondering if the drama would ever stop.

How much of this stuff will I live through?

In the aftermath of Theo versus Larry, the Red Sox were without a general manager — at least for a time. Epstein resigned from his post, leaving the Sox with an oligarchy headed by baseball lifer Bill Lajoie and Sox executive Craig Shipley, a former player now regarded as an excellent evaluator. Under the watch of Lucchino, Lajoie and Shipley executed a succession of major maneuvers that included the departures of center fielder Johnny Damon (via free agency to, of all teams, the Yankees) and prized young shortstop Hanley Ramirez in a trade with the Florida Marlins that brought pitcher Josh Beckett and third baseman Mike Lowell to Boston. The two also acquired second baseman Mark Loretta. In acquiring the heady Loretta, the Sox had parted ways with backup catcher Doug Mirabelli, whose place in the Red Sox organization was quite specific.

For five years, he had served as Wakefield's personal catcher.

Wakefield was disappointed at the departure of Mirabelli, whom he regarded as a big part of his success over the past five years. *Dougie knows how I think, and he knows how the pitch moves.* Red Sox officials had expected Wakefield to be disappointed, so they had taken the preemptive strike of calling Wakefield ahead of time to inform him of their decision and to ensure that he would have a say in finding Mirabelli's replacement. Wakefield nonetheless called Mirabelli and expressed his sadness at seeing his batterymate go. He also had some concern about his next catcher's ability to deal with the inevitable frustration of catching the knuckleball.

The experience with Varitek in Game 5 of the 2004 American

League Championship Series had proven that, and Varitek was someone Wakefield *trusted,* someone with whom he had shared a clubhouse for years.

"I had the ability, I guess," Mirabelli said when asked to explain his knack for handling the knuckler. "Most of all, I have God-given hands that were pretty good. I have good hand-eye coordination and the ability to relax in tough situations. When you think your energy could be flying through the roof, I had the ability to relax in those situations, and I think that's important for catching the knuckleball. It can move so much that if your hands and arms are tight, you're going to have trouble."

To their credit, Red Sox officials did not take the issue lightly, remaining quite aware of the problems that a knuckleballer could cause for his own catcher. First and foremost, the Sox knew that in order for Wakefield to be as effective as possible, he had to possess the confidence that the pitch would be caught. Beyond that, there was the issue of passed balls, which had nearly cost the Red Sox their season during Game 5 of the 2004 ALCS against the Yankees.

In fact, from 1995 through 2006, during the first 11 years of Wakefield's career with the Red Sox, Boston had totaled a major league–leading 277 passed balls, 110 more than the next-closest team, the New York Yankees. During that span, Boston's total was more than twice the league average of 125–130 passed balls per team. With Wakefield on the staff, the Red Sox had averaged 25 passed balls per season, the large majority of which occurred with Wakefield on the mound. And yet, the most astonishing part of these numbers was that the Sox passed-ball totals had dwindled to 97 over the last five years of that span, an average of slightly more than 19 per season that spoke volumes for Mirabelli's abilities as a receiver. Mirabelli's uncanny knack for tracking the knuckler and catching it was a skill that baseball people often referred to as *soft hands.*

In the six years before Mirabelli arrived, with Wakefield on the staff, the Red Sox averaged exactly 30 passed balls per season. With Mirabelli behind the plate, the number dipped to a little more than 19, a difference that translated into a savings of just under 37 percent.

Wakefield knew as well as anyone that whatever Doug Mirabelli lacked with his bat — the catcher generally hit for a notoriously low average but did have some power — he more than made up for with his glove.

Nonetheless, with needs throughout their lineup, the Red Sox made offense a priority, a move they soon came to regret. The original plan was to have Wakefield work with John Flaherty, a veteran catcher who was moving from starter to backup late in his career. For an assortment of reasons that included both an inability and an unwillingness to grapple with the knuckler, Flaherty instead opted to *retire*. After catching Wakefield for two innings in a spring game, he learned that chasing around the knuckler "wasn't something I wanted to do" and that, "if you're not fully committed to doing that, then you're not going to do a good job." The responsibility then fell on youngster Josh Bard, whom the Sox had acquired in a trade that also delivered outfielder Coco Crisp from the Cleveland Indians. The hope had been that Bard might someday replace an aging Varitek as the Boston starter.

For Bard, the knuckleball experiment was an utter disaster. Never having been asked to handle a knuckleballer before, the likable young man was charged with a whopping 10 passed balls in his first four games with Wakefield. As Bard seemed to be shuttling to and from the backstop on a regular basis, Wakefield found himself having great compassion for his catcher, who was doing his absolute best to rise to an extremely difficult challenge. *It's not his fault,* Wakefield repeatedly told both himself and anyone else who would listen. Baseball history was spotted with great catchers who had wanted nothing to do with the knuckleball. Johnny Bench, for instance, once told the coaching staff at an All-Star Game that he preferred that someone else catch knuckleballer Phil Niekro. Bard had been thrust into an impossible situation, Wakefield realized, and the knuckleballer was willing to nurture his new young catcher for the benefit of the long term.

Mirabelli, too, had experienced great difficulty with the knuckleball at the outset, but made adjustments as he went along. The first was to use an oversized glove, which many other catchers had done. Another involved shifting his body toward the second baseman so that he could rotate to his right more easily. Most importantly, Mirabelli had to completely alter his standard for success and throw out conventional catching wisdom that no longer applied.

But it all took time.

"The hardest part is not really knowing what the knuckleball is going to do. It's so deceptive," Mirabelli said. "I've often told Wake, 'I think the knuckleball, by definition, is a wild pitch,' because that's really the whole premise behind it. You don't know what it's going to do. If it was consistent, it would get crushed because hitters eventually would figure it out.

"I remember when I first got traded to Boston, I was playing catch with him in the outfield, and I was pretty confident in my ability to catch the ball," Mirabelli continued. "I was like, 'Okay, I've got this down.' I caught him in the bullpen, and I was like, 'Okay, no problem.' Then the game started. We were in Toronto and the dome was closed, and for whatever reason, that thing always moved more in domes. It was moving like I've never seen. It's uncontrollable. Now my anxiety is going up, my back and arms are stiffening up, and I couldn't catch the thing. I think I had two passed balls right away, and every time I came in [to the dugout] I apologized to him. I was mentally exhausted that year.

"Right away, I had to throw away the notion that I was never going to have passed balls," Mirabelli went on. "That was hard for me to handle. As a defensive catcher, that's a big adjustment. Guys were stealing, and I wasn't throwing them out — things like that. As a player, you never want to be embarrassed. That was a hard thing to deal with at first."

Red Sox officials believed that Bard, too, would eventually solve the mystery of the knuckler, but they lacked the one thing Mirabelli initially had: time. They felt pressed to find a solution. When word came from San Diego that the Padres were frustrated and disappointed with Mirabelli's early performance and attitude — Wakefield's former catcher missed Boston — Epstein and his former boss, Padres general manager Kevin Towers, worked out a very simple trade: Bard for Mirabelli, backup catcher for backup catcher, a deal the Red Sox quickly made just as the New York Yankees were set to arrive at Fenway Park for the opener of a series in which Wakefield would be pitching.

Only in a baseball-obsessed city like Boston could a backup catcher return to the team, on a chartered jet, greeted by a police escort prepared to take him to Fenway Park.

Whether by circumstance or coincidence, Wakefield's fortunes — and those of the team — took a dramatic turn for the better upon Mirabelli's return. Wakefield was 1–4 with an above-average 3.90 ERA through his first five starts without Mirabelli, largely owing to wretched run support during a stretch in which the Red Sox lost games by scores of 3–0, 5–1, and 7–1. But as soon as Mirabelli showed up just before the first pitch and donned his equipment, then scurried out to home plate without even warming up, everything changed. Wakefield went seven strong innings in a 7–3 victory over the Yankees, and the knuckleballer began a stretch during which he ripped off three wins a row.

As rapidly as it had dissolved, karma had been restored.

"I do think Mirabelli, with how good he is at it, is taken for granted sometimes," Epstein said of the catcher, whom the general manager also referred to as "the best knuckleball catcher on the planet" amid the comical drama. "He makes it look easy, so he becomes like the umpire or the third-base coach [who is good at his job]. You don't notice. That's a good thing. But he's pretty darn good at it."

Indeed, Mirabelli's receiving skills were a gift. The key to catching the knuckler, Mirabelli often said, was to wait and *react* to the pitch rather than to jab at it, a mistake that many catchers made. Mirabelli's glove almost seemed to be moving backward when he caught the pitch — that is, away from Wakefield — as if he were attempting to catch an egg without breaking the shell.

After going 14–11 before Mirabelli's return, the Red Sox almost immediately started playing better baseball and caught fire in June, at one point ripping off 12 straight wins and 14 of 15 to improve to 49–29, a record that earned them a four-game lead in the American League East. And then, slowly, they began to fall apart. The Red Sox already were playing poorly when they were hit by a rash of injuries at midseason, two factors that contributed to a damaging five-game series sweep at the hands of the hated Yankees — at Fenway Park no less — in mid-August. The Sox stumbled to an 86–76 finish that left them in third place in the division, marking the first time in Epstein's young career as a GM when the team he built failed to make the postseason.

Wakefield was among those Sox players who ended up on the disabled list, derailed by a back injury later diagnosed as a stress fracture in his ribs. He was never sure how the injury occurred. What he did know was that he was in pain every time he pitched. He labored through the pain for a short period, but when the problem intensified he needed to take time off. By the time Wakefield returned in the middle of September, the fate of the 2005 Red Sox had long since been decided, and he was badly out of rhythm, posting a 7.52 ERA over a span of four starts, all of which produced Red Sox losses. A season that got off to a fast and promising start had been derailed just as quickly, Wakefield finishing with a 7–11 record and 4.63 ERA in just 140 innings, an innings pitched total that matched the lowest of his Red Sox career to that point. Wakefield also felt that his won-lost record did not accurately reflect how he had pitched. Among the 45 American Leaguers who threw at least 140 innings that season, only two had worse run support.

During the off-season, predictably, there were questions about the direction the Red Sox suddenly seemed to be headed in following their World Series win two years earlier, a theme that trickled down to the individual players. *Was 2004 a case of one and done?* For Wakefield, the obvious issue was his age, particularly following a season when he had suffered the first major injury of his career and celebrated his 40th birthday (in August).

True to knuckleballing form, Wakefield recommitted himself to his conditioning. Phil Niekro, after all, pitched his last game when he was 48. And Doug Mirabelli knew as well as anyone that Tim Wakefield had plenty left in the tank, that his partner possessed far more fire and competitiveness than anybody was ever willing to give him credit for.

"It's funny because he has this competitiveness in him as much as anybody," Mirabelli said. "He loves to compete. He loves to fight. He always had this chip on his shoulder that he didn't throw 99 miles per hour, but that he would prove he was just as good. And he could compete from a stats standpoint with a lot of those guys.

"I remember we were in a team meeting one time, and Pedro [Martinez] stood up and said, 'I've got a lot of respect for Wake because he goes out on the mound and fights. If he doesn't have a good knuckleball he ain't got shit, but he fights.' Pedro absolutely meant it as a compliment," Mirabelli said. "[Wakefield] was the ultimate competitor and a very caring person."

And while most of the Red Sox already knew that, they would soon get another firsthand look at what Tim Wakefield could do.

In Boston the 2007 baseball season will go down as one of the most unusual in Red Sox history for one very simple reason: almost nothing went wrong. Fortified during an off-season in which club ownership and management committed in excess of $200 million to long-term contracts for outfielder J. D. Drew, shortstop Julio Lugo, and Japanese pitching import Daisuke Matsuzaka, the Red Sox burst from the gate with a near-perfect blend of pitching, defense, offense, youth, and experience. The club was a certifiable wrecking machine, posting a 36–15 record in its first 51 games, a pace that would have translated into 114 victories over the course of a 162-game schedule.

Wakefield had no idea at the time that the season would produce a second World Series title in the span of four seasons.

Or that he would be faced with the supreme sacrifice along the way.

For the first time in months, Wakefield felt entirely healthy when he took the mound at the start of the season — and it showed. With Mirabelli still behind the plate, Wakefield allowed a total of nine earned runs in his first seven starts. Though he was just 4–3 during that span — two of his losses were by scores of 2–0 and 3–1 — Wakefield had a sparkling 1.79 ERA. Once a knuckleballer who threw other pitches at the most predictable times, he now had fully morphed into a more complete pitcher who, while still relying largely on the knuckleball, would throw fastballs, curveballs, and cut fastballs in far more unlikely scenarios, a transformation that had gradually taken place over the course of a career that was still, incredibly, evolving.

At 40, Tim Wakefield saw his age as a *benefit,* fulfilling the prophecies set forth by Niekro.

Use the uncertainty to your advantage.

If you learn to command this pitch, you can pitch until you're 45.

At their peak, the 2007 Red Sox led the American League East by a stunning 11½ games as late as July 5. Although the lead would shrink dramatically in the final weeks of the season, the Red Sox were never in danger of missing the playoffs. Wakefield completely hit his stride in the final stages of the year, ripping off a span of 11 consecutive starts during which he went 9–2 with a 3.69 ERA. The possessor of a 7–8 record before the streak, Wakefield was 16–10 by the end of it, a run that grew additionally impressive when catcher Kevin Cash seamlessly stepped in and replaced Mirabelli, who had been sidelined by a calf strain. This time the results didn't change with the change in catchers. In Cash, the Red Sox and Wakefield both had found an invaluable insurance policy, another catcher with soft hands and the gumption to take on the knuckleball, a reassuring development given the events of October 2004 and beyond.

If Doug isn't back there for some reason, we'll still be fine.

By offering Cash a pointer or two on how to handle Wakefield's knuckler, Mirabelli helped the new catcher make a swift transition. Like Mirabelli, Cash was a light-hitting, soft-handed receiver who had some power, but the knuckleball tested his skills to the nth degree. Mirabelli suggested, among other things, that Cash turn his body slightly toward the right side of the infield, as if he were squared up with the second baseman, a tip that paid immediate dividends. Wakefield reached the final month of the season pitching some of the best baseball of his career — for a team that had been destined for the playoffs for months.

And then, once again, the knuckleballer learned that he was susceptible to unpredictable dips and turns.

Wakefield's shoulder began bothering him, a problem that persisted throughout the month and affected his delivery, undermining his command of the knuckleball. Though his last outing of the season was a relatively good one, he went 1–2 with an 8.76 ERA in September. The

Red Sox suddenly were faced with an uncomfortable decision: would they include Wakefield on their active roster for the first round of the playoffs against the Angels? This dilemma immediately prompted comparisons to 1999. Wakefield himself wondered, *Are they going to do it to me again?* The team's decision to leave him off the active roster for the 1999 ALCS against the Yankees had scarred him, inflicting a wound that had never truly healed. As surely as Wakefield remembered, so did Epstein and Francona, though they had had nothing to do with Wakefield's dismissal from active status eight years earlier.

Because of a change in baseball rules, the decision would be different for the Sox than it had been in 1999. Earlier, had Wakefield been injured during the series against the Yankees, the team would have lost his services for the balance of the series and been unable to replace him unless or until they reached the next round, in that case the World Series. With this rule in place, Sox officials had all but entirely eliminated Wakefield from their decision-making about the playoffs roster. But now teams in the playoffs were allowed to replace injured players in the middle of a series, and so the decision was slightly more complicated. The team would sacrifice little by trotting Wakefield out to the mound, but the price for the pitcher was considerable.

If Wakefield had to be replaced, he would be ineligible for the *next* round — the ALCS, against whom the Sox would face the Yankees or Cleveland Indians. Wakefield thus had to decide whether he wanted to pitch earlier in the playoffs or later — assuming the Sox won. He came to the obvious conclusion with team officials during a meeting at the end of the regular season.

He sat out the first round.

"We made [the decision] as a team," Wakefield said. "Trust me, it was a hard decision to make when I was sitting in that office. It's hard to take yourself out of the equation sometimes. Instinct says, 'I'll do it, give me the ball and I'll do whatever you want me to do,' but in a short series with the rules changing, I didn't want to hurt us."

As it turned out, the decision proved to be a good one for both the player and the team: the Red Sox wiped out the Angels in three consecutive games while Wakefield benefited from the additional rest. It was the best of both worlds for everyone. After the Indians defeated the Yankees in six games, Boston and Cleveland were set to face off against one another in the American League Championship Series, by which point Wakefield's shoulder had sufficiently improved for him to give pitching a try. Francona lined up his rotation so that Wakefield would take the ball in Game 4, following Josh Beckett, Curt Schilling, and Daisuke Matsuzaka, in that order. The Game 4 start meant that Wakefield would get just one start in the series, but the knuckleballer was on board for a very simple reason.

Realistically, he couldn't pitch more than that.

Wakefield was proud of his versatility and resiliency throughout his career — on short rest, between starts, whatever the situation called for — and so it was a most unusual situation he found himself in late in 2007. Suddenly, he could not bounce back as quickly. Making even a regular turn was out of the question. Once able to pitch on as little as two days of rest, Wakefield now needed closer to 10 days between starts "to recoup." The injury had been diagnosed as a strain in the back of his shoulder — a common injury for pitchers that could result from wear and tear — and it had robbed Wakefield of one of his greatest strengths: durability. Nonetheless, he could still pitch — or try to — though the problem typically intensified as a game progressed.

Still, it was worth a shot.

Having taken over first place in the division on April 18 and swept the Angels in the first round of the playoffs, the Red Sox found themselves in an unusual situation after winning Game 1 of the Cleveland series but losing Games 2 and 3: they were behind. Wakefield had little doubt about the team's ability to come back, and he took the mound in Game 4 with a good deal of confidence. Matched against Cleveland craftsman Paul Byrd — a soft-throwing right-hander who had built a solid career on smarts and guile — Wakefield held the Indians scoreless through four innings. The Indians then rallied in the fifth, chasing Wakefield from the game when five men reached base during a span of seven hitters that staked Cleveland to a 2–0 lead.

Going into the game, Francona knew that he would have to watch Wakefield closely, paying close attention to the pitcher's delivery, facial expression, and mechanics. *Other people may not know how much he's hurting, but I do.* That fact prompted Francona to lift Wakefield earlier than usual — Byrd, too, was pitching well — but the move back-fired when reliever Manny Delcarmen entered and allowed a three-run home run to Jhonny Peralta that gave the Indians a bulging 5–0 advantage. The Indians tacked on a pair of additional runs to take a 7–0 lead en route to a resounding 7–3 victory that gave Cleveland a 3–1 series edge and eliminated any remaining margin of error for the Red Sox.

With one more loss, Boston's season would be over.

Having played with the Red Sox prior to 2004 and gone through that year's comeback against New York, Wakefield now recognized the change in the team's psyche and mentality. *We're not dead yet. We came back against the Yankees when we were down by more, and we can do the same to Cleveland.* The Red Sox had an extremely high level of confidence when playing at Fenway Park, and they believed that they still had every chance to win the series if they could just get through Game 5 in Cleveland, a contest in which they had one very big factor in their favor.

Josh Beckett.

Now in his second season after being acquired from the Florida Marlins, Beckett was coming off a 20-win regular season and was positively dominating in his first two starts of the postseason, both victories. Like many of the staff aces who pitched for the Sox during Wakefield's career — Clemens, Martinez, Schilling — Beckett was a fierce competitor. Wakefield respected that about him. He saw Beckett as having a maturity beyond his years, a presence that relatively few young players possessed. Wakefield would watch with great pride as Beckett slowly matured into a leader of the pitching staff over the course of their careers together in Boston, and he respected the way Beckett went about his business: the young right-hander *expected* to win, but made no excuses when he lost.

When Wakefield awoke on the morning of Game 5, he was in agony. Overnight — as he knew it would — the pain in the back of his shoulder had intensified. The start against Cleveland had been his only outing in 17 days, and Wakefield knew that such acute pain in his shoulder was not a good sign.

"The next day," he said, "I couldn't pull the covers off me when I woke up."

Knowing he would not be able to pitch again in the series, Wakefield watched as Beckett dominated again in Game 5, pitching the Red Sox to a 7–1 win that sent the series back to Boston. Back at Fenway Park, the Red Sox vanquished the Indians in Games 5 and 6, winning by scores of 12–2 and 11–2. The victories brought Boston's advantage over the final three games of the series to a mind-numbing 30–5, a total that actually increased to 33–5 when taking into account the fact that the Red Sox had also scored the final three runs of Game 4.

Collectively, it was as if the Red Sox were coasting along until that moment when they actually needed to, well, play.

Okay, time to get serious.

With another trip to the World Series now a reality—this time the opponent would be the Colorado Rockies—the Red Sox had only two days to catch their breath and begin preparing for Game 1, to be played at Fenway Park on October 24. For Wakefield, the two-day respite offered an opportunity to assess the health of his shoulder and the strength of his arm, both of which had both him and team officials concerned. Everyone agreed that he should try to throw from a mound in between the ALCS and the World Series—in what is typically referred to as a *side session*—and the results were poor. With pitching coach John Farrell at his side, Wakefield labored to get the ball to the plate. His shoulder ached. Though he had taken a cortisone injection in September, the problem now was worsening again, to the point where Wakefield wondered whether he could pitch even once in a seven-game series, let alone twice.

"I could hardly play catch," Wakefield said. "It was still bothering me. I was trying to throw a side, and I had to cut it short because I couldn't even reach the plate. [Red Sox officials] told me they wanted me to pitch Game 2 and Game 6, if possible, and I told them, 'I don't even know if I can pitch Game 2.' It sucked. I wanted to pitch, but I was also worried. What if I tried to warm up and I couldn't go? Then what? I couldn't look the other 24 guys in the face if that happened."

With media members eagerly awaiting Francona's announcement with regard to his pitching plans for the series, Wakefield met with his manager, pitching coach, and assorted team officials, including the medical staff, to discuss his fate. Because of the inflammation in his shoulder, doctors said, Wakefield could suffer lasting damage to his shoulder if he elected to pitch. It was yet another thing to consider. Wakefield wanted to pitch not only in the World Series but in the future, and he also wanted to do what was best for the team first. He was stuck. Recognizing Wakefield's contributions to the organization and maintaining respect for his status as a veteran, Sox officials effectively put the matter in Wakefield's hands.

If you want to try, we'll let you try. It's the last round of the playoffs anyway. We can replace you without any real penalty. You have the right to make this decision.

Indeed, if Wakefield was unable to pitch, the Sox had Jon Lester on standby to pitch in his place, though that would require a reshuffling of the rotation. Nonetheless, the Sox had the pitching and the patience to let Wakefield decide. Lester's presence certainly made his decision easier, but that was not what concerned the knuckleballer. Again, Wakefield was unsure if he could pitch *one* game, let alone two. If he could not warm up, the pitching plans for Game 2 would be thrust into a state of chaos because the Red Sox would not be able to replace him until *after* the game. The same was true if he had to leave the field during the game because of injury or ineffectiveness. This was the *World Series*, after all, and one game or one pitch could make the difference in the outcome, something Wakefield knew all too well from the experiences of 2003 and 2004.

If I pitch and get hurt — and if that costs us the World Series — I'm not sure I can live with that.

And so Tim Wakefield did what he almost always did.

He thought of the group first.

And he pulled the plug on himself.

• • •

The 2007 World Series, like the one in 2004, was a landslide. The hottest team in baseball, the Colorado Rockies were entering a best-of-seven set with the Red Sox having won 21 of their 22 previous games in the regular season. The Rockies won 14 of 15 to end the regular season before sweeping their way through the first two rounds of the playoffs, at which point they encountered a long layoff as they waited for the Red Sox and Indians to play out the ALCS.

When the Rockies finally returned to the field, they encountered a Red Sox team that was hotter.

With the rotation now shuffled to accommodate Lester, who would go in Game 4, the Red Sox won by a 13-1 score behind the steamrolling Beckett in Game 1. In order, Schilling, Matsuzaka, and Lester then closed out a series in which the Red Sox outscored the Rockies by a 29–10 margin, bringing Boston's lopsided scoring edge to an incredible 62–15 over the final 67 innings of the postseason. Lester pitched 5⅔ scoreless innings in Boston's 4–3 victory in Game 4, a game in which Wakefield joined the large majority of onlookers rooting for a young man who was one of the brightest prospects in the Red Sox system.

Like many of the Red Sox, Wakefield took a particular interest in Lester, a highly regarded prospect who had joined the major league team in 2006. Late that same year, Lester had been diagnosed with large cell lymphoma, a treatable form of cancer. A native of Tacoma, Washington, Lester spent the subsequent winter being treated at the Fred Hutchinson Center in Seattle, then returned to the Red Sox in 2007. The team brought him along slowly. From the very start, Wakefield liked Lester's work ethic and attitude, and he found the young man to be understated and respectful, different from some of the brash young players coming up from the minor leagues. *This kid gets it.* Wakefield had spent countless hours visiting children in Boston-area hospitals during his career with the Red Sox, and he had lost his grandfather, named Lester, to cancer.

Throughout Lester's Game 4 performance, Wakefield said nothing to him during the course of the game. Baseball etiquette generally calls for pitchers to be left alone in the middle of an outing, and so Wakefield stayed away, silently pulling for Lester from the dugout.

Attaboy, Jon. Keep it going. Only when Lester was lifted from the game, with 17 outs to his credit, did Wakefield rise from his seat and climb to the top steps of the dugout, where he greeted his young replacement with a handshake and a hug.

You've made us proud.

In the immediate aftermath of the victory at Coors Field in Denver, Wakefield celebrated with his teammates on the field, just as the Sox had done in St. Louis. Longtime Sox veteran Mike Timlin placed his arm around Wakefield and, in plain sight of television cameras, commended his teammate for doing the right thing and making the ultimate sacrifice. The image further enhanced Wakefield's rightful reputation as a *team guy,* not a *me guy,* and the expression on Wakefield's face and his watery eyes delivered a clear message to Red Sox fans who had long since learned what he stood for.

You have no idea how hard this was for me.

In Boston, during the victory celebration that followed, the Red Sox once again rode duck boats through the city streets to reward a fan base that had gone, seemingly overnight, from destitution to an embarrassment of riches. Devoid of a World Series championship for 86 years, the Red Sox now had won *two titles in four years.* The significance of the fact that the Red Sox had a cast of young players who had performed well in the series — from Lester and Matsuzaka to second baseman Dustin Pedroia to center fielder Jacoby Ellsbury — was impossible to overlook. The Red Sox were not about their past anymore, but about the future.

Wakefield took a great deal of pride in that development. During his career, the Red Sox had changed.

For the better.

Though Wakefield had pitched in just one game during the postseason — Boston went 11–3 in the playoffs, the same record the team posted in 2004 — Red Sox fans hardly overlooked him, applauding him for his decision to effectively withdraw from the World Series. The signs carried by some fans that declared him the "unsung hero" of the 2007 Red Sox made Wakefield very proud. He had been in Boston for 13 seasons, longer than any other member of the Red Sox, and he had immersed himself in the community. He had never claimed to be a superstar. He tried to show up every day and do his job, to invest in the community, to become one of *them*, and the support shown by Red Sox fans in the aftermath of the World Series assured him that they understood, that they recognized his sacrifices, and that they had accepted him as readily as he had accepted them.

At that moment, Tim Wakefield was a man who, after spending much of his career feeling alienated because of his affiliation with the knuckleball, felt as if he truly belonged.

Twelve

●

I don't want anybody to panic. I'm not pitching. I'm just throwing out the first ball.

— Phil Niekro, prior to a ceremonial appearance at the World Series

FROM ROGER CLEMENS to Mo Vaughn to Nomar Garciaparra to Pedro Martinez, Tim Wakefield had seen a succession of superstars leave the Red Sox by one method or another. He could hardly have been surprised when Manny Ramirez joined the list.

Ramirez's time in Boston had had its share of controversial events, though most of them were disputes with management stemming from Ramirez's general unhappiness in Boston. Wakefield never had a single problem with the slugger. Ramirez was not the kind of player who developed close relationships with teammates, but Wakefield generally found him to be a positive presence on the field and in the clubhouse, where Ramirez's feats and antics could be, to say the least, entertaining. As a right-handed hitter, in Wakefield's eyes, Ramirez was peerless. As for his comedic value, that often spoke for itself.

Once, during a tense game with the Los Angeles Dodgers, Ramirez dropped a routine fly in shallow left field, allowing the tying run to score in a game the Red Sox had led, 1–0, with two outs in the top of the ninth inning. Upon returning to a dugout where the tension was palpable, a self-deprecating Ramirez quietly placed his hat and glove on the bench, then sarcastically wondered aloud whether he had just cost himself a Gold Glove. Wakefield and the rest of the Red Sox exploded with laughter. (The Sox then went on to win that game, 2–1.) Moments like that became customary with Ramirez during his time in Boston, and Red Sox officials, players, and fans alike were willing to chalk up Ramirez's shenanigans to nothing more than *Manny being Manny.*

And yet, Wakefield was among those who noticed a change in the player in 2008, when Ramirez's frustrations over his contract status reached a new level and he became so unhappy in Boston that he was involved in a pair of physical altercations.

The first, in early June, came during a game between the Red Sox and Tampa Bay Rays at Fenway Park. Wakefield was seated in the dugout, not far from Ramirez, when Kevin Youkilis returned to the dugout after a frustrating at-bat. Known for his volatility, Youkilis began slamming equipment, and Ramirez chastised his teammate for childish behavior. Wakefield sensed tension building. *Uh-oh.* Ramirez and Youkilis suddenly began shoving each other before Wakefield leaped from the bench and wedged himself between his two teammates, all as television cameras caught the Red Sox in a *boys-will-be-boys* moment that turned out to be so much more.

Indeed, the incident would not be the last time that season Wakefield sprang from his chair to wonder what silliness Ramirez was up to now.

Only a few weeks later, Wakefield was sitting at his locker prior to a game with the Houston Astros when he heard shouting from what players sometimes referred to as the *food room*, an area that effectively served as the kitchen. *What the hell is that?* Again, Wakefield got up from his seat. This time a flock of teammates had beaten him to the spot: Wakefield found Ramirez being held away from 60-something traveling secretary Jack McCormick, whom Ramirez had angrily pushed to the ground during a heated dispute. Ramirez's request for more tickets had been denied on a day when McCormick's supply was decidedly thin.

The matter was quickly settled, but Wakefield, like most everyone else around the Red Sox, saw this incident as being entirely different from past episodes of *Manny being Manny.*

He really wants out this time.

Indeed, for all of Ramirez's behavioral flare-ups during his time in Boston, almost everyone agreed on two points: Ramirez generally had remained harmless, and the team, overall, was not affected. Wakefield was not the only one who found it astounding that Ramirez could continue to enter the batter's box and hit as if nothing at all out of the ordinary had just taken place. Once coupled with Ortiz, in fact, Ramirez became part of such a potent tandem that it was impossible to mention one without the other. During the five full seasons Ramirez and Ortiz were full-time lineup mates — from roughly June 1, 2003, to May 31, 2008 — the Red Sox scored 4,475 runs, second in all of baseball to only the New York Yankees (4,499). They *averaged* 5.5 runs per game. The Sox had won two World Series and been to the playoffs four times, and the performance of their dynamic duo in postseason play was positively mind-numbing.

And yet, personality-wise, Ortiz and Ramirez could not have been more different. Wakefield found that somewhat amusing. Where Ramirez would withdraw from the team, Ortiz was a much softer sort who engaged with people. Most people on the team, including Wakefield, became friendly with Ortiz. "Big Papi" did not give his manager headaches, did not antagonize management, and was far more apt to put his arm around a frustrated teammate than confront him in the dugout, as Ramirez had done with Youkilis. Wakefield saw Ramirez and Ortiz as being complete opposites.

The only thing they really have in common is that they can hit.

By the end of July, albeit for reasons beyond anyone's control, even that was no longer true. Ortiz was on the disabled list with a wrist injury. And so, on July 31, 2008, in a move that was shocking on some levels and entirely unsurprising on others, the Red Sox executed a three-team trade with the Los Angeles Dodgers and the Pittsburgh Pirates that sent Ramirez to the West Coast (and not so coincidentally, the National League) while bringing talented, hardworking outfielder Jason Bay to Boston. The deal may have sent ripples throughout major league baseball, but Wakefield was hardly surprised when he learned about the trade from media reports on a day when the Red Sox had no game scheduled.

I think we all saw this coming.

While Ramirez's departure signified the end of yet another era in Boston, Wakefield wondered if it also triggered the start of a new one, particularly with the Red Sox in another race for the playoffs and, perhaps, a World Series championship. He had played with Clemens, Vaughn, and Garciaparra, all of whom had been drafted by the Red Sox. During his time with the team, Martinez and Lowe had been brought in and then cast off. Schilling, as it would turn out, had pitched his last game in the 2007 World Series—a shoulder injury would force his retirement later in 2008—and now Ramirez had come full circle during his time in Boston, too.

Incredibly, Tim Wakefield and his unpredictable knuckleball had become the hub around which the Red Sox carousel had been turning for years.

He had outlasted them all.

When he arrived for the start of the season, before the Ramirez drama, Wakefield had known there would be questions. He was approaching his 42nd birthday. A shoulder injury had prevented him from pitching down the stretch in 2007. Wakefield had spent the winter reconditioning himself, and time had worn away some of the versatility he once possessed as a knuckleballer.

I'm just not as durable as I used to be.

Wakefield opened some eyes that year when he said that one of his goals was to "make my 32 starts and give the club 200-plus innings," but that objective was not so far-fetched. Only a few years earlier, when Wakefield had totaled 225⅓ innings during a 2005 season in which he celebrated his 39th birthday, he had joined a group that, since 1980, included just 27 pitchers who had compiled at least 225 innings at the age of 38 or older. Of those 27, nine—or one-third of them—had been knuckleballers. By then, everyone knew that knuckleballers constituted maybe 1 percent of all pitchers in baseball at any given time, yet depending on where one drew the line, they could constitute an amazing 33 percent of a list like this one.

Tim Wakefield was feeling every bit his age—he was now a father of two—but he also had history on his side.

And even Wakefield himself admitted that he began giving thought to his legacy.

"I wanted to get to 200 wins, and I wanted to maybe tie or break Cy Young's and Roger Clemens's record for all-time Red Sox [victories]," Wakefield said, "but I didn't know if it was possible."

Not long after the July 31 trading deadline, Tim Wakefield's shoulder flared up again, in essentially the same area that had ailed him at the end of the previous season. The problem reached an apex during an August 6 game at Kansas City that produced an 8–2 Red Sox victory and in which Wakefield contributed six strong innings for his seventh win of the season. To that point in the season, Wakefield had been *averaging* 6⅓ innings per start, compiled 147 innings, and posted a 3.67 ERA, numbers suggesting that, when healthy, he was still quite effective.

The Red Sox, fearing a flameout like the one that had derailed Wakefield the previous season, immediately pulled the plug on him and gave him a cortisone injection in hopes of preempting a larger issue. Wakefield was all too eager to comply. He did not want to go through the prior season's pain again. Meanwhile, the Red Sox were having other issues with their pitching staff — a not uncommon problem for teams that advance deep into the playoffs a year earlier. Ace Josh Beckett was ailing, and the innings were beginning to pile up on every Red Sox pitcher. As the Red Sox had learned in 2005, if the pitching staff's postseason sacrifices were going to come due, it was likely to happen late in the year, when fatigue invariably became a factor.

Wakefield ultimately missed only 20 days before returning from the disabled list, a far shorter absence than the previous season. He returned for an August 26 start against New York at Yankee Stadium, pitching five innings in a 7–3 victory for the Red Sox. At the time, Wakefield knew that trip was likely to be his last to Yankee Stadium: the Yankees were scheduled to move into a new ballpark beginning in 2009, and it was unlikely that Boston would face New York in the playoffs because, quite simply, the Yankees weren't going to qualify. The Tampa Bay Rays and the Red Sox, in that order, were running first and second in the American League East, and both seemed destined for the postseason. Oddly enough, the Yankees were on the outside looking in.

New York was where it had all happened for Wakefield — the home run to Boone, the comeback in 2004, the nadir of his Red Sox career and the subsequent redemption. Wakefield had come to love the trips to New York. He appreciated the history of the park. He had been a *part* of that history. He regarded Yankee Stadium, like Fenway Park, as a "cathedral," as "hallowed ground." It was playing in New York and Boston especially that reminded him of just how privileged he had been to have a professional baseball career and to get a chance to play in those places.

Wakefield kept a pair of baseballs as mementos from his final game at the Stadium. Clubhouse attendant Lou Cucuzza gave Wakefield a handful of dirt from the playing field. Wakefield wondered whether the younger members of the Red Sox really appreciated Yankee Stadium as much as he did, but then he realized: how could they? He himself had *pitched* in Game 7 in 2003. He had *celebrated* following Game 7 in 2004.

The start on August 26 was Wakefield's 25th and final career regular or postseason appearance at Yankee Stadium, where he went 7–8 with a 3.90 ERA. His 115⅓ innings at the Stadium during that span were more than anyone else on the team. Wakefield had recorded precisely 346 outs during his career at the most storied baseball stadium in American history, no small achievement for a man who had been released by the Pittsburgh Pirates 14 seasons earlier.

I've outlasted Yankee Stadium, too.

As it turned out, Tim Wakefield's hopes for the 2008 season were somewhat optimistic. He failed to make 32 starts, and he failed to pitch 200-plus innings.

But he came pretty darned close.

By the time the Red Sox wrapped up a fifth postseason appearance in six seasons, Wakefield had totaled 30 starts and 181 innings while posting a 10–11 record and 4.13 ERA. Now 42, he finished second to only 24-year-old left-hander Lester in both starts and innings pitched.

Wakefield's totals, in fact, were quite comparable to Beckett's, who finished 12–10 with a 4.03 ERA in 174⅓ innings during a season in which the workload from 2007 indisputably caught up with him, wore him down, and sidelined him.

Earlier in the 2008 season, Beckett had turned 28.

Because of additional open dates in the first round of the playoffs, the Red Sox needed only three starting pitchers against the Los Angeles Angels, who by then had become a familiar opponent. Lester, Beckett, and Matsuzaka were Terry Francona's choices, a decision that left Wakefield sidelined — at least for the first round. Matsuzaka had enjoyed a productive season during which he went 18–3 with a 2.95 ERA, though he had posted those numbers in fewer innings than Wakefield and along the way had earned a rather dubious distinction: among major league starting pitchers *in history* who had won at least 18 games, nobody had ever done so while recording fewer outs than Matsuzaka. For Wakefield, year after year, it was as if the Red Sox regarded the knuckleball as having a "low battery" warning — a pitch that had enough life to make it through September but needed to be shelved once the biggest games of the year arrived. *It's good enough to get us there, but dangerous to us now.*

Wakefield had long since grown accustomed to that line of thought.

The Red Sox prevailed over the Angels in four games of a first-round series that were decided by three runs, two runs, one run, and one run, respectively. The Red Sox were underdogs in the series — the Angels had won 100 games during the season — and so the series again highlighted the club's change in karma: the Red Sox, who historically so often lost when they should have won, were now *winning* when they should have *lost.*

With a seven-game series now looming against the younger, hungry Tampa Bay Rays, Wakefield was scheduled to pitch Game 4, a responsibility that grew in importance with the Red Sox facing a 2–1 series deficit. Though the Sox won Game 1, Tampa had rebounded with resounding victories in Games 2 and 3 by the combined score of 18–9, the latter game a 9–1 victory over Game 1 playoff starter Lester. The Rays were hot when Wakefield stepped up to the mound at Fenway

Park for Game 4, and they kept up the pace against Wakefield, who was starting for the first time in 16 days. Tampa raced to a 3–0 lead in the first inning on home runs by Carlos Pena and Evan Longoria, then added two more runs in the third on a homer by Willy Aybar. His team reeling from one Tampa haymaker after the next, Francona lifted Wakefield in favor of youngster Justin Masterson, who stymied the Rays only briefly in what eventually became a 13–4 Tampa win.

Though Wakefield was disappointed and frustrated by the outing, he was also wise enough to know that the Rays were rolling — *They're red hot,* he thought — and might be impossible to stop.

What Wakefield did not know at the time was that the game might have been the last postseason outing of his career.

Picking up right where they left off in Game 4, the Rays teed off on Matsuzaka at the start of Game 5, racing to a 5–0 lead after three innings and once again forcing Francona into his bullpen in the early innings. By the middle of the seventh inning, the score was 7–0 in favor of the Rays. For Wakefield, the series felt eerily similar to Boston's first-round meeting with the Chicago White Sox in 2005, when the White Sox swept the Red Sox and advanced to the ALCS and, later, the World Series. The Rays were hitting everything thrown to the plate, no matter who threw it, no matter where. The Red Sox had nine outs remaining in their season when the seemingly impossible happened.

They rallied for an 8–7 win.

Scoring eight times in the final three innings — four in the seventh, three in the eighth, one in the ninth — the Red Sox forced the series back to Florida for a sixth game. Again, the Sox had won when they should have lost. Boston claimed Game 6 at Tropicana Field in St. Petersburg to set up a decisive Game 7, a seemingly impossible achievement given how weary and battered the Red Sox were. Beckett was pitching hurt. Closer Jonathan Papelbon was exhausted. The Red Sox were playing in their second ALCS in 13 months — their fourth in six seasons — and each time the series had followed a similar pattern. In 2003 the Sox trailed in games 3–2 before forcing a seventh game (the Aaron Boone game) in New York; in 2004 they had trailed the Yankees 3–0 before winning the next four; in 2007 the Sox trailed the Indians 3–1 before ripping off three straight wins; and now, in 2008, the Sox had trailed the Rays in games 3–1, and trailed in Game 5 by a 7–0 score *in the seventh inning*, only to come back and again force a final, decisive, seventh game.

Wakefield, a member of all those teams, took a great deal of pride and satisfaction in how they played the game.

Take it to the limit.

In the end, the 2008 season proved more like 2003 than 2004 or 2007, though it was devoid of the late-game dramatics that resulted in Wakefield facing Aaron Boone. Sox starter Lester pitched quite well only to be outdueled by Rays right-hander Matt Garza, who was brilliant. Late in the game, likable Rays manager Joe Maddon summoned rookie left-hander David Price into the game in a key situation, and the fireballing Price whipped a called third strike past Sox outfielder J. D. Drew to end a Red Sox threat with the bases loaded. The 3–1 Tampa victory ended a long, grueling Red Sox season.

In retrospect, in summoning an unproven young pitcher into a critical situation, Maddon had made a bold, admirable decision that helped raise his profile and standing throughout a baseball world that already regarded him as a creative, unconventional thinker.

Less than a year later, Maddon would prove that again.

And this time to no one who would appreciate it more than Tim Wakefield.

Tim Wakefield had 164 career victories for the Red Sox when he reported to spring training in 2009, and so the math was simple. Wakefield needed 29 wins to overtake Cy Young and Roger Clemens atop the team's all-time list for wins, a number that would require at least two seasons of production, more than likely three. Over the previous three years, Wakefield had averaged 11 wins a year. At that same pace, he would be able to break the club record in 2011.

That would also be the season in which Wakefield would celebrate his 45th birthday, the age Phil Niekro had suggested from the very beginning was within the realm of possibility.

That would be perfect.

Much to Wakefield's delight, the season began in a fashion that exceeded even his own plans and expectations. After a solid season debut in which he suffered a loss but allowed three runs in six innings — the definition, by major league standards, of a *quality start* — Wakefield went 4-0 with one no-decision in his next five outings (all Red Sox wins). He then lost one, won two, lost two, won four. By the time July dawned, Wakefield was 10-3 with a 4.18 ERA and the Red Sox were a sensational 12-3 in his 15 starts, the kind of bottom-line performance that every pitcher covets. Wakefield always had believed that his primary responsibility to the Red Sox was to make his starts and to "suck up" innings — to collect those precious outs — and that the rest would take care of itself. If he did his job, the team would win the majority of his starts. He would get his share of wins. The victories were a by-product of effort, not the other way around, and so Wakefield tried not to put too much emphasis on the individual victories.

And yet, in the real world, Wakefield knew that perception was everything. When people talked of pitchers from the past, they talked about things like *20-win seasons* and careers in which pitchers *won 300 games*. The bottom line was deceiving, to be sure, but the bottom line was often what people focused on.

Much to his surprise, as the Red Sox neared the conclusion of the first half of the season, Wakefield found himself being discussed as a candidate for the All-Star Game, an honor he had never achieved during his career. For that reason, it meant something to him. Wakefield and his wife, Stacy, had planned to spend the All-Star break vacationing with their two children — Trevor, then five, and four-year-old Brianna — a customary respite that he, like most players, longed for amid the relentlessness of the major league schedule. The All-Star break was a time to get away. And yet, as people spoke about his potential candidacy for the All-Star Game — some argued that Wakefield might even be considered to *start* the game, an enormous honor — Wakefield found himself hoping that he would be selected and in fact wondering why it had never happened before. He felt that it was an honor he had certainly earned.

On the day Major League Baseball announced the rosters for the

All-Star Game in St. Louis in a made-for-television selection show aired about 10 days before the game, Wakefield went about his standard pregame business in the weight room at Fenway Park. Starting positional players are *elected* to All-Star rosters through fan balloting, but backups and pitchers are *selected* through a more intricate process that involves player balloting and managerial decisions. Sometimes the choices fell exclusively to the All-Star team manager to make, as Terry Francona had twice experienced. The presence of the Red Sox in the World Series in 2004 and 2007 had earned Francona the right to manage the All-Star team in each of the following seasons, a role that was both an honor and a responsibility. Frequently it was a no-win situation as well.

Politics and restrictions also played a big part in the election process — officials from Major League Baseball could get into the act and "advise" the manager on his selections — and all these factors frequently combined to prevent the best players from being honored.

Wakefield knew all of this, and he knew, too, that the knuckleball worked against him. Without the knuckleball, he was already one of those players deemed to be "on the bubble." Wakefield's best chance seemed to be through the intervention of American League manager Joe Maddon, the Tampa Bay skipper who might use one of his manager's picks on the knuckleballer. But in choosing Wakefield, Maddon might leave himself open to criticism and second-guessing by fans and officials in the numerous markets that had an equally worthy pitcher who was, well, *not* a knuckleballer.

And so, as Wakefield went through his pregame routine, he was unsure of what to expect when pitching coach John Farrell entered the weight room and told Wakefield that he was wanted in Francona's office "after he talked to the other guys." Wakefield was unsure what that meant. *Other guys? What other guys? And about what?* Wakefield nodded to his pitching coach, his mind searching for the possible cause of a trip to the manager's office. *What could this possibly be about?* The All-Star Game never crossed his mind as Wakefield walked toward Francona's office. The door was closed as Wakefield approached — a sign that he would have to wait, that the manager was in the middle of other business and needed privacy. When the door finally opened, a group of Red Sox players that included first baseman Kevin Youkilis, second baseman Dustin Pedroia, outfielder Jason Bay, closer Jonathan Papelbon, and Beckett emerged from a meeting with the manager, all toting informational packets distributed by their manager that highlighted their responsibilities at the All-Star Game. Unsure if he was going or not, Wakefield didn't know what to make of this group, though he was developing a pit in his stomach.

If I were going, wouldn't I have been in the meeting with those guys?

Francona, keeping a stoic face, asked Wakefield to take a seat. Wakefield simply couldn't get a read on his skipper. Francona began to speak calmly and then simply could not hold back his excitement, his happiness, his enthusiasm. *You're going to the All-Star Game, Wake. Joe Maddon picked you.* Francona, in typical fashion, had orchestrated the entire process as a prank, inviting the other five Red Sox All-Stars into his office separately so as to deliberately string Wakefield along. He convinced the players to go along with the prank and got Farrell's collusion in the scheme as well. And he kept a straight face right up until Wakefield was sitting in his office — at which point Terry Francona, incapable of keeping the secret any longer, broke into a knowing laugh.

"Knowing the voting and how it works, I know that it's tough. But if there's ever a year [Wakefield] deserves it, it's now," Francona said. "He's going to show up in St. Louis next week, and when they introduce his name he's going to be one of the proudest guys — and he should be. He's very worthy."

Wakefield wasted little time notifying Stacy, for whom the message was simple. *Remember that trip we go on every year? Well, this year we're going to St. Louis.*

For Wakefield, being selected to the All-Star Game was a validation of his career, an appreciative acknowledgment of the sacrifices he had made. He had never considered himself a superstar. He believed in the concept of a team, and he knew that his own role in particular as a team member had required sacrificing the kind of individual statistics that lead to honors like selection to the All-Star Game. It had always been a trade he was willing to make to do his job more effectively.

But in 2009, finally, he had the chance to do both.

"You go and play professional baseball and always want to make an All-Star team. I had opportunities, just never got a chance," Wakefield said. "I think I appreciate it more now knowing how hard it is to be picked. If it had happened a lot sooner, I still would have appreciated it, but not as much."

Maddon, as expected, drew criticism for the selection, something he accepted and just as easily dismissed. *In my line of work, it's just part of the job.* Maddon had consulted with major league officials during the process, but the ultimate decision rested with him. By the middle of 2009, Tim Wakefield was in his 17th major league season and had never been to an All-Star Game. Not in 1995. Not in 1998. Not in 2005 or in 2007. Wakefield's opportunities were dwindling, and Maddon essentially admitted that Wakefield's selection to the team went beyond the wins and losses of any one season, that Tim Wakefield was, for lack of a better term, *a special case.*

"Wakefield is having a good year, obviously, pitches in Boston, and he's had a tremendous body of work throughout his entire career," Maddon explained. "I just felt that getting him on a team was the right thing to do."

As it turned out, Wakefield did not appear in the game, though that was hardly the point. Being there was what truly mattered. Wakefield attended all of the All-Star Game festivities he could — the parties, the Home Run Derby, the game itself — and he relished every moment. The introductions felt like the World Series to him. He met President Barack Obama. Maddon had told Wakefield ahead of time that the knuckleballer would be his emergency plan — that is, the American League team's final pitcher if the game went to extra innings — and Wakefield, as always, graciously accepted the role. *Whatever you need me to do, skip.* He watched as the American League defeated the National League, ensuring home-field advantage if the Red Sox had the privilege of playing for a title again, and he felt more than ever that all of his contributions to the Pirates, to the Red Sox, and to baseball had been noticed all along.

Maybe people have been paying closer attention than I thought.

• • •

For any successful knuckleballer, longevity comes at a price. The longer the career, the more persistent the dips and turns. The turbulence always endures.

Shortly after the All-Star break, while throwing a side session in Toronto in preparation for an upcoming start, Wakefield felt pain in his lower back and had to cut short his workout. Within days, the problem had worsened to the point where the club had to place him on the disabled list. Through consultation with team doctors, Wakefield learned that he had a fragmented disc that was pressing on a nerve. The doctors told Wakefield that the only way to correct the problem was through surgery, which, if performed immediately, would leave open the possibility of coming back for the postseason. But given the club's needs in the interim, Wakefield instead agreed to a cortisone injection that would alleviate some of the pain and might allow him to contribute effectively in the shorter term.

Wakefield remained out until late August, when he returned to pitch seven strong innings in a 3–2 Boston win over the Chicago White Sox, but he was unable to pitch again until 10 days later, on September 5. His next start came 16 days later, on September 21. After that, he didn't pitch again for another nine days, on September 30. All in all, Wakefield made just four starts after the All-Star break, none closer than nine days apart. The nerve irritation in his back caused him to lose more than 50 percent of the strength in his left leg. He couldn't run. He couldn't bike. And with each outing, the problems seemed to intensify.

Every time I throw, the problem gets worse.

Intent on returning at full strength in 2010, Wakefield approached the Red Sox about having back surgery immediately so as to have as much time as possible to rehabilitate before spring training. Fearing the potential for a mishap during the playoffs that would require Wakefield to pitch anyway, the club asked him to delay the procedure. Wakefield complied. After he finally had the surgery on October 21, 2009, the doctors expected him to make a full recovery, but they also gave no guarantees.

Amid continuing speculation about his future — he was, after all, 43 by then — Wakefield reminded himself, and others, that he had pulled himself out of contention for a playoff spot only two years earlier, in 2007, before the American League Championship Series. *Lots of people thought I was done then, too.* Wakefield spent the subsequent winter strengthening and rehabilitating his right shoulder, then went on to win 10 games while making 30 starts and pitching 181 innings in 2008. He made the All-Star team in 2009. Now he was experiencing back problems that he regarded as merely another bump in the road, no matter how many others regarded his latest ailment as perhaps the *coup de grâce* that would effectively end his career.

Of course, Wakefield had other designs, though Red Sox officials now clearly had their doubts, too. Despite having exercised the re-generating option on Wakefield's contract on an annual basis since its inception, Sox officials contacted the pitcher's agent, Barry Meister, about reworking Wakefield's deal again after the 2009 campaign. While Red Sox general manager Theo Epstein was publicly stating that the Red Sox had concerns about an escalating payroll and the club had to do some creative accounting to avoid eclipsing a $170 million payroll threshold that would result in having to pay what baseball calls the *luxury tax,* Wakefield saw the discussions with the team in an alto-gether different light. *They're putting me on the clock.* At this stage of his career, Sox officials indicated, they were placing Wakefield's ceiling in 2010 at roughly 100 innings. In their minds, he did not have the same value anymore. The pitcher's regenerating option was thus replaced with a finite, two-year deal valued at a guaranteed $5 million — $3.5 million in 2010 and $1.5 million in 2011. Because of major league rules, the deal allowed the Red Sox to list Wakefield's salary at $2.5 million (the average over the length of the contract) instead of $4 million (the value of his original option), but such a savings was relatively trivial for a franchise worth nearly $1 billion. The way Tim Wakefield saw it, the Red Sox were accomplishing something altogether different.

They've drawn the finish line for me.

But I can still break the record for wins.

On many levels, the 2010 season proved to be an enormous disap-pointment for Wakefield, producing just a 4–10 record and a 5.34 ERA. Still, in the aftermath of back surgery, Wakefield remained entirely healthy from the beginning of the season to the end, amassing 140 innings — a whopping 40 percent more than the club had projected for him. *You guys were wrong about that one.* The Red Sox jettisoned him to and from the bullpen with such regularity that Wakefield was reminded of the Joe Kerrigan years. Without any consistency in his routine, he did not pitch well and became increasingly frustrated. Neither a starter nor a closer, he was stuck in the netherworld between the two. The Red Sox seemed to use him only when their starter had failed and they faced a significant deficit — what veteran baseball people call *mop-up time,* meaning that a pitcher has to be summoned solely to clean up someone else's mess.

After 16 years with the Red Sox, Tim Wakefield wasn't sure if he wanted to clean up messes anymore. He believed he could still pitch, but he had no way of convincing the Red Sox of that, and he had no desire to pitch anywhere else. He wanted a more meaningful role — in the middle innings perhaps — and his success throughout his career in filling gaps suggested that he could succeed. In Wakefield's mind, the *long man* or *mop-up* role was an entry-level position in the major leagues, a place for a young man to prove himself and earn greater responsibility. It was not a grazing pasture for a veteran. Wakefield felt like the club regarded him as nothing more than an insurance policy for the starting rotation, and yet the club simultaneously employed him in a role that made it difficult for him to be effective.

I want to pitch, but I want to stay in Boston.

He was stuck.

Late in the year, with the Red Sox grinding through an injury-filled season that ended when they missed the playoffs for just the second time since the start of the 2003 season, the team was playing in Oakland when general manager Theo Epstein approached Wakefield about a meeting. Wakefield's unhappiness had been obvious, though he often wondered if club officials misinterpreted his stance. *I don't mind pitching in relief. I just feel like you never really gave me a chance.* Wakefield arrived in the cramped clubhouse at the Coliseum and changed into his uniform, then strolled down a narrow corridor and into a shoebox of a manager's office, where he and Epstein sat, behind closed doors.

The Red Sox had five starting pitchers under contract through at least 2012 — Beckett, Lester, Matsuzaka, newcomer John Lackey, and youngster Clay Buchholz — and Wakefield could do the math as easily as anyone. He was on the outside looking in. Wakefield sat and listened as Epstein delivered his message, leaving little doubt that Wakefield was truly near the end and faced a decision.

"When players get to the end of their careers, they envision something in the way of a parade," Epstein told him. "For most guys, it doesn't end that way."

Wakefield listened, yet wondered.

Why not? Why can't it end well for everyone? Why does it have to be that way? Maybe they want me to retire. Maybe they're going to release me.

By the time 2010 ended, Wakefield had 179 career wins with the Red Sox, 13 short of Clemens and Cy Young, 14 short of number one on the team's all-time list. Overall, including his time with Pittsburgh, Wakefield had won 193 games, just seven shy of a tidy 200. Wakefield had been in this kind of position many times before in his career — "I feel like I've been in survival mode for 19 years," he noted — and he had persevered before. He had quit his first college team and been granted a second chance. He failed as a positional player in the minor leagues and was given a second chance. He succeeded and then failed with the Pirates, only to receive a second chance in Boston. And his time in Boston had been filled with a succession of unpredictable dips and turns, from Kevin Kennedy and Jimy Williams to Joe Kerrigan, Grady Little, and Terry Francona. Wakefield had started and relieved, won and lost, and endured most everything in between, pulled along by the mystifying pitch that had been responsible for all of his accomplishments.

At that point, Wakefield seriously considered retirement. He felt as if he had spent the entire year — as he had spent his entire career — trying to prove himself. He entered spring training believing that he was going to be a starter. Instead, he ended up as a reliever and insurance policy for the preferred starting five. The entire series of events had frustrated him, failed to meet his expectations, and yet, physically, he felt better than he had in some time. In 2011 he would celebrate his 45th birthday, and Wakefield knew that Phil Niekro had pitched until he was 48.

Tim Wakefield had to decide whether he wanted to risk being disappointed again.

In the immediate aftermath of any season, the clubhouses at every stadium in the major leagues look the same: with open cardboard boxes and rolls of packing tape scattered about the room, the scene very much resembles a college dorm during the last week of spring semester when students repack their belongings and return home for the summer. Players seal up their belongings in boxes and put those boxes in the care of team personnel, who then ship them out. Red Sox players shake hands and embrace one another, saying a permanent *good-bye* to some, an optimistic *see you later* to others. When they walk out the clubhouse door and into the real world, many of them are cherishing the chance to lead normal, private lives, even if only for the next three or four months.

Tim Wakefield had long since learned that moving day was no time to make decisions, that he usually needed more distance from the season to make rational, prudent choices. Still, this case was different. The team's fade from contention, along with his own move into an unfulfilling role, had given him weeks and months to examine how he felt. Wakefield remembered something that seemed especially relevant now: an excerpt that a friend had sent him from a speech by Teddy Roosevelt.

"It is not the critic who counts; not the man who points out how the strong man stumbles, or where the doer of deeds could have done them better. The credit belongs to the man who is actually in the arena, whose face is marred by dust and sweat and blood; who strives valiantly; who errs, who comes short again and again, because there is no effort without error and shortcoming; but who does actually strive to do the deeds; who knows great enthusiasms, the great devotions; who spends himself in a worthy cause; who at the best knows in the end the triumph of high achievement, and who at the worst, if he fails, at least fails while daring

*greatly, so that his place shall never be with those cold and timid souls
who neither know victory nor defeat."*

With that in mind, Tim Wakefield's decision became easier.

I'm not a quitter.

Wakefield had decided that he was going to continue wearing a major league uniform until the Red Sox told him he could not. If the Red Sox did not want him, that would be their choice. He wanted to make a final run at Clemens and Cy Young, and a run at 200 victories. Whether he actually attained the record would be largely irrelevant. His legacy had already been forged. But what Wakefield had always done, unfailingly amid the knuckleball's bumps and dives, was put in the effort.

I've been through this many times before.

And so, once more, Tim Wakefield prepared himself to pitch. He positioned the fingernails of his right index and middle fingers into the leather cover of a baseball, into the major league logo just inside the horseshoe, unsure of exactly what the knuckleball might do and uncertain as to where it would take him.

Tim Wakefield was certain of only one thing.

He was still willing, as always, to go along for the ride.

Acknowledgments

•

APPROPRIATELY, OVER A period of years and like the knuckleball itself, the plans for this project unexpectedly changed direction on more than one occasion. In the end, *Knuckler* landed safely in the hands of many capable people who were all eager to help harness it, an outcome for which both the author and the writer could not be more grateful.

Any and all credit for this book must begin with Houghton Mifflin Harcourt editor Susan Canavan, who demonstrated extraordinary patience through both a negotiation process and a production process that the author and writer took to the very last pitch, with two outs and the bases loaded in the bottom of the ninth. She embraced this idea from the very beginning and painstakingly pored over a manuscript that was greatly improved through her suggestions and criticisms. Her work was nothing short of brilliant. Rare are those people who make pride the driving force behind their effort, and Susan treated this book as if it were her very own — which, in many ways, it was. We cannot possibly thank her enough for that.

Representatives Kim Zayotti of Blue Sky Entertainment and Scott Waxman of the Waxman Literary Agency demonstrated an especially

ACKNOWLEDGMENTS

high level of tolerance during the negotiations, a process that most everyone generally finds stressful. To their credit, the deal got done, and they, too, should be especially proud of what came of it.

Thanks are also due to Cindy Buck for her excellent copy editing.

The research for *Knuckler* began 15 years ago when the author and writer simultaneously landed at Fenway Park. Neither could have imagined the story and relationships that would develop over the years. During that period of time, the Red Sox rose to prominence as one of the premier franchises in baseball and Fenway Park became one of the more desirable workplaces in the game. The entire Red Sox organization — from ownership to the volunteers — helped create an environment that fostered growth, success, and passion. Without that, the Red Sox fan base would not be what it is today — one of the best on the planet — and there would not have been any incentive to tell this story and many, many others.

We can never thank you enough, Red Sox fans, for caring so much.

A cast of people, knowingly or unknowingly, helped fill the inevitable gaps that came up along the way. Over the last two decades or so, baseball coverage in Boston has reached unmatched heights, and the work done by those assigned to the Red Sox by the *Boston Herald* and the *Boston Globe* was an invaluable resource. Those people are too many to name, but anyone who wrote about the Red Sox or Wakefield during that time contributed to this work in some way. Of particular value was a profile done by longtime baseball writer Gordon Edes on Woody Huyke, the man who came up with the idea of turning Tim Wakefield from a fledgling minor league first baseman into a historic knuckleball pitcher. Sportswriters Glenn Miller (of the *Fort Myers Press*) and John Perrotto (of BaseballProspectus.com) helped with those parts of Wakefield's career for which the writer was not present.

Of great value, too, were *The Knucklebook* by Dave Clark and *The Physics of Baseball* by Professor Robert Adair of Yale, works that offer perspective, humor, and insight into the most fascinating pitch in baseball.

The list of those who offered their cooperation in telling Tim Wakefield's story reads like a who's who in baseball over the last several decades, and we cite them here in no particular order. Les Hall, who coached Wakefield in college, provided invaluable background on Wakefield's career at Florida Tech, from which relatively few official accounts remain. The knuckleballer's parents, Steve and Judy Wakefield, proudly recounted their son's development as an athlete and, just as importantly, as a person. Pittsburgh Pirates director of media relations Jim Trdinich served as a liaison to Chuck Tanner, the longtime skipper who managed knuckleballer Wilbur Wood when both were with the Chicago White Sox. (Tanner later managed the Pirates, but before Wakefield reached the majors.) The esteemed Jim Leyland generously took time from his schedule with the 2010 Detroit Tigers to discuss the early years of Wakefield's career in Pittsburgh. Joe Torre, who is almost certainly headed for the Hall of Fame, similarly took time from his season with the Los Angeles Dodgers to offer his insights on both Wakefield and Phil Niekro, with whom Torre was paired as a catcher for the Atlanta Braves.

And then there was the innovative Jimy Williams, the man who was bold enough to employ Tim Wakefield as a closer during the 1999 season and who always has placed great value on things that others do not. The knuckleball is just one of the many specialties that Williams has championed over the years.

Put those four managers together — Tanner, Leyland, Torre, and Williams — and you get 11,781 games of managerial experience. Add in the contributions of longtime baseball evaluator and executive Bill Lajoie, who has spent more than 50 years in professional baseball, as well as affable commissioner Allan "Bud" Selig, and you have roughly 250 years of baseball experience from which to draw.

We cannot thank these men enough for sharing their wisdom on the knuckleball and all things baseball over the years.

Still, because the knuckleball is the ultimate specialty, true experts were required. Both Wilbur Wood and Phil Niekro were remarkably gracious and generous with their time to help this project, each spending long stretches on the phone to share experiences and insights. Only the seasoned knuckleballer truly knows what any other knuckleballer feels. Niekro went above and beyond any reasonable expectation by agreeing to contribute the foreword for this work, with no compensation, further fortifying the belief that knuckleballers are true team players and among the selfless talents in professional sports. Thank you so much, Phil. You, too, *Wilbah*. We hope this work will call further attention to the many contributions each of you has made to the game.

Wakefield's career with the Red Sox intersected with those of many others, and the list of teammates who contributed to his success is far too long to include here. Nonetheless, for a pitcher who believes in and understands the concept of a team, a formal measure of gratitude must be expressed to all of them. For this project, former Red Sox manager Dan Duquette and current Red Sox general manager Theo Epstein willingly gave their time. Catcher Doug Mirabelli, who caught Wakefield during the prime of the knuckleballer's career with Boston, was as patient and understanding with this process as he was with the knuckler itself. That is no small contribution, and something for which the author and writer are extremely grateful.

And finally, a special thanks from the author and writer to their respective wives and children, who know better than anyone what sacrifices must be made to accommodate anyone who works in or around the world of professional sports.

Tim Wakefield
Autumn 2010

Tony Massarotti
Autumn 2010

TIM WAKEFIELD'S CAREER STATISTICS

YEAR	Tm	Lg	W	L	SV	SVO	G	GS	CG	IP	H	R	ER	HR	BB	SO	ERA
1992	Pit	NL	8	1	0	0	13	13	4	92.0	76	26	22	3	35	51	2.15
1993	Pit	NL	6	11	0	0	24	20	3	128.1	145	83	80	14	75	59	5.61
1995	Bos	AL	16	8	0	0	27	27	6	195.1	163	76	64	22	68	119	2.95
1996	Bos	AL	14	13	0	0	32	32	6	211.2	238	151	121	38	90	140	5.14
1997	Bos	AL	12	15	0	0	35	29	4	201.1	193	109	95	24	87	151	4.25
1998	Bos	AL	17	8	0	0	36	33	2	216.0	211	123	110	30	79	146	4.58
1999	Bos	AL	6	11	15	18	49	17	0	140.0	146	93	79	19	72	104	5.08
2000	Bos	AL	6	10	0	1	51	17	0	159.1	170	107	97	31	65	102	5.48
2001	Bos	AL	9	12	3	5	45	17	0	168.2	156	84	73	13	73	148	3.90
2002	Bos	AL	11	5	3	5	45	15	0	163.1	121	57	51	15	51	134	2.81
2003	Bos	AL	11	7	1	1	35	33	0	202.1	193	106	92	23	71	169	4.09
2004	Bos	AL	12	10	0	0	32	30	0	188.1	197	121	102	29	63	116	4.87
2005	Bos	AL	16	12	0	0	33	33	3	225.1	210	113	104	35	68	151	4.15
2006	Bos	AL	7	11	0	0	23	23	1	140.0	135	80	72	19	51	90	4.63
2007	Bos	AL	17	12	0	0	31	31	0	189.0	191	104	100	22	64	110	4.76
2008	Bos	AL	10	11	0	0	30	30	1	181.0	154	89	83	25	60	117	4.13
2009	Bos	AL	11	5	0	0	21	21	2	129.2	137	67	66	12	50	72	4.58
2010	Bos	AL	4	10	0	0	32	19	0	140.0	153	92	83	19	36	84	5.34
TOTALS			193	172	22	30	594	440	32	3071.2	2989	1681	1494	393	1158	2063	4.38
TOTALS AL			179	160	22	30	557	407	25	2851.1	2768	1572	1392	376	1048	1953	4.39
TOTALS NL			14	12	0	0	37	33	7	220.1	221	109	102	17	110	110	4.17

ABBREVIATIONS

Tm   Team
Lg   League
W   Wins
L   Losses
SV   Saves
SVO Save opportunities
G   Games
GS   Games started
CG   Complete games
IP   Innings pitched
H   Hits allowed
R   Runs allowed
ER   Earned runs allowed
HR   Home runs allowed
BB   Walks
SO   Strikeouts
ERA Earned run average

DETAILED BREAKDOWN

GENERAL	W	L	SV	SVO	G	GS	CG	IP	H	R	ER	HR	BB	SO	ERA	AVG	OBP	SLG
Home	102	78	13	17	305	221	18	1593.2	1595	850	757	198	522	1030	4.28	.259	.324	.420
Away	91	94	9	13	289	219	14	1478.0	1394	831	737	195	636	1033	4.49	.248	.331	.412
Starter	183	158	0	0	440	440	32	2775.1	2728	1543	1371	357	1045	1812	4.45	.255	.329	.419
Reliever	10	14	22	30	154	0	0	296.1	261	138	123	36	113	251	3.74	.238	.315	.390
vs. NL	29	29	4	4	96	74	7	497.2	493	263	238	50	217	278	4.30	.261	.341	.404
vs. AL	164	143	18	26	498	366	25	2574.0	2496	1418	1256	343	941	1785	4.39	.253	.325	.418
vs. AL East	70	52	9	13	209	152	6	1064.1	1000	570	495	143	398	721	4.19	.247	.322	.414
vs. AL Central	60	43	4	8	154	114	9	818.2	789	437	382	103	281	586	4.20	.251	.318	.406
vs. AL West	34	48	5	5	135	100	10	691.0	707	411	379	97	262	478	4.94	.263	.336	.439
vs. NL East	19	15	3	3	59	42	4	284.0	277	145	131	21	120	159	4.15	.258	.336	.380
vs. NL Central	1	2	0	0	8	8	0	47.0	44	20	17	7	17	34	3.26	.249	.332	.401
vs. NL West	9	12	1	1	29	24	3	166.2	172	98	90	22	80	85	4.86	.269	.353	.445
Pre-All Star	100	95	16	19	337	241	11	1702.1	1652	920	815	195	675	1127	4.31	.253	.330	.407
Post-All Star	93	77	6	11	257	199	21	1369.1	1337	761	679	198	483	936	4.46	.255	.324	.427
Interleague	15	17	4	4	59	41	0	277.1	272	154	136	33	107	168	4.41	.255	.329	.409

W   Wins
L   Losses
SV   Saves
SVO   Save opportunities
G   Games

GS   Games started
CG   Complete games
IP   Innings pitched
H   Hits allowed
R   Runs allowed

ER   Earned runs allowed
HR   Home runs allowed
BB   Walks
SO   Strikeouts
ERA   Earned run average

AVG   Opponents batting average
OBP   Opponents on-base
      percentage
SLG   Opponents slugging
      percentage

DAYS REST &	W	L	SV	SVO	G	GS	CG	IP	H	R	ER	HR	BB	SO	ERA	AVG	OBP	SLG
Start 0–3 Days Rest	13	15	0	0	34	34	3	203.1	217	133	123	38	72	133	5.44	.271	.337	.484
Start 4 Days Rest	94	74	0	0	216	216	20	1397.0	1334	759	666	169	505	921	4.29	.250	.322	.408
Start 5 Days Rest	54	45	0	0	132	132	4	817.0	825	455	413	107	324	530	4.55	.261	.336	.428
Start 6+ Days Rest	22	24	0	0	58	58	5	358.0	352	196	169	43	144	228	4.25	.255	.333	.402
Relief 0 Days Rest	0	2	5	6	21	0	0	32.2	28	9	6	3	11	28	1.65	.235	.301	.336
Relief 1 Day Rest	3	4	3	5	34	0	0	63.2	60	44	42	12	38	52	5.94	.254	.364	.470
Relief 2 Days Rest	3	4	3	7	37	0	0	70.1	63	32	30	5	27	64	3.84	.247	.328	.369
Relief 3–5 Days Rest	3	3	8	9	48	0	0	98.1	89	44	37	14	28	84	3.39	.237	.295	.411
Relief 6+ Days Rest	1	1	3	3	14	0	0	31.1	21	9	8	2	9	23	2.30	.191	.256	.255

MONTHLY	W	L	SV	SVO	G	GS	CG	IP	H	R	ER	HR	BB	SO	ERA	AVG	OBP	SLG
April	26	23	4	4	81	61	4	432.2	397	216	192	45	185	279	3.99	.240	.323	.383
May	29	31	3	4	108	74	2	525.2	542	304	277	62	233	337	4.74	.267	.350	.426
June	31	34	6	8	111	79	4	544.2	534	303	261	63	198	367	4.31	.256	.327	.416
July	37	25	6	6	94	70	8	500.0	485	256	233	70	169	366	4.19	.253	.319	.423
August	38	28	1	3	93	75	8	520.1	505	295	266	81	175	357	4.60	.252	.317	.430
September	29	29	0	1	97	76	6	513.0	493	285	246	65	188	328	4.32	.252	.328	.409
October	3	2	2	4	10	5	0	35.1	33	22	19	7	10	29	4.84	.246	.295	.470

POSTSEASON TOTALS

All statistics according to STATS, Inc.

YEAR	Rnd	Tm	Lg	W	L	SV	SVO	G	GS	CG	IP	H	R	ER	HR	BB	SO	ERA
1992	LCS	Pit	NL	2	0	0	0	2	2	2	18.0	14	6	6	4	5	7	3.00
1995	Div	Bos	AL	0	1	0	0	1	1	0	5.1	5	7	7	1	5	4	11.81
1998	Div	Bos	AL	0	1	0	0	1	1	0	1.1	3	5	5	0	2	1	33.75
1999	Div	Bos	AL	0	0	0	0	2	0	0	2.0	3	3	3	0	4	4	13.50
2003	Div	Bos	AL	0	1	0	0	2	1	0	7.2	6	5	3	0	3	7	3.52
2003	LCS	Bos	AL	2	1	0	0	3	2	0	14.0	8	4	4	1	6	10	2.57
2004	LCS	Bos	AL	1	0	0	0	3	0	0	7.1	9	7	7	1	3	6	8.59
2004	WS	Bos	AL	0	0	0	0	1	1	0	3.2	3	5	5	1	5	2	12.27
2005	Div	Bos	AL	0	1	0	0	1	1	0	5.1	6	4	4	1	1	4	6.75
2007	LCS	Bos	AL	0	1	0	0	1	1	0	4.2	5	5	5	1	2	7	9.64
2008	LCS	Bos	AL	0	1	0	0	1	1	0	2.2	6	5	5	3	2	2	16.88
PLAYOFF TOTALS				5	7	0	0	18	11	2	72.0	68	56	54	13	38	54	6.75
DIV TOTALS				0	4	0	0	7	4	0	21.2	23	24	22	2	15	20	9.14
LCS TOTALS				5	3	0	0	10	6	2	46.2	42	27	27	10	18	32	5.21
WS TOTALS				0	0	0	0	1	1	0	3.2	3	5	5	1	5	2	12.27
TOTALS AL				3	7	0	0	16	9	0	54.0	54	50	48	9	33	47	8.00
TOTALS NL				2	0	0	0	2	2	2	18.0	14	6	6	4	5	7	3.00

Rnd Series
Tm Team
Lg League
W Wins
L Losses

SV Saves
SVO Save opportunities
G Games
GS Games started
CG Complete games

IP Innings pitched
H Hits allowed
R Runs allowed
ER Earned runs allowed
HR Home runs allowed

BB Walks
SO Strikeouts
ERA Earned run average

Index